Appleby College Women's/Parents' Association
History
1928 - 2003

By Margaret I. Bennett

® **Appleby College**

ISBN: 1-894933-53-2

Table of Contents

Dedication and Acknowledgements

This book is dedicated
To
My husband, Mark Bennett'64
And
Our Children
Sarah, Michael'99, Emily'03, and Madeleine'06
They all contributed, one way or another, be it making meals, editing from across the miles, assisting at the computer, chauffeuring, no mom at the lake, no mom anywhere - just at the computer, all in all the never ending Appleby College Women's/Parents' Association History. It is finally, a fait accompli, my darlings, thank the Lord.

Acknowledgements:

A special thank you
To the Editors
Dede Hacking and Michael Desroches'62
Dede for modern English usage, and more,
Michael for historical accuracy, and more.

Thank you
To
Dorothy and Edward Leonard
of Emerald Presentations, Oakville,
for the layout.

Thank you to the many others who contributed:

Nancy and Jim Baillie'37, Marsha and Aubrey Baillie'63, Rusty Baillie'66,
Colleen Baumler, Diana and John Berriman, Carol Budd, Mary Coleman, Isabel Collins,
Liz Denyar, Midge and Michael DesRoches'62, Mary Dewar, Jill Edmonson,
Cindy Galway, Anita Griffiths, Dede Hacking, Mary Haddon, Jackie Haroun,
Maggie Hayes (Larock), Libby Heisey, Margaret Hodgins, Pearl Lande, Guy McLean,
Sharon Maich, Barbara McCarter, Jane Minkhorst, Melanie Molyneaux, Andrew Moore,
Sandra Mussi, Betty Newlands, Susan Nicholas, Rosalind Nightingale, Patti Parke,
Carmen Peirce, Laurie Salvi, Karen Shields and Don Stewart.
Please forgive me any errors or omissions as to contributors and/or content. Margaret Bennett

The Appleby College Women's/Parents' Association has a history that is as rich as the school's itself, and it has been a pleasure to watch its evolution from a small group of dedicated mothers to an association that touches every Appleby parent's life.

The Parents' Association's impact can be seen in a myriad of fundraising initiatives, with proceeds going towards projects and programmes specifically designed to benefit Appleby students. Of course, the PA does much more than fundraising for the school. Members can been seen at outreach events; volunteering at the lost and found, Turnover Shop and College Shop; welcoming new parents at social events; and organizing volunteers and events such as the Christmas House Tour and the fall Grade Parties. The PA president also meets with the Board of Governors, participating in the decisions that move the College forward.

In the spring of 2003, a team of educators from the Canadian Educational Standards Institute visited the College as part of its accreditation process, and had much to say about the value and commitment that Appleby parents bring to the school. In its evaluative report, Appleby's volunteer "army" was described as "caring, global citizens," and their enthusiasm in enhancing life at Appleby was seen as a tangible strength to the school. This commitment is something that I have seen here on a daily basis, as the Parents' Association takes on yet another successful fund or friendraiser, bringing ever more parents into the fold of enthusiastic volunteers and participants.

The people involved with the Parents' Association are too many to thank, but this book recognizes the gift of their time and passion, ensuring Appleby's success. Margaret Bennett must, however, be singled out for congratulations for this history, which is no small undertaking. I sincerely appreciate the time that she has put into a project of this magnitude, crossing generations and continents to collect its stories, photographs and historical information. The care that has gone into the description of the Parents' Association's last 75 years is certain to be reflected in its flourishing future. Happy 75th to the Parents' Association!

With sincere thanks,

Guy McLean
Headmaster

About the Author

Following in the footsteps of her mother-in-law, Mrs. H. G. Bennett, who served on the Women's Association Executive Committee from 1956-1962, Margaret Bennett has been a committed parent volunteer at Appleby since her son Michael'99, entered the final grade four class at Appleby to the present (her youngest daughter, Madeleine'06, is a current student). While it is not the Association's way to sing the praises of individual volunteers, suffice it to say that Margaret's sense of history, attention to detail, and inclusiveness will be long remembered. These qualities also particularly suit her to the task of writing this history. Margaret has spent months poring over the Association's scant records and collecting reminiscences from those familiar with its earlier years. We are truly fortunate that she accepted the invitation in 1998 to undertake this project. We are especially grateful that she has seen the project to completion in time for the Association's 75th anniversary.

AGM, 1994, Guest Speaker, Priscilla de Villiers
with Margaret Bennett (Mark'64)

LADY BAILLIE
A LITTLE HISTORY

Lady Baillie

In 1877, Canada was ten years old and Bracebridge, Ontario, was a very small village. On September 17th, 1877 Edith Julia White was born in Bracebridge to Emily (neé Bridgeland) and Aubrey White. Emily was from England and Aubrey from Ireland. Sadly, Emily died after bearing her fourth child in 1879. Of her four offspring only two survived, Nelly and Edith. Being widowed with two small children would be a hardship for any man, fortunately Aubrey married Mary, Emily's sister.

"…a young Irish lad named Aubrey White, who was later to become a captain on the Lakes, then to be occupied in lumbering, later Crown Lands agent and soon thereafter being called to Government headquarters in Toronto, where he was appointed Deputy Minister of Lands and Forests for Ontario. A cairn in Mr. White's memory was erected by the Department of Lands and Forests in 1965 at High Falls."[1]

Aubrey's appointment took place in 1882. Edith was five years old at the time of the move. She was educated in Toronto and spent many years there. As a girl she summered on Chief Island on Lake Muskoka. She graduated from the Toronto Conservatory of Music with the degree of A.T.C.M.

Edith met and married Frank Baillie in Toronto. They were wed on June 8th, 1900. They had five children Marion, Edith, Aubrey, Frank and Jim.

Frank was as industrious as Edith's father, Aubrey. He organized and manufactured aeroplanes and munitions in Canada during World War I. He was knighted for his diligence, business acumen and general service during the War.

Lady Baillie was community minded thanks to the example of her father. Not only was she a giving woman but she was also lots of fun, warm and hospitable, and no stranger to tragedy.

"…and on the next curve on Lakeshore Road was 'Lisonally Farm'[♥], the home from the First World War years of Sir Frank and Lady Baillie. Here there was literally not a dull moment. There were horses to ride and a large swimming 'tank' as it was called then, with a convenient bungalow for changing. A fine *en-tout-cas* tennis court was undoubtedly partly responsible for the outstanding tennis played by daughter Marion and her family and friends. This excellent court, when not in use otherwise, was generously made available to the rest of us, regardless of our skill! A very large sun-room along the west side of the house was one of our favourite places for dancing. Lady Baillie's house burned down later on, and was replaced by another on the same site …"[2]

In January 1921, Sir Frank died prematurely leaving a young widow Edith and five young children. Marion was 20 years old, Edith 17, Aubrey 13, Frank 8 and Jim 3. It is amazing what Lady Baillie accomplished in the years following her husband's death. She certainly proved to be a woman well ahead of her time. She had been active while her husband was alive but continued in a more sustained way afterward.

At the time of Sir Frank's death, Lady Baillie and her children lived in Toronto, they spent time on the farm, weekends and such. Aubrey was already enrolled in

---

[1] Early Days in Muskoka, by George Boyer, 1970.
[♥] Lisonally Farm was their Oakville home.
[2] Oakville, A Small Town 1900-1930, Francis Robin Ahern, 1981, The Oakville Historical Society.

1920 Photo, Lady Baillie with son, Jim[37]

Lady Baillie with son Aubrey[27]
travelling by train

Lady Baillie enjoyed
boating & fishing

Appleby School. In 1922 Lady Baillie enrolled Frank and in 1927, young James. The family did not move to Oakville until 1939. That did not stop Lady Baillie from achieving at Appleby or elsewhere.

In 1927 she rallied the Appleby parents to ensure that a covered rink would be built for the boys. It was important that they be able to play hockey and be able to skate plainly and simply. After successfully accomplishing this she went on to launch the Women's Association of Appleby School. Much of what she did for Appleby is enumerated in the following history. Many other accomplishments are not.

Lady Baillie was a religious woman and it is reflected in her accomplishments. She took quite literally the Biblical dictum to develop one's talents and to share them. In 1948 some of what she did was listed:

"Early in the late war she threw her energies into war work. She was president of the Oakville Women's War Services League, which was later amalgamated with the Red Cross. For six years from 1941 until 1947 she was president of the Oakville and District Red Cross Society, and during her presidency served as a member of the Executive Committee of the Ontario Division of the Red Cross Society. During the war she was chairman of the Red Cross Donor's Clinic in Oakville, and also served as chairman in no less than three Victory Loan Campaigns. She was instrumental in providing a recreation room on Colborne Street for patients at the Oakville Convalescent Retraining Centre, and organized a series of weekly entertainments for the patients at that establishment. It was under Lady Baillie's chairmanship that a community fair was held in Oakville. She also headed the committee in charge of a drive for clothing for the Russian war victims.

"Lady Baillie is a member of White Oak Chapter, I.O.D.E., and is a former chairman of the board of the Oakville and Trafalgar Hospital Association. In 1945 she received the award of merit from the Oakville Lions Club for outstanding service to the community.

"Keenly interested in work on behalf of the blind, Lady Baillie was for ten years president of the Women's Auxiliary of the Canadian National Institute for the Blind, and was a member of the Council of the Institute for six years. She is now honorary vice-president of the Women's Auxiliary and holds the same position in the Institute itself. She is also an active member of the Halton County Advisory Board of the Institute.

"For many years Lady Baillie has been an admirer of the Salvation Army and its welfare work, and has given liberally of her time to promote this work. She has acted as convenor of the women's team in campaigns to raise funds for this organization. She was one of the original honorary presidents of the Junior League of Toronto, and still holds office as honorary president."[3]

Remember this was only 1948, Lady Baillie continued to contribute to the community for seventeen more years. She was an active member of St. Jude's Church and the Women's Guild. Lady Baillie was a charter member of the Oakville-Trafalgar Memorial Hospital. In 1949 she organized the Oakville-Trafalgar Memorial Hospital

---

[3] The Oakville Record Star, 1948, Article courtesy of The Oakville Historical Society.

Edith Baillie &
Audrey Mussen (sister),
1949

Lady Baillie, at Home

Women's Auxiliary and served as its president until 1954. She was involved with the Oakville United Appeal, the Victorian Order of Nurses, and was president of the Junior League of Hamilton.

Undoubtedly a woman of this stature would have helped many anonymously and independent of the organizations she belonged to. She truly was way ahead of her time.

She was not an 'all-work' and 'no-play' type of gal. She played bridge, fished and golfed. There was nothing shabby about anything she did. "One of Lady Baillie's outstanding interests is golf, at which she is adept. She has held the women's senior golf championship of Canada, and also the Canadian women's senior golf championship for grandmothers, the latter for two consecutive years. She is a life member of no less than three golf clubs, the Oakville Golf Club, the Toronto Golf Club, and the Ladies' Golf and Tennis Club of Toronto. She is also a member of the Lambton Golf Club. She was the first president and one of the organizers of the Ladies' Golf and Tennis Club, the first club in Toronto to be operated on a nominal fee basis."[4]

With all of this involvement, Lady Baillie never tired of the Women's Association. She attended meetings until her death.

Lady Baillie has one surviving son, Jim and his wife Nancy. She has a great number of grandchildren and great grandchildren. Many of her descendents have and will attend Appleby College. A number of them have and do serve Appleby College. She set an incredible example and standard for all of them and for all who serve in her organization – The Parents' Association of Appleby College.

---

[4] The Oakville Record Star, 1948. Article courtesy of the Oakville Historical Society.

Lady Baillie, 1960

HISTORY
AT A GLANCE

McCraney's Creek, May, 1913
View from Lake Ontario

Covered Rink, c 1930
This was a natural ice rink, provided largely through the efforts of Lady Baillie in 1927. The rink collapsed from the weight of snow on the roof in 1945; luckily, no one was injured.

In 1928, when Lady Baillie called together a few friends to inaugurate the Women's Association, Appleby was but a fledgling school. Appleby School was seventeen years old. The property (32 acres) housed only the barn, Colley House (referred to as Main House or School House), Powell's House and the covered rink. Not only did students reside in Colley House, they also attended classes in that building and took their meals in the basement. The Chapel was a work in progress.

Lady Baillie had rallied the parents in 1927 and with their support was able to provide the school with a covered rink. The rink provided great pleasure and sport until 1945 at which time it collapsed. It is always said 'blessedly', no one was on the ice or near the rink at that time. "'All of us woke up to a horrible crunching sound,' Pearce Bunting[47] remembers. What the boys heard was the noise of Lady Baillie's covered rink collapsing to the ground. The accident brought on by the weight of snow on the roof, …"[5]

In 1928 Lady Baillie probably felt the strength and support of the parent body with the dream of a rink having been realized. She called together friends and discussed and thrashed out the details of a Women's Association. The first Annual Meeting of the Association was held in Powell's House on May 23rd, 1929. Of the ten members present we could imagine, from the stationery, that Lady Baillie and Mesdames Ambrose, Davis, Guest, Marlatt, McLeod and Osler were there with three others. Their goal for the year was to raise funds to complete the chapel. This would have been the school year 1928-1929.

In the next year, two standard brass lamps were gifted to the Chapel from the Women's Association. These would be the first of many donations, by the Association, to the Chapel and the school itself. The Association was formed "to further the welfare of the school and add to the comfort of the Masters and boys."[6]

The women also helped in recruiting students for the school. "It was suggested by Lady Baillie that all the members should talk about the school and in that way try to get new boys, as that was the most important thing for the school just now."[7]

In 1934 John Guest[*] retired as Headmaster of Appleby School and Percy Wickens took over. Mr. Wickens had only three years as head of Appleby. He died of cancer in 1937. He had been diagnosed several months before his death but did not let on to anyone that he was ill. John Bell took over and remained Headmaster until 1968. He left his imprint on the school. The Chapel was named in Dr. Bell's honour. It is important to the history of the Women's/Parents' Association that the head of school be named. He played and plays an important role in the operation of the Association. In fact, without his blessing the Association could not operate. It has been noted that in other independent schools parents' Associations do not enjoy the freedom of operation that the Women's/Parents' Association has and does enjoy at Appleby College.

The parents have had and continue to have a feeling of being at home on campus. The women were always able to sell jewellery in the foyer (today in the shop), decorate and provide for rooms of the buildings as they were erected, and to update them as they aged. The Chapel has been home to many a mother serving on the Chapel Guild. For a

---

[5] The Appleby Story, by Jack Batten.
[6] The Argus, Volume 36, June 1929.
[7] The A.C.W.A. minutes, June 17th, 1938.
[*] The John Guest Hall (the dining hall) was named in his honour.

Appleby School Women's Association

HON.-PRES. MRS. J. A. M. BELL
HON.-PRES. LADY BAILLIE
PRES. MRS. DONALD BENSON
VICE-PRES. MRS. E. F. OSLER *Mrs Little*
HON. SEC. TREAS. MRS. HENRY HILL

COMMITTEE :

MRS. E. H. AMBROSE   MRS. ALFRED BUNTING
MRS. W. D. ROSS   MRS. HUGH DENISON
MRS. B. P. ALLEY   MRS. J. W. LITTLE

List of GGifts given to the School;

Year	Gift	Amount
1930	Altar Curtains for Chapel	123.26
1931	Curtains for Stage in Gymnasium	99.50
	Standard Brass Lamps in Chapel	320.00
1932m	Beams at Chapel Roof	243.00
	Tinted Window in Chapel	80.00
	Cupboard in Chapel	59.20
	Credence Bracket	27.50
	Grilles	20.00
1933	Contribution to Dramatic Club	75.00
1934	" " "	66.40
	Tiling Shower Baths	357.00
1936	Curtains, Rugs, Painting etc.	250.00
	Potato Peeler	100.00
1937	Decorating Interior of Hospital	331.81
	Electric Equipment for Hospital	28.00
1938	New Lights for School & Powell's House Reading & Dining Rooms	200.00
	Cassocks for School Choir	75.00
	Book Cases for Reference Books	38.15
1939	Finishing work on Pews in Chapel	235.00

1940 75 Folding Chairs + books for library   150.00
50 annually voted for Reference Books.

1940 List of Gifts to the School from 1930 to 1940

number of years all the Executive Committee meetings have been held at the school. Afternoon bridge has been played in the dining hall on a Thursday afternoon for a number of years.

In the 1930's funds were given for the dramatic club, lamps for the entrance to the school, another chapel window, covers for the beds, chairs, library books, paint, curtains, table cloths, a used industrial potato peeler, cushions and on and on. The women would see a need and fill it.

At this point two meetings were held annually, one in the spring, the other in the fall. If at all possible the meetings were held at the school. Space was limited so meetings were also held in the homes of Association members and the Headmaster's home. Minutes were written or typed and took only a page or two while today they take as many as five to ten pages or even more depending on the verbosity of the members (or was it truly the advent of computers which allowed much greater expression than the manual or even electric typewriter?). It is interesting to note that from the earliest minutes until the early 70's the women referred to each other rather formally as Mrs. Alfred Bunting, Mrs. Jack Little and so on. By the mid-70's it was Mary or Betty.

In 1941 the name of the school was changed from Appleby School to Appleby College. This designation was in use at the other independent boys' schools. In fact, Appleby College had been a common usage so much so that in the minutes of the Women's Association of the 1930's the Association was at times called Appleby College Women's Association rather than Appleby School.

In the 1940's much was provided for the school. Pews were installed in the chapel, "Mr. Bell then spoke to the meeting. He thanked the members for their gift to the chapel in the form of a cheque to be used to furnish the gallery with proper pews. He explained that it was quite inadequate at present and that only the day boys used. (sic) He felt that more parents would come to the Sunday Evening Service if there was more room. It was badly needed also for the Carol Service and other services. The pews are to be put in steps for better vision. They had already been ordered and he hoped to have them installed within the month. Mr. Bell also thanked the Association for a jig saw, a power saw and other tools which Mr. Partridge had been able to order last year. There was also a dark room for amateur photographers, with Mr. Cushley in charge. ..."[8] And bedspreads were provided, movies for viewing on Saturday nights were purchased, a movie screen, more chairs and books were given, lighting, prayer books, choir gowns, and a multitude of other gifts. Funds were given towards cadet uniforms, reference books, for the hospital, for the junior common room. For a number of years $50.00 was given annually for reference books and $30.00 for movies.

Dances were held. "Mrs. Hart gave her report on the two dances given during the year, one in June at the end of the School term, and the other during the Christmas holidays. Both of these were very successful and great enthusiasm was shown by the boys."[9]

A mother-son tea was held annually. "The mother-and-son tea was discussed and decided upon. It was decided that this should be in the fall, regardless of domestic

---

[8] The A.C.W.A. minutes, May 9th, 1946.
[9] The A.C.W.A. minutes, May 15th, 1942.

Powell's House Rink, *Undated Photo*

Campus, circa 1940
Looking from the west bank of McCraney's Creek, a view of the main playing field, with the covered rink in the background among the trees.

12

problems. [This refers to a shortage of staff.] That sandwiches and cakes could be supplied by the mothers."[10]

The staff was thinly spread because it was war time. A number of masters and staff members went to war, as did a number of Old Boys. The Memorial Classroom Building was built in 1949; but it was not until "May 11, 1956 after the cadet corps' annual Inspection Day, David Guest, son of the school's first Headmaster and James Osler's brother-in-law, unveiled a tablet in memory of the Appleby dead in World War Two. The tablet is on the south wall of the entrance to the classroom building. There are twenty names on it."[11]

In 1945 Lady Baillie donated a stained glass window to the Chapel in appreciation of all the school had done for her three sons. (See back page and cover.)

In the 1950's, the Women's Association continued to support the school. The school had grown and enlarged in many areas. "Mr. Bell reported there were 181 boys in the School, which is filled to capacity. Dr. Neathy is leaving. The library [not the library of today but one located above the foyer of the classroom building] is almost completed, though books are very badly needed.

"Mr. Bell thanked the Association for its generous contribution to the Library furnishings and went on to say that he is well aware the tuck shop is not attractive, but evergreens are to be planted to hide it.

"The hospital has been refloored and redecorated. One of the fathers arranged the surfacing of three tennis courts, a welcome addition to the school grounds.

"Generally fine performances were given by the School Choir during the year and the Cadets won a special trophy to be presented at the Inspection."[12]

Many more purchases were made for the school by the Association. Many of these were the technology of the day, a gramophone, a record player and a slide projector. The usual donations were made for research materials for the library, games for the boys and other extras.

The first Bursary, $300.00, was given to the school in 1953. To this day the Bursary is supported by the Parents' Association. In 2003, the Bursary donation was $30,000. It is interesting to note that from the small association that Lady Baillie and friends birthed has grown a large and prosperous association. But it is an association that walks in the same footsteps and follows the same motto as those in 1928 did; an association that has great regard for its history and its founder, Lady Baillie.

The year 1953 saw the Coronation and the Appleby Choir travel to England for the ceremonies. "It was voted to plant a tree, the gift of the Association to the School, in commemoration of the Coronation.

"The tree was dedicated by the Headmaster on the evening of May 10th, following which ceremony Dr. and Mrs. Bell, Mr. Bott and the members of the Choir departed for England. The good wishes of the Association go with them all for a successful trip, and the members are happy in the knowledge that the Choir boys of Appleby College will bring credit to their School and to Canada."[13]

---

[10] The A.C.W.A. minutes, May 15th, 1942.
[11] <u>The Appleby Story,</u> by Jack Batten.
[12] The A.C.W.A. minutes, May 11th, 1951.
[13] <u>The Argus,</u> June, 1953, Number 61.

1956 Play: "Lost: A Smallish, Brownish Dog" *by H.C. Hardwick*
*The Women's Association was involved for many years in helping Appleby's Dramatic
Society with costumes and make-up. Remeber that boys played girls' roles in those days.*

Through the fifties, as through all the years, where there was a need the Women's Association filled it. "Mr. Hardwick of the staff asked for help with the costumes for the plays to be held Mar. 17, 1956. The costumes are now too expensive to rent. The senior play needs women's dresses, the junior play several costumes. Mrs. Curran suggested we scan our wardrobes for suitable costumes and meet at her house Feb. 15. At that time a letter be proposed to send to all the mothers in the Association for clothes to begin a costume wardrobe that could be stored in the gym for future use."[14] At a subsequent meeting "The President told how the executive had cooperated on planning and making the costumes for the plays and particularly thanked Mrs. Bennett for her effort."[15]

The new gymnasium was opened and the April 9th, 1956 meeting was held there. Often raffles were held at the meetings. At the general meetings a school blazer would be raffled and often the centre pieces on the tables.

The women hoped to have a bridge club at the school as they do today. "Mrs. Wace the President opened the meeting with an explanation of why we did not have the bridge party suggested at the fall meeting. The gym was not available at any time for our use."[16]

"Canon Bell suggested that one of the two following projects might be undertaken:-

1. The purchase of two finely made chairs for the entrance hall of the office & class room building, the seats & backs of these chairs, it was hoped might eventually have hand worked needle point coverings designed with the Appleby Crest.
2. The donation of six or eight bed side tables for the hospital. Approximate cost per table $35."[17]

The chairs were purchased in England and many readers will remember them in the foyer of the classroom building. They are on campus and are treasured.

At this time the Executive Committee began to hold monthly meetings as well as the two general meetings. As today, the Headmaster often addressed the Executive Committee. "Cannon Bell commented on the following changes on the grounds. The Snider property has been purchased, and the Young cottage has been winterized. Sarge* will soon be living on the grounds. Also the cottage occupied by Mrs. Bath will be used for workmen.

"A very nice gift for the Chapel of two pews was made by Mr. Wm. Grant+, in memory of Mrs. Grant. They have one son Ian Grant at the school.

"We received a tennis practice board from Mr. Smye.

"The school has been admitted to the Ontario Teachers Superannuation Scheme♥. This applies to masters who are certificated. The Annuity at the time of retirement is good and enables us to employ masters who won't lose their pension.

---

[14] The A.C.W.A. minutes, October 28th, 1955.
[15] The A.C.W.A. minutes, April 9th, 1956.
[16] The A.C.W.A. minutes, March 25th, 1957.
[17] The A.C.W.A. minutes, October 22nd, 1957.
* Sarge was Sergeant Major Clark the head of the Cadet Corps.
+ Mr. Wm. Grant'29 was the father of Ian'60 and grandfather of Fraser'87 and Heather. (Fraser and Heather both teachers at Appleby).

MEMBERS ARRIVE FOR APPLEBY WA MEETING
Mrs. William Tate, Mrs. G. A. Wilson, Mrs. George Broomfield

Appleby WA Annual Meet Hears Reports, Headmaster

OAKVILLE — Representatives of women's associations of Ridley College, St. Catharines, St. Andrew's College, Aurora, a n d Trinity College School, P o r t Hope, were guests of Appleby College Women's Association at its annual meeting at the College Wednesday. Nearly 80 women were present altogether.

Canon J. A. M. Bell, headmaster of Appleby, addressed t h e meeting on the many changes in educational methods now taking place, and the new qualifications required for university entrance. He complimented organization on the manner in which it is supporting the college.

The retiring president, M r s. J. R. Winchell, reviewed the work of the association during the past year. The association awarded a $500 bursary, purchas-

ed drums and a mace for the Cadet Corps, and a pair of candleabra for the dining-room in memory of the late L a d y Baillie, a generous contributor to the college.

The following officers w e r e elected for the year: Honorary vice-presidents, Mrs. J. A. M. Bell, Mrs. J. S. H. Guest; Past president, Mrs. J. R. Winchell; President, Mrs. D. W. Newlands; vice-president, Mrs. G. L. Waters; Secretary, Mrs. J. W. Baillie; Treasurer, Mrs. H. W. Angus; Committee, Mrs. J. A. Botterell, Mrs. C. N. P. Blagrave; Mrs. W. J. H. Disher, Mrs. K. B. MacNaughton, Mrs. R. L. Onkey.

Mrs. T. H. Jamieson represented t h e Appleby boys w h o fought overseas.

Article in Oakville Daily Journal-Record, April 14, 1966

"Forecasting the Future:-

"We would like to have a new dining room in Georgian style such as Ferguson Hall at U.C.C., new kitchens and dining room large enough to seat 200 or 250. This would teach the boys to eat properly, not just 'feed'. It is desirable to have three houses instead of two, and we would like a new residence♣ on this side of the road. The chapel should be enlarged some day. Mr. Guest built the chapel and raised the money to buy furniture, etc. for it. We will do a little bit at a time.

"We are working with 'your sons'. A boy must be aroused and stimulated, and mothers learn to 'take it'. Far too many people have never become mature, and learned to 'take it'. One must be able to face life rich or poor, with a calm view point. Nobody can always win, or have his own way. One can find happiness either way."[18] At a later meeting "The Canon then spoke to us on the aims of Appleby and the duty and responsibility of the parents and the home to give a full, well rounded educational training to our young people."[19] The tone of the fifties can be felt in what Canon Bell had said.

At this time the women sold ash trays, matches and lighters. Today this would be scandalous. Times have certainly changed. This would seem almost contradictory to Canon Bell's words (if they were uttered in the nineties or later), but one must remember that smoking was socially acceptable everywhere in the fifties.

This decade finished with a progress report on the school to the women by Dr. Bell. "Highlights—220 pupils registered and 17 staff members. A scholarship was won by Peter Wright to Western University. We are all very proud of that. A new Junior School has been set up under Mr. Merritt and is working very well. A new addition has been completed to Mr. Dewar's house♦ and new classrooms are in the process of being built. Miss Sanderson, the school nurse is leaving Christmas to be replaced by Mrs. King.

"Future plans for a new dining hall are now prepared and Dr. Bell said his dream was to have the 50th Anniversary dinner of Appleby College held in that new hall in 1961."[20] All things worked out and Dr. Bell realized another dream in the '60's.

The Women's Association continued its altruistic work. Bursaries were given annually, supplies for the hospital, for dances, and for the Chapel were provided. Even a billiard table was purchased with the Women's Association (W.A.) paying for over half of it. The first field trips were instituted under the leadership of Mrs. B. H. Collins, Jr. New mothers were always made welcome. "Mrs. Baillie offered to have a sherry party at her house for members of the Executive and mothers of new boys."[21]

♥ Cindy Galway, daughter of Canon Bell, said that her father did not qualify for the pension but it was a good thing for those who did. He pursued this in their interest.

♣ Some students were housed across the lakeshore, eventually faculty members were housed there until the turn of the century at which time (2002) the property was sold.

[18] The A.C.W.A. minutes, November 1st, 1957.

[19] The A.C.W.A. minutes, April 8th, 1959.

♦ Powell's House, the south end was added to.

[20] The A.C.W.A. minutes, October 30th, 1959

[21] The A.C.W.A. minutes, September 26th, 1961.

Dr. Bell and Miss Chamberlain on the occasion of their retirement party

Miss Chamberlain & Ian Newlands '78

The women wanted to serve sherry prior to the general meetings and they sought permission from Dr. Bell. This was graciously permitted, in fact, Dr. and Mrs. Bell would often host the new mothers in their home prior to the general meeting.

In September the dining hall began to function, "the noon meal on the first day was served on schedule in the John Guest Hall to 225 students and eighteen staff members."[22] On November 25th, 1961 the John Guest Hall was officially opened. Around the same time New House[*] was opened "That weekend saw a mass trek of boys across the campus, boys carting beds, furniture and possessions to their spanking new quarters. It was a giddy time for the students, as it was for a handful of masters who reshuffled their responsibilities. Bill Joyce moved from Colley House to New House as its first housemaster. Tom Menzies shifted from Powell's to replace Joyce in Colley, and David Smith, the newest man on the job, recently married, even more recently a father, took up residence in Powell's as its housemaster."[23]

Appleby was and is very much a large family, parents, faculty and staff. There were and are many beloved characters in this family. This is just a glance, so only a couple can be mentioned. Hilda Chattaway, the cook for many years was much loved and is warmly regarded by old boys and their parents. She even had a residence named after her. (This was the top floor of Colley House which housed the junior boys and is no longer in existence as such.) Hilda contributed greatly to the school, at times through the W.A. She did not want anyone to know of her generosity. She was pleased to give but did not want it recognized.

Miss Chamberlain, fondly referred to as 'Chaimby' was also well regarded. She taught the 'little boys' and was dubbed "the sweetheart of the Junior School."[24] Mrs. D. Newlands recalled hosting a retirement party for Dr. Bell and Miss Chamberlain. At the party Mrs. Newlands learned that it was 'Chaimby's' birthday and that she had never had a birthday party in her life. Mrs. Newlands, Dr. and Mrs. Bell and the others in attendance, their hearts touched on hearing this, made her retirement party also her first birthday party.

On March 14th, 1965 Lady Baillie died. To say that the school lost a friend would be an understatement. Lady Baillie gave so much and for so long. She never lost her interest in her baby, the Women's Association or the much loved Appleby College. Lady Baillie presided over the W.A. for ten years and served for many more never losing touch. She attended practically every Annual Meeting right up and into the sixties. She was remarkable, a gift in herself to the Appleby Family. To this day she is remembered by many. Many who never knew her but are familiar with the legendary lady she was.

After her death, life continued as always at the school, the students attended class, the faculty and staff carried on as usual, the women continued to work diligently following in Lady Baillie's footsteps. The women wanted to give a fitting memorial in her memory. They chose a pair of silver candelabra, inscribed 'In Memory of Lady

---

[22] The Appleby Story, by Jack Batten.

[*] New House was later renamed Walker House in honour of Sir Edmund Walker, Appleby's patron and first Chairman of the Board.

[23] The Appleby Story, by Jack Batten.

[24] Ibid.

George Wright and Dave Newlands

Miss Chamberlain, Nancy Baillie (Jim '37), Peter Baillie '68, Ned Larsen

Baillie'. To this day the candelabra are used at the school, biennially on the tea table for House Tour, and on many other occasions.

The Chapel was enlarged. "When the architects, masons and carpenters laid down their tools, Bell and everyone else at the school pronounced the chapel a triumph, and on Sunday, December 17, 1967 when the boys moved from the gym where services had been held during construction into the chapel for a carol service, the sounds of the singing were, for John Bell, as sweet as he'd ever heard. The first full service in the chapel came on January 10, 1968, the snowiest day of the winter, and two months later, on March 3, the Right Reverend Walter Bagnall came to the chapel for the most significant service of all. On that day, he dedicated the building for all time in the name of the man who most merited it. The building became the John Bell Chapel."[25]

In 1968 Dr. Bell resigned. He had served the school for thirty one years. He was honoured in many ways. "When Bell retired in 1968, he was already laden with recognition. His old college, Trinity, has awarded him a Doctor of Divinity many years earlier. And he left Appleby with all sorts of tangible indications of the respect and affection he had attracted from students, masters and old boys. The non-teaching staff presented him with two dozen crystal tumblers, the boys gave him a refectory table, and the masters surprised him with a pair of sterling silver book ends that carried engravings of the Appleby crest and the signatures of all the staff members. From the Appleby Women's Association, Bell received money to buy a color television set. He got a generous cheque from the old boys, and from the Board of Governors came a coffee table made out of wood taken from an oak tree that had grown on the Appleby grounds. Dr. and Mrs. Bell retreated with their gifts to a comfortable bungalow in Oakville that the Board had purchased with the Headmaster's retirement in mind."[26]

Mrs. Bell shared a great deal with Dr. Bell in regard to the school. She often held Association meetings in their home, hosted the mothers while the sons and fathers dined. She entertained parents, faculty and staff jointly with her husband. Their home was open often to the Appleby family as is Joanne and Guy McLean's today. (All of the Headmasters and their wives have graciously and often entertained members of the Appleby Family.)

The sixties finished with the women completing the décor of the New House common room, repairs to the billiard table and such. The Bursary was given as had been done every year since 1953. A charge was made for the annual luncheon so that monies intended for the boys would not be spent on lunch. Everyone was adjusting to the new Headmaster, E. R. (Ned) Larsen. (Ned Larsen served Appleby from 1968-1980.)

The seventies saw the school gifted with "eleven acres on Rabbittnose Island in the north arm of Lake Temagami, land which came to the school through its great friend, Bruce McLaughlin."[27] The school also received an arena; "a home at last for Appleby hockey, cost $200,000 and opened for play on February 6, 1970. Gairdner [J. S. (Jock) Gairdner] presided over the official ceremonies which were followed in the usual fashion by a game between the Old Boys and the Firsts. As they had at the opening of the

---

[25] The Appleby Story, by Jack Batten.
[26] Ibid.
[27] The Appleby Story, by Jack Batten.

1995 Book Fair and Pot Luck Luncheon
Ken Dryden, author and hockey great, signing books

Round Square, 2000
Lunchtime Volunteers

covered rink in 1927, the Old Boys came out ahead, this time by an 8-4 score."[28] The school also received the gift of a swimming pool. "At the Old Boys' luncheon on Saturday, November 1st, 1969, the Headmaster announced that Dr. Norman B. Keevil, his son, Dr. N. B. Keevil Jr. ('43-'47) and Mr. Leslie A. Allen had generously donated this new athletic facility to us. Dr. Keeveil Sr. has three boys presently at the School; Norman Jr. has one son, currently in Grade Eight as has Mr. Allen (son, John).

"One of the lower Tennis courts will disappear to make room for the new pool, which will be attached to the south side of the Gymnasium. The new building will incorporate a pool 25 yards long, and changing facilities which will be used for visiting teams in all sports."[29]

The arena and pool were only a small part of the happenings on campus. The Raymond Massey Library and the science labs were opened in 1973. "The school grounds received a beauty treatment. And, most significantly, the Science and Resources Centre came into existence. Construction on the centre got under way in February 1972, and by the following Thanksgiving, it was opened to reveal three spacious labs and enough resource material in books, films, tapes, journals, maps, slides and flat pictures to satisfy the needs of all the inquiring young minds in all the grades of Appleby students."[30]

Naturally the Women's Association sold hockey shirts, swimming trunks and other necessities for rink or pool and provided books for the library. Each successive decade became busier at the school. There were more students enrolled, more faculty and staff. The mothers were more involved trying to keep up with the ever expanding needs of masters and students.

The first Country Fair was held in the fall of 1975. This was an enormous undertaking, demanding a great deal of the mothers' winter, spring and summer time. The first fair generated over $5,000 in profit. But more than money was made. Many friendships formed (this was true in all the years of the Women's/Parents' Association) and much fun was had. It has often been said that the resume a volunteer could put together (particularly an Appleby volunteer) would be astounding.

The first Appleby Cookbook, Bon Appetit Appleby was published; another major project that would be replicated in 1993 with A Taste of Appleby, and again in 2003 with another new cookbook. As always great fun was had, much was learned and treasured friendships were built.

During these years the Women's Association met the needs and wishes of students and Headmaster. Bursaries, trophy cases, screen and projector, library books and dozens of other items were donated to the school. Family picnics were held to the enjoyment of so many.

In the 1980's the first Art Auction/Dinner Dance was held with great success. More such evenings would follow. The Fall Fair continued with great enthusiasm but the women realized that with much less effort (Art Auction/Dinner Dance) a good deal of money could be raised. The first Art Auction generated over $8,000, the last Fall Fair over $13,000 but with such great effort and so much of everyone's summer time. The

[28] The Appleby Story, by Jack Batten.
[29] The Appleby Quarterly, January 1970, Vol. 2 – No. 1
[30] The Appleby Story, by Jack Batten.

Pot Luck, 1997
Campbell MacKay and Gale Salema

Bookers Evening, 1997
Author Naoko Matsubana
with David Boyd,
Appleby's In-House Author

Fall Fair was discontinued after 1983 and a pot luck luncheon was held in the fall. This luncheon was attended by mothers and faculty members. It proved to be much fun and a wonderful way of mixing. It is still held in 2003 with great attendance and amusement. For several years in the nineties it was held in conjunction with a book fair. As the school aged (the younger grades were done away with) there was less interest in a book fair.

In 1988 the Women's Association celebrated 'The Bursary Ball'. The Association was 60 years old and it seemed a wonderful way to celebrate. A silent auction was held, dinner and dancing. It was most successful bringing in over $57,000 for the Bursary Fund and great friendship and fellowship for the committee and a fun evening for the guests.

The first Parent Handbook was created in the 80's. This handy guide is still in use today. It has been revamped a number of times and is no longer a parent publication but does have Parents' Association input.

The 80's saw the opening of the Bookstore on campus. This was innovative, convenient and a real money maker. The Bookstore served the school for over ten years and generated thousands of dollars of revenue and more important thousands of hours of volunteerism. The volunteering brought much warmth and personality to Appleby. The hours shared in that Bookstore add greatly to the history of the Women's/Parents' Association. So many friendships were formed while working in the Bookstore or indeed anywhere on campus. So much of the Association is a sharing with others and a caring for Appleby. The seeds that Lady Baillie planted blossomed into such a huge organization of altruism yes but friendship, fellowship and so much more.

During each decade much more occurred at the school and within the Association than is glimpsed here. This is merely to inform the reader of the overall goodwill of the Association. In the Comprehensive History section, more detail is given.

Colley House was renovated in the '80's and the Women's Association was quick to decorate and furnish the common room. The Nicholas Arts Centre was opened in 1985. More land was acquired in 1987 and again in the 90's.

In 1986 the school celebrated its 75th anniversary. Headmaster, Alexis Troubetzkoy, (he served from 1981-1987), wrote "Let us rejoice, also, in our present. We have one of the finest and certainly most beautiful school plants in Canada, a student body and teaching staff of exceptional quality and varied, well developed programmes which enhance the totality of training the boy is offered."[31] The Premier of Ontario, David Peterson, wrote "A great debt of gratitude is owed to all those who have contributed to the outstanding success of the College since its founding in 1911. It is my sincere hope that it will continue to make a significant contribution to the optimum development of the young men of the province for many years to come."[32] And finally, Peter Cameron[48], Chairman of the Board, 1980-1985, said "More remarkable, perhaps is the increasing success of the programmes and fund-raising of the Women's Association, at a time when a majority of Appleby mothers hold part-time jobs. There may have been a day when Appleby was run by the Chairman of the Board and the Headmaster. The

---

[31] The Quarterly, 75th Anniversary Souvenir Edition.
[32] Ibid.

*Linda Hatch preparing Chapel
for House Tour 2000*

October, 1997 - United Way - 5K Walk
*Many Appleby parents and pets participate in the Oakville Independent
Schools' Parent / Teacher 5K Old Oakville walk for the United Way*

vigorous, growing School of the 1980's seeks the participation of many. Parents enrolling their sons at Appleby join a community which depends on their participation in the School and offers a variety of avenues by which this may be accomplished."[33] The Women's Association helped with the year long celebrations.

The 80's brought the school several Headmasters. Jack Dickens was acting Headmaster from spring 1980 until spring 1981 at which time Alexis Troubetzkoy returned to Appleby as Headmaster. Alexis Troubetzkoy had been a master at the school in the late 60's. He went on to head Selwyn House (Montreal) in 1971, until he was called back to head Appleby College. In 1987 Alexis Troubetzkoy left for the Toronto French School and Guy McLean was named Headmaster. "In making the announcement in late July, Board Chairman Pearce Bunting said: 'Mr. McLean has shown leadership, scholarship and administrative ability, coupled with a thorough knowledge of Appleby's mission and goals. These qualities make him an excellent choice as a leader for the school.'"[34]

The 1990's heralded much change at Appleby, the first alteration being the renaming of the Women's Association to the Parents' Association. The school went co-ed in the early '90's and saw the end of grades four through six. The Association never missed a beat. It continued to look after the needs and wants of the students and the Headmaster. "Maggie Larock thanked all the volunteers who worked so diligently throughout the school year. She reviewed the activities of the Women's Association, including the Fall Grade Parties, Friday the 13th Barbecue, November Pot Luck, Canadian Tire Money Blitz, Tuition Draw, as well as all the volunteer efforts in the College Shop, Library, Bookstore, Telephone Committee, Fulford Cup Debates, and the Board Auction."[35]

The auction was and is a Board initiative but the parents truly run it hand in hand with Appleby's faculty and staff. The Auction Committees are listed in the appendix.

There was tremendous growth at the school in the '90's with the opening of the Student Health Centre, Athletic Therapy Centre, Baillie House, new faculty housing, the artificial turf and the bubble, new Powell's House and the Colin W. Beasley[*] Technology Centre. There were changes to the infrastructure, the birth of the e-school and much more. Change can cause controversy. Guy McLean said, "For each generation, each class, and even each student, the traditions and characteristics which form the core of the Appleby experience will be unique. It is our nature that we choose to remember our personal experiences as special, even when they are not always positive. As Appleby changes and evolves, for most associated with the school in the past, the new is viewed through the lens of personal experience and history. It is a challenge for any of us to watch dispassionately as something which played such an important role in our lives evolves to meet the needs of current and future generations of students. Change is both necessary and inevitable, but it must be achieved in a context that recognizes the contributions of those who came before, and values the traditions of the past, as well as the new traditions being established today for future generations. …

---

[33] The Quarterly, 75th Anniversary Souvenir Edition.
[34] The Appleby Quarterly, August 1987, Special.
[35] The A.C.W.A. minutes, May 2nd, 1990.
[*] Colin W. Beasley, a generous parent.

House Tour Tea
Nancy Baillie (Jim '37) & Marion Ferris (Frank Baillie '31)

Pot Luck, 2000
Standing: Judith Nestmann, Barbara Carrick, Deb Sewell, Sandy White, Jill Edmonson
Seated: Cherie Duval, Catherine Raaflaub, Judy Mills, Sue Baillie (Rusty '66)

Pot Luck, 2000
Standing: Diane Boston, Ann Veel, Oddny Cook
Seated: Maureen Collins, Deborah Sibbald, John Berriman, Mary Anne Sarne, Jane Muddiman

"Appleby, like most great institutions, is a school led by its traditions, not bound by them. Whatever your memories of Appleby or your opinion of the changes which have transpired since your days as a student, I hope you will come back to campus this spring and rediscover pride and spirit in your Appleby College."[36]

Through all the change the Parents' Association carried on with great strength and determination to fill the needs as they arose. The needs of the school became greater. With the introduction of an e-school there was an ever growing need for technological additions to the school. CD-Roms, computer labs, printers, Physical-Education software, thousands of dollars for computer equipment and more in the technology sector was given by the Parents' Association. The traditional donation to the Bursary was honoured and its minimum in the 90's was $15,000 annually, on one occasion $25,000.

The Association has never been idle. In 1992 the first House Tour was held to great acclaim. The most recent House Tour (2002) generated more than $50,000. Once again it was not a case of only money but also the wonderful goodwill generated for the school and the great sharing that took and takes place with the parents and all those involved.

The Interguild Annual General Meeting was held at Appleby for a second time. The women had hosted them in the 80's and once again in the 90's. This too generated great goodwill for the school and a tremendous sharing with the parents and staff involved.

The Parents' Association pledged $100,000 to Powell's House in 1996-1997 and completed that pledge in 2000-2001. There were numerous other gifts made by the Association.

The Association continues to give as it has always done, the areas of giving have expanded but so too has everything about Appleby. The 90's were years of great change, challenge and accomplishment.

The Parents' Association and Appleby College entered the new century faced with the challenge of hosting the Round Square Conference, a formidable task. As always the Appleby family rose to the occasion and surpassed their expectations. "More than two year's planning came to fruition when delegates began arriving on campus from all over the world on Day 1 of the conference. All those who worked hard on their individual committees held their collective breath in those first few days, but it was soon clear the hours and hours of preparation were well worth it."[37] Nothing has rivaled the success of this conference or will soon do so for some time. Everyone involved or in attendance was most impressed with the smooth running of the Appleby family with its best foot forward.

Today the campus boasts 59 plus acres of land, the chapel, four residences, dining hall, health centre, therapy centre, gymnasium, classroom building, science labs, library, the arts centre, the technology centre, the bubble[*], the arena, the pool, the barn and the staff houses. The Parents' Association continues to carry out the mandate that Lady Baillie penned in 1928 "to further the welfare of the school and add to the comfort of the

---

[36] The Appleby Quarterly, April 1995, Volume 17/Number1.
[37] The Appleby Quarterly, Winter 2000, Volume 22, Issue 2.
[*] The artificial turf is covered in the winter and makes for more athletic space.

AGM, 2003
Aubrey Baillie'⁶³ and Nancy Baillie (Jim'³⁷)

AGM 2000
Standing: Stefa Williams, Karen Bergin, David Paul, Vicki Lydall
Seated: Bev Paul, Mags Shorey, Vicki Kennan, Jeannie Osmak

Masters and boys." In 2003 read that as the teachers and students. It is still the wonderful organization which Lady Baillie started but it has evolved from an infant to a full grown and wonderfully mature adult. It will continue to grow with the spirit and love with which Lady Baillie and friends imbued it 75 years ago. They would be proud.

New Appleby College Gates, 2003

COMPREHENSIVE HISTORY

Appleby School Women's Association

HON.-PRES. MRS. J. S. H. GUEST
PRES. LADY BAILLIE
VICE-PRES. MRS. E. F. OSLER

COMMMITTEE:

MRS. E. H. AMBROSE   MRS. W. S. DAVIS
MRS. W. T. MARLATT   MRS. J. B. McLEOD

Assoc. 1929

Some friends of Appleby School have decided that an association of women such as other schools have, would further the welfare of the school and add to the comfort of the Masters and boys.

Such an association has been formed with the name "Appleby School Women's Association." It has been proposed that all mothers and sisters of Appleby School boys, past and present, should be invited to join, also wives and daughters of old boys.

The object of this Association is to provide funds to improve the equipment of the school by adding to the furnishing of the houses and the hospital, and to assist in beautifying the chapel.

I hope that you will consent to become a member of this Association. There are no obligations except an annual subscription of $5.00.

Will you kindly send this fee to the address given below and let us know what you think about the Association?

We intend to hold a meeting on the annual Sports Day in May, and hope that all members who have enrolled by that time will be present to elect new officers and give suggestions.

Yours truly,

Address:-

Lady Baillie,
    Appleby School,
        Oakville, Ont.

Edith Baillie
President

*1929 Letter from Lady Baillie outlining the creation of the
Appleby College Women's Association*

This history is based mainly on the minutes of the Association, <u>The Argus</u>, <u>The Appleby Quarterly</u> and the recall of a number of members of the 'Appleby Family'. From 1928 to 1932 the minutes were either not kept or they were misplaced. We have a few sketchy notes from these early years. In fact Lady Baillie met with friends in 1928 and decided to form an Association "to further the welfare of the school and add to the comfort of the Masters and boys." This is attested to in a letter written by Lady Baillie to the mothers of the boys. I gather that after her initial meeting with friends they had stationery drawn up and decided how they would operate. This was outlined in the same letter of 1929. "...all mothers and sisters of Appleby School boys, past and present, should be invited to join, also wives and daughters of old boys." There would be an annual fee of $5.00 and the first meeting would be held on the annual May Sports Day.

1928-1929   *Headmaster – John Guest 1911-1934*
President   **Lady Baillie**

- First annual meeting held in Powell's House on May 23rd, 1929.
- The newly formed Association had 70 members.
- Their goal, for the year, was to raise funds to complete the Chapel in time for school opening in September.

In speaking of the Chapel, in 1929 it was written, "Although the fact it will stand as a permanent memorial to those who gave their lives for their country gives it special significance, yet it is hoped that all will realize what an important place it will take in the School, and will make a special effort to aid the Women's Association in their effort to ensure that the completed building shall be as beautiful as possible."[38]

1929-1930
President   **Lady Baillie**

- Provided the Dramatic Club with a beautiful new curtain for the front of the permanent stage in the gymnasium.
- Placed two handsome standard brass lamps in the Chapel.
- Continued to use Association funds to make the Memorial Chapel even more beautiful.
- They encouraged boys and Old Boys to have their mothers and sisters join the Association as soon as possible.

1930-1931
President   **Lady Baillie**

- "It was agreed that the Association (W.A.) should present to the school, standard lamps to be placed on the pillars recently erected at the main entrance from the highway."[39]
- The Association would order another window for the Chapel.

---

[38] The Argus, Volume 36, June 1929
[39] The Argus, Volume 40, June 1931

The Annual Meeting of the Appleby School Women's Association will be held in the Library of Powell's House at 2.00 p.m. on Saturday, May 16th, before the beginning of the Annual Games. It is hoped that all members will make a special effort to be present, and that any mothers or sisters of Appleby boys, who have not yet joined the Association, will take this opportunity of doing so, and will be present at the meeting.

Subscriptions ($5.00) for 1930-31 are now due and may be sent to the President, Lady Baillie, at Appleby School.

Notice of Annual Meeting, 1931

1931-1932

President   **Lady Baillie**

- Meeting held in the Reading Room of Powell's House.
- A fund was to be started for the Chapel organ.

1932-1933

President   **Lady Baillie**

- The meeting was held once again in Powell's Reading Room.
- $75.00 to be given to Mr. Wickens for Dramatic Club expenses.
- Planned on hosting an informal tea in the form of an informal meeting to keep members interested.

1933-1934   *Headmaster – Percival Wickens 1934-1937*

President   **Lady Baillie**

- 78 letters were sent requesting present and back fees – 12 paid, 14 resigned and 52 did not answer. It was decided to write once again and ask for fees.
- "It was with regret we heard of the resignation of Mr. Guest who has been such an excellent Headmaster for so many years. It was also felt that there was no one who could carry on more capably than Mr. Wickens."[40]
- Spent $300.00 on new bed covers in the School colours.

1934-1935

President   **Lady Baillie**

- *A point of interest – in the minutes of 1935 the Association is referred to as The Appleby College Women's Association not The Appleby **School** Women's Association as it was previously referred to. The name Appleby College was not officially adopted by the school until 1941.*
- $175.00 was spent on chairs and some library books.
- Mrs. W. G. Thompson presented the school with a much needed Encyclopedia.
- It was suggested that fees be reduced from $5.00 to $2.00 because so much was expected from members. Lady Baillie suggested that Associates (members other than parents) pay $1.00. *(Often the women were asked for funds on top of the membership fee.)*
- It was decided that there should be two meetings a year, one in the fall, the other in the spring.
- Brass plates were placed in the Chapel to bear the names of those who donated special gifts to the Chapel.
- The showers and bathrooms were improved.

---

[40] The A.C.W.A. minutes of May 12th, 1934

1937

Appleby School Women's Association

HON.-PRES. MRS. J. S. H. GUEST
PRES. LADY BAILLIE
VICE-PRES. MRS. E. F. OSLER

COMMITTEE :

MRS. E. H. AMBROSE   MRS. W. S. DAVIS
MRS. W. D. ROSS   MRS. J. B. McLEOD
MRS. B. P. ALLEY   MRS. A. F. JENNINGS

The Annual Meeting, held last February in Toronto at Lady Baillie's house, was well attended.

It was decided to enrol Associate Members in addition to the Sustaining Members. Whereas the subscription for Sustaining Members is five dollars annually, that for Associate Members will be one dollar. Membership will be open to all mothers and sisters of past and present pupils, wives of masters and Old Boys and any others who would be willing to take an active part in the work of the Association. A committee was formed under Mrs. H.W. Weis to organise the decorating of the Library, the Prefects' Room, the Masters' Room and the Headmaster's office. A grant of $250 was made to this committee to cover the cost of material, curtains, paint, etc., and to provide new cushions. This work has been carried out most satisfactorily and Mrs. Weis and her Committee have been well supported by an enthusiastic group of Associate Members, who have made curtains, cushion covers, table covers and so on. A letter expressing deep appreciation of the work done by this section of the Association has been received from the Headmaster.

A grant of one hundred dollars towards the new potato peeler was approved.

Subscriptions for 1936, not yet paid, should be forwarded at once to Mrs. D.F. Benson, 30 Roxborough St. E., Toronto.

Balance Sheet for 1936:

Income	Expenditure	
By Subscriptions - $450.93	Mrs. Weis and her Committee -	$250.00
	Potato Peeler -	100.00
	Printing -	1.00
		351.00
	Cash in Hand -	99.93
		450.93

Report to Members, 1937

38

- *It was written in the Argus of 1935 that "The Association is an entirely independent organization and was formed originally to be free to use its funds in providing some things which the school authorities would not feel called upon to budget for in the ordinary way."*
- Assigned a New Mothers representative to welcome and inform them.

1935-1936
President   **Lady Baillie**

- Meeting held at home of Lady Baillie in Toronto.
- The Associate members were asked to give their time sewing etc.
- New chairs and/or a piano were not wanted at this time.
- A committee was formed to approach the school about new curtains, fresh paint, table cloth in the masters' sitting room, a rug, anything necessary to make the school more attractive.
- It was voted to give the committee $250.00.
- Perhaps Mr. Wickens would allow some of the boys to help spruce up the school.
- $100.00 was given towards a new or second-hand potato peeler.
- Executive Committee members are to wear name tags at Sports Day and other School events.
- Lady White♥ donated $15.00 towards a Reference Library.

1936-1937
President   **Lady Baillie**

- Meeting held at home of Lady Baillie.
- Lady White gave Mr. Wickens two lovely rugs, one for his office.
- The potato peeler was purchased.
- $212.00 was spent on painting the hospital.*
- An organ was needed in the Chapel. An organ without pipes would cost $2,000.00. There was discussion how funds should be raised.
- Suggested to the Board that the second Floor of School House *(now called Colley House)* be painted.
- The Reading Room in School House, or Senior Common Room as it is now called, was entirely redecorated, all soft seating and chairs reupholstered in comfortable leather. Very attractive curtains were made by members.
- A billiard table cover was made.
- New cushions and curtains were also made and placed in the Prefects' room, the Masters' room and the Headmaster's office.
- Mr. Wickens stated "The A.S.W.A. are keeping up the splendid work they have done for a number of years: as we go to press the Association is having the School hospital decorated inside. All the rooms are being painted and blinds and curtains

---

♥ Perhaps Lady White was a relative of Lady Baillie. There is no documentation as to who she was.
* Hospital, infirmary and health centre are synonymous. This was/is the place on campus where one sought/seeks medical attention.

Dr. Bell
Late 1930's

Campus Life? circa 1930

are being placed in the windows. At a recent meeting it was decided to make a special effort to assist the School in obtaining an organ for the Chapel as soon as possible. Approximately $2,000.00 remains to be collected to make it possible to go ahead with the work."[41]

- The project for the year was to have the hospital entirely decorated.
- *Of interest's sake – the fees for boarders were $750.00 per annum and for day boys $180.00 per annum.*

1937-1938   *Headmaster – John Bell 1937-1968*

President   **Lady Baillie**

- The June 17th, 1938 meeting was held at 'Lisonally Farm', the Oakville home of Lady Baillie.
- Mrs. Holden donated $50.00 to help with the hospital decorating.
- Lady Baillie gave new curtains and rods for the dining room. *(The dining room was not The John Guest Hall we know today but was an earlier dining room in the basement of School House (Colley House)).*
- Wishes for next year   1: book shelves were needed for School House reading room on which would be placed reference books. These shelves were made to match the existing book shelves but had glass doors.

    2: lights for School House reading room and semi-indirect lighting at a cost of $55.00

    3: 2 lamps and semi-indirect lighting for Powell's House reading room at a cost of $33.00.

    4: The dining room needs 6 lights, semi-indirect lighting at a cost of $107.40.

    5: Ten cassocks for Junior choir boys at an approximate cost of $100.00. They would be double breasted dark blue with light blue cords.

    6: Painting $100.00.

    7: Floor tile for the kitchen at a cost of $85.00.

    After some discussion item numbers 4 and 5 were deferred, the other items would be looked after.
- Lady Baillie suggested that parents of new boys be advised of the Association and that a list of accomplishments to date be drawn up and forwarded to new parents.
- The first Telephone Committee was established.
- Mr. Wickens had cancer and passed away.[42]
- Mr. J. A. M. Bell was appointed Headmaster thus Mrs. Guest was no longer Honorary President. Mrs. Bell became the Honorary President.
- Mrs. D. F. Benson was named the President of the Women's Association. "Mr. Bell thanked Lady Baillie and congratulated Mrs. Benson he hoped she would carry on in her mother's footsteps.'"[43]
- Lady Baillie elected Honorary President. (now there were two!)

---

[41] The Argus, Volume 45, February 1937

[42] Information learned from Michael DesRoches'62 , Appleby Archivist

[43] The A.C.W.A. minutes of June 17, 1938.

Appleby School Women's Association

Mr. Bell has invited the Women's Association to hold their Annual Meeting at a Luncheon at the School at 1 o'clock (D.S.T.) on Friday, May 12th, (half term week-end.)

A prompt reply is requested to—
Miss Lightbourn, in care Appleby School, Oakville.

Your subscription for 1939 is now due and may be paid at this meeting. $1.00 Associate, $5.00 Sustaining.

Invitation to Luncheon, 1939

Cadets in Navy Uniforms
Late 1930's

- *A point of interest – "On July 7 Lady Baillie entertained Old Boys and their wives from 6:00 to 8:00 o'clock on the lawns of her home "Lisonally Farm", Oakville to meet Reverend and Mrs. Bell, the newly appointed Headmaster and his wife."*[44] *There were 100 in attendance.*

1938-1939

President   **Mrs. D. F. Benson**♥

- The meeting was held at the school with a lunch.
- The kitchen floor had been tiled. It was paid for with money from the Blue Bombers Rugby (football) Team from Winnipeg.[45]
- The members discussed having a speaker at their annual meetings.
- Ridley College Women's Guild invited two representatives from the A.C.W.A. to attend their Annual Meeting on Friday, May the 19th. The women agreed that the President and another member should attend. *(This would be the precursor of Interguild which would be formed in 1989, "with the goal of sharing information for the betterment of all member schools."*[46] *Today the President and other Executive members attend. The Association pays for two representatives to attend and the others pay their own way. At one time, as in 1939, this was a gratis invitation but as the years went by and costs rose it seemed expedient to have extra delegates pay their own way.)*
- It was decided that each year the two members who have served the longest on the Committee should retire and allow two new members to be elected.
- An organ and screen were installed in the Chapel thanks to Lady Baillie, Mr. J. D. Carruthers and Mrs. Walker. *Of interest – a new pipe organ is being installed in the Chapel and will be ready to be played in the fall of 2003.*
- New pews were needed for the Chapel at a cost of $235.00 and a new Union Jack was needed.
- It was agreed that the Annual General Meeting (A.G.M.) be held on the first day of half term week-end. That would be the May long week-end.

1939-1940

President   **Mrs. D. F. Benson**

- The Annual General Meeting was held prior to the Cadet Inspection. There were 43 members in attendance.
- Mrs. A. P. Mills donated a new Union Jack to the school.

---

[44] The Argus, Volume 46, March 1938

♥ Marion Benson, eldest daughter of Lady Baillie.

[45] Cindy Galway (Mrs. J.) said that the Blue Bombers Rugby Team stayed in Burlington at the Pig and Whistle in the summer and practiced on the Appleby playing fields. This generated some funds.

[46] Guildlines, 4th issue, Spring 1995, Letter from Rosemary McIntosh – Trinity College School, President of Interguild. Edited by Sue Baillie (Rusty '66) – St. Mildred's Lightbourn School and Appleby College, Sandy McDonald – Havergal College and Mags Shorey – Appleby College

Appleby School Women's Association

HON.-PRES. MRS. J. A. M. BELL
HON.-PRES. LADY BAILLIE
PRES. MRS. DONALD BENSON
VICE-PRES. MRS. E. F. OSLER
HON. SEC. TREAS. MRS. HENRY HILL

COMMITTEE :

MRS. E. H. AMBROSE   MRS. ALFRED BUNTING
MRS. W. D. ROSS   MRS. HUGH DENISON
MRS. B. P. ALLEY   MRS. J. W. LITTLE

At the annual meeting of the Appleby Women's Association which was held in June at the home of the President, Lady Baillie, the following changes were made in the committee: -

Mrs. Guest resigned as Hon.-Pres., and Mrs. Bell was elected to take her place.
Lady Baillie resigned as Pres., and Mrs. Benson elected as President.
Mrs. Osler was appointed as Vice-President.
Mrs. Hill was appointed as Hon.-Sec.-Treas.
Mrs. Bunting, Mrs. Hugh Denison and Mrs. Little were new members appointed on the committee.

Receipts		Expenditures	
Membership Fees	$ 389.62	Reg. A. Cozens, Gen. Electrician, Lights, wiring &c., Powell's and School House, Reading Room & Dining Room -	$ 200.00
		Duty on Cassocks -	15.85
		J. Whipple & Co. Ltd., Cassocks	75.35
		Book Cases -	
		H. Parnaby	22.20
		Davis & Doty	12.21
		J. Mathias	3.75
	$ 389.62		$ 329.36
	329.36		
Balance, Oct. 12th	$ 60.26		

The fees for 1939 are now due and cheques should be made payable at par in Oakville and sent to Mrs. Henry Hill, Hon.-Sec.-Treas., Colborne Street, Oakville.

Meeting Record, mailed to members of the Women's Association, 1939

- Mrs. J. B. Holden gave a lathe and jigsaw (fret saw mentioned in one spot) for the workshop.
- The pews were installed in the Chapel.
- Donated $50.00 for books for the reference library and expect this to become an annual donation.
- 50 chairs would be purchased and an oriental rug for Mr.[*] Bell's office.

1940-1941
President   **Mrs. D. F. Benson**

- Provided a new billiard table cover for the Main House (Colley House).
- $50.00 given for reference books for the library.
- Additional money used for entertainment for the boys. (No elaboration or explanation given as to amount of money or type of entertainment.)
- A dance committee was formed.
- Dr. Bell informed the W.A. that the English boys needed spending money – this would be looked after by the Association.

1941-1942
President   **Mrs. D. F. Benson**

- The Annual General Meeting was held on May 15, 1942. There were 33 members present. Due to inclement weather the meeting was held in the skating rink.[47]
- A Christmas and a June dance were held for the boys. These were very successful and would be carried on in years to come.
- $50.00 was given for reference books.
- 60 new Indian print bedspreads were provided.
- $30.00 was given to purchase movies for the boys.
- $50.00 for the hospital.
- $50.00 for the Junior Common Room
- Mr. Bell addressed the W.A. as he did every year. "He took this opportunity of thanking Mrs. Benson for her untiring efforts in the past, and also thanked Mrs. Hart, Miss Stone, Mrs. Green and Mrs. Slater for their work in connection with the school dances. He remarked how nice it was to have Lady Baillie living near again, as she had always taken such an active interest in the school. Mr. Bell thanked the Committee for the new spreads in the boys' bedrooms, and also for

---

[*] Mr. Bell is referred to as Mr. Bell, Dr. Bell and Canon Bell – Cindy Galway, daughter of Dr. Bell, explained that he was awarded an Honorary Doctorate of Divinity from Trinity College in 1951, University of Toronto and was made a Canon by the Niagara Diocese of the Anglican Church, 1956.

[47] Mrs. D. M. Dewar (wife the assistant Headmaster and House Master of Powell's House at that time) stated that the skating rink was located in the field by Powell's House. *As a matter of interest – Mrs. Dewar said that boys would skate and come into her home, two by two, for hot chocolate as they came off the rink or those who were flooding the rink overnight would do the same.* The rink was provided by Lady Baillie in 1927. It provided a great deal of pleasure and sport.

Mimi Home,
In Front of Old Gym
Early 1940's

Mimi Home & Cindy Galway
(Daughters of Dr. Bell)
Near Colley House Tennis Courts, 1940's

the new reference books in the library, the latter being probably one of the best gifts they receive. He said that last year the books were mostly for smaller boys and he hoped that in the future they might be able to get some on travel or biography. He expressed a desire to have the parents bring him any suggestions or criticisms which would be beneficial to the boys' welfare."[48] Dr. Bell also stated that there would be a church parade on May 24th because the Inspection had been rained out.

- It was found that the English boys did not need spending money after all.
- *Of interest – A mother and son tea was held annually.*
- $15.00 was collected for a gift for Miss James[49] to thank her for all her thoughtfulness.
- Mrs. D. Benson resigned and Mrs. R. R. Hart was elected the next President.

1942-1943
President   **Mrs. R. R. Hart**

- Annual General Meeting held at the home of Mrs. J. Bell, there were 20 members present.
- Mother and son tea had not been held in the fall.
- 3-$5.00 Eaton credit slips (gift certificates) had been given to Miss James.
- $50.00 for the reference library.
- About 40 Cadet Corps uniforms were in bad condition and needed to be replaced. Mr. Bell had been given two grants to assist in getting new ones but could use some more financial help. It was decided to give $100.00 towards cadet uniforms. Mrs. Hart told the gathering that "the Officers inspecting the Cadet Corps were full of praise and said 'We have never seen the head of a Cadet Corps taking Command for one hour and forty-five minutes in such perfect manner as was done by Bremner Green.'"[50]
- $30.00 would be given annually for movies for the boys as long as this need existed.
- "Other donations for this year were big lights, posters and a pair of curtains for the Junior Common Rooms. An electric freezing room. Dishes-instruments and new linoleum for the Hospital floor."[51]

1943-1944
President   **Mrs. R. R. Hart**

- Annual General Meeting held in Toronto at the home of Mrs. H. W. Weis. There were 33 members present.

---

[48] The ACWA minutes May 15, 1942
[49] Mrs. D. M. Dewar said that Miss James was "head of the kitchen in Colley House – she was not a dietician but was a school matron." As the school matron, Miss James was in charge of all the school's domestic services.
[50] The ACWA minutes May 21st, 1943
[51] Ibid

JEWELRY PRICE LIST

Appleby Crests - Sterling	$3.10
Tie Tack - Sterling	3.55
Pin - clutch back, Sterling	3.25
Bracelet with charm, Sterling	10.50
Charm - Sterling	6.90
Charm - 10K. Gold	18.50
Cuff Links - Sterling	10.75
Cuff Links - Metal gilt	7.85
Key Ring - silver metal	3.50
Rings:	
Sterling	11.25
Sterling with blue stone	19.75
10 K. Gold	33.95
10 K. Gold with blue stone	42.50
Wallet - brown leather	4.50
Parker Jotter Pen	10.75
Parker Jotter Pen - smaller	8.25
Zippo Lighter - engraved with	
School Crest	5.00

(5 weeks delivery)

Plus 5% Sales Tax on all items.

A note regarding rings.
      When an order is received for a School ring,
Miss Wethey in the School office will size your son's finger.

      Since our jewelry "business" is small,
we have been asked by our suppliers to facilitate matters and
place our orders four times a year - therefore, jewelry should
be ordered with the following dates in mind:-

          October 15th
          November 15th
          February 15th
          May 1st.

      Orders may be placed by mail. Please include
cheque at the time of your order. (Be sure to add 5% Sales Tax
to prices quoted.) Cheques are to be made payable to Appleby
College Women's Association and sent to:
          Mrs. B. B. Green
          1335 Cambridge Drive,
          Oakville, Ontario.
          845-6074

      Jewelry will be on display and orders may be
placed at the Women's Association Autumn Meeting.

Jewellery Price List, circa 1970's

- Suggested that Head Boys from other Colleges be invited to the dances, with Mr. Bell's approval.
- A stained glass window for the Chapel had been given by Lady Baillie in appreciation of the influence the College had on her sons. (see back cover)
- Life membership was begun. For a fee of $25.00 one could become a life member and receive the Association and College mailings. *Today the fee for Life Membership is $50.00.*
- $50.00 given for reference books.
- $30.00 donated for movies.
- A movie screen was donated.
- W.A. would like a reporter to be present at all W.A. activities.
- There was a discussion on smoking and the possibility of a smoking room but the members felt this should definitely not be considered.
- Thanked Miss James, the cook, Miss Niblett, the nurse and the Misses Marsden for sewing and all the extra things they did for the boys. A silver collection was to be given to them and a fund was to be started by the boys.
- *Of interest – Mr. Bell spoke and said that there were 89 boarders and 24 day boys, of these 18 were from England. Cubs were started at the school under the leadership of Mr. Gladman, there were 30 of them. The first musical evening was held at the school. There were 550 old boys at this time and 275 of them were in uniform. There were plans for an addition to Powell's House – that would have been to the Master's residence.*

1944-1945
President   **Mrs. C. B. Green**[♥]

- As it was war time there was a shortage of help at the school and it was decided that a Fall Annual General Meeting would be more suitable to everyone involved.
- The meeting took place in November at the home of Mrs. J. Bell.
- The Association sponsored the dances over the year. The December 1944 dance was held at the Oakville Club and it was a Cadet Corps dance. For the December 1945 dance they invited Cadet Corps officers from the other schools.
- $50.00 for reference books.
- $30.00 for movies.
- It was decided that some money be given for Manual Training (carpentry) at the school.
- A representative was assigned for each class to advise parents of upcoming rugby games so they would get out and support the teams.

1945-1946
President   **Mrs. F. Milligan**

♥ Edith Green, second daughter of Lady Baillie.

<u>Constitution</u>

1946

Name: Appleby College Women's Association.

Object: To enable the mothers to take an active interest
           in the comfort and well-being of the boys through
           co-operation with the Headmaster. To provide
           extra equipment such as books, films, etc.

Members: Mothers and sisters of boys attending the School;
           mothers, wives, ~~and~~ sisters of Old Boys, *and friends of the School*

Fees: The Fees are two dollars per annum, payable in
           October. Life Membership - $25.00.

Officers: Hon. President
           Hon. Vice President
           President
           Vice President — *2nd Vice Pres.*
           Secretary
           Treasurer
           A Committee of six to be elected at the Annual
           Meeting, leaving one vacancy to be filled in
           the fall.

           An absence of any member of the Executive from
           three consecutive meetings automatically creates
           a vacancy. *No member shall hold the same office for more than two years.*

Meetings: The Executive shall hold a meeting during the first
           two weeks of April. The Annual Meeting to be held in
           the spring after this meeting. The Fall Meeting of
           the Executive shall be held during the first week in
           October and the General Meeting to be held during
           the same month.

Banking: The funds must be deposited under the name of the
           Appleby College Women's Association. Cheques to be
           signed by the President and Treasurer.

Appleby College Women's Association Constitution, 1946

50

- The Annual General Meeting was held in May at the home of Mrs. J. Bell. There were 32 members present.
- Association voted to refurnish the Chapel gallery. Pews were installed with the capacity of 45 people at a cost of $616.00.
- A simple constitution was drawn up and circulated to the parents and would be discussed at the Fall Meeting.
- It was decided to have a 2nd Vice-President and a Secretary.
- Mothers and wives of old boys who lost their lives in the war were made honorary Life Members.

1946-1947
President   **Mrs. F. Milligan**

- The Constitution was adopted.
- Each member was asked for $2.00 in talent[52] money. This money went towards curtains or furnishings for the new building.
- Mr. Bell thanked the Association for the pews for the Chapel gallery, this would allow more to attend the Carol Service. Mr. Bell also had the plans for the new addition, this would be what we know today as the classroom building.
- The annual monies were donated - $50.00 for reference books and $30.00 for movies.
- 2 dozen Prayer Books and Hymn Books were donated.
- At the end of the meeting box lunches were distributed. The women felt that the boys' Tea Dance which was taking place on the same day should take precedence so they settled for box lunches.

1947-1948
President   **Mrs. H. P. Bellingham**

- Annual General Meeting was held in the Powell's House Common Room, there were 43 present.
- The Prayer Books which were to come from England were held up for 6 to 8 months.
- Mr. Bell suggested an attendance book be purchased and kept for signing by each member attending meetings. (This was used until the AGM April 2, 1970.)
- A report of the meeting was sent to the Globe and Mail for insertion in the Social Column and the Fall Meeting was advertised in the same paper in the Announcements Column. It was felt that publicity should be sought for the school.
- $50.00 for reference books was held as requested by Mr. Bell.
- Each member must raise $25.00, $5.00 each year for the next five years. These monies would be used for the furnishing of a room in the new classroom building.

---

[52] Money earned through bake sales, bridge parties or whatever held by individual members.

James'³⁷ & Nancy Baillie, 1946

Sports Day, 1948

In addition to this each member was expected to raise $5.00 for the pews in the Chapel.

- Association members were sent lists of all mothers of boys at the school.
- $30.00 for movies.
- School dances were sponsored, decorated and paid for by the W.A.
- A radio was provided for small boys in School House (Colley House)
- The Treasurer's books to be audited annually, this to be added to the Constitution.
- Mr. Bell addressed the Association and spoke of the past 10 years. *Of interest – Mr. Bell said that $130,000.00 was in hand for the new [classroom] building and they hoped to begin construction in July 1948.*

1948-1949
President   **Mrs. H. P. Bellingham**

- The Annual General Meeting was held at the home of Mrs. J. Tomlinson on May 13th, 1949. It was felt that a change of venue was in order.
- It was suggested that a history of the Association be written.
- Since $70.00 was spent on the dance. Sandwiches were made at Mrs. Bell's home to keep costs down. "For future dances it was thought that as the school is in a better position as far as help is concerned that a donation to the orchestra might be sufficient."[53]
- Flowers had been sent to the bereaved family of Sergeant Major Clarke[54], the head of the Cadet Corps.
- Miss James had been very ill, flowers were also sent to her.
- Mesdames Pethwick and Tomlinson each donated a much needed choirboy cassock.
- Presented Hilda Chattaway[*] with a handbag as a going away gift. She was traveling to England for a holiday.

1949-1950
President   **Mrs. J. Tomlinson**

- Purchased bonds with monies in the 'Building Fund'[55] until such time as they would be needed.
- *Of interest - Lady Baillie "pointed out that 1949 was the 21st year of the organization. Lady Baillie had been present at the first meeting in 1928 and read a report from the Argus relating to it, and went on to recount the great pride felt by the original members in their first achievements, such as supplying curtains for certain rooms, cassocks for the choir, and getting the showers tiled. The first*

---

[53] The ACWA minutes April 19th, 1949
[54] Sergeant Major Clarke had been associated with the school for 29 years, from 1920 to 1949.
[*] Hilda was the much loved cook. Mrs. Dewar said that she arrived at the school in 1928.
[55] 'Building Fund' was a phrase which Lady Baillie disliked. She felt that the WA should provide furnishings. The Building Fund became the Library Fund, this would provide furnishings for the library. The A.C.W.A. minutes, October 28th, 1949.

Lady Baillie & Family, 1946

meeting was only attended by five members, the attendance today being 72. Lady Baillie spoke of the development of the Association and stressed the point that all the activities are well worthwhile."[56]

- *Another point of interest – "Mr. Bell paid a warm tribute to the late Mr. Colley, whose sudden death was a great loss to the College. It had been decided to rename School House 'Colley House' as a memorial tribute to the great services rendered by Mr. Colley during his 35 years residence."[57]*

- New pews for the Chapel were acquired at a cost of $822.96.

- The Association would use the library funds to furnish a temporary library until the new library would be completed.

- Struck a committee to source 2 chesterfields, 6 large chairs, 6 smaller chairs, and 1 large table.

- Allotted $500.00 to the Furniture Committee. It would be up to this committee, in accord with Mr. Bell, to choose furnishings for the library.

- Mrs. Tomlinson resigned, for personal reasons. Mrs. H. G. Pepall became President and presided over the May 26th meeting. This meeting was held at Mrs. Pepall's home in Erindale.

- Thanked Miss Lightbourn (worked in the front office) in recognition of the constant assistance given by her to the Association.

- "Mrs. Bellingham drew attention to the fact that at one time it had been decided to affix a plaque to any donation from the Appleby College Women's Association to commemorate the gift, this had not been done in all cases, the Executive agreed in future to attend to this matter."[58] *(To this day there has been discussion and consideration of placing a plaque on all contributions by the A.C.P.A. On occasion it has been done and at other times has fallen by the wayside.)*

1950-1951
President   **Mrs. H. G. Pepall**

- The Furniture Committee reported that Mrs. Pepall donated 1 chesterfield and they purchased the second. Mrs. Brouse donated 6 chairs, Mrs. Bull gave 2 tables and they purchased fabric for curtains.

- Mr. Bell addressed the assembly. He said how much books of all kinds were needed by the College. He thanked the Association members for all of their continued good work. He especially thanked those who donated furniture for the library.

- Mrs. Curran donated a map for the library.

- The Spring Meeting of the W.A. was held at the home of Mrs. R. G. Wace.

- The hospital was re-floored and redecorated.

---

[56] The A.C.W.A. minutes, October 28th, 1949.
[57] Ibid.
[58] The A.C.W.A. minutes, May 26th, 1950.

Chapel Choir, 1951 - 1952

The Womens' Association regularly provided new cassocks for the choir. Note the brass standard lamps on either side of the altar. These were among the first gifts the Womens' Association made to the Chapel and the School

- Mr. Bell showed a fabric that had been especially designed for Appleby, suitable for curtains and bedspreads.[59]
- All Masters' wives were to be honorary members of the Association and were welcome at all meetings.
- A radio-gramophone was to be purchased for the school.

1951-1952
President   **Mrs. H. G. Pepall**

- Mr. Bell wrote that he would prefer structural frames for outdoor basketball rather than a radio-gramophone. It was voted to proceed with this.
- $270.00 was put aside to purchase a tape recorder for the school.
- $300.00 donated to the school for the purchase of library books.
- Mrs. Russell donated a subscription to National Geographic and Mrs. Curran a subscription to Canadian Geographic.
- W.A. would donate $25.00 annually for the purchase of periodicals as approved by Mr. Bell.
- Mr. Bell addressed the meeting. He thanked the women for all they had done. He said the school was full to capacity with 186 boys – 22 new boarders and 15 new day boys. The dining room had been redecorated in the summer and had new curtains made of 'hop-sacking'. Mr. Bell went on to say that the ladies had all opposed the use of 'hop-sacking' but it was a great success. He spoke of a new Fire Protection Scheme that had been installed in Powell's House and the infirmary. "There are bells and a siren on every building and work has started on Colley House. Tennis Courts have been laid, and the back fence erected. The Special Platoon of the Cadet Corps did well in front of Princess (Queen) Elizabeth."[60] He also said that Junior Matriculation would now be called "Ontario Secondary School Graduation Diploma."
- 43 members attended the annual Spring Meeting at the home of Mrs. Pepall.
- $200.00 was set aside to purchase an electric stove for Mesdemoiselles James and Niblett who were retiring at the end of the school year.
- The Association would provide ice cream cones for the boys on Sports Day as long as the Headmaster agreed.
- Dr. Bell addressed the membership and his comments are *of interest – after all of his thanks to the members he said "The School has had a good year, the senior boys worked well and became adjusted to the idea of a certain standard of conduct, plus personal appearance. The Hockey Team gave a good account of itself, and there were 65 entries in a total of 71 Boxing bouts. The Choir won first place at the Kiwanis Festival, and was broadcast over CBC on Easter Sunday evening.*
  "Dr. Bell said both he and Mrs. Bell had greatly enjoyed their trip to Winnipeg and Calgary, at the instigation of the Board of Governors.

---

[59] Mrs. D. M. Dewar said it came in a number of shades and had the Appleby grey hound on it and was used for many things including clothing.
[60] The A.C.W.A. minutes, November 2nd, 1951.

Mrs. T.R. Deacon, 1953

Mrs. Deacon, President of the Women's Association, unveils a commemorative plaque at the base of a maple tree planted on the brow of the hill west of Colley House to honour the Corontation of Queen Elizabeth II. The ceremony took place on May 7, 1953, with the members of the Coronation Choir in the background.

" The Headmaster emphasized that education was a term of approximately twenty-five years. The most important lessons are:
1. *learning to think*
2. *expression in writing and words*
3. *to accept responsibility*
4. *and <u>most</u> important self-discipline."*[61]

1952-1953
President   **Mrs. T. R. Deacon**

- New cassocks were ordered from England at a cost of $250.00. These would be worn by the boys for the Coronation Tour.
- Suspended the Library Fund until the new library was completed. The temporary library was well furnished.
- The annual fee was once again raised to $5.00.
- Lady Baillie was presented with a corsage at the annual Fall Meeting in recognition of all that she had accomplished for the school and because it was the 24th anniversary of the Association.
- A publicity committee was set up under the direction of Mrs. Holden. Newspapers were to be approached and articles on the school submitted to them.
- Lady Baillie presented Dr. Bell with a barometer "as a token of our esteem since this year is also his 25th anniversary at Appleby College."[62]
- *Of interest-The Association Executive members were interested in perhaps having a day boy prefect be appointed, this question was addressed to Dr. Bell. Dr Bell responded "Prefects are chosen by the Headmaster, in consultation with the Housemaster. Any VIA or Grade 13 student is eligible, provided he has the qualifications necessary to fulfill the duties of a Prefect."[63] Continuing in the minutes it stated that "Dr. Bell would like to make it quite clear to the Members of the Women's Association, that there is no discrimination between Resident and Day pupils in sports, academics, privileges, or any honour to which the Headmaster, at his discretion, feels a student is entitled."[64]*
- "It was suggested that Mrs. Jamieson, in view of her many years of devoted interest in the welfare of Appleby College, be asked to accept an Honorary appointment on the Executive as representative of the Mothers of boys who served Overseas. This motion was adopted unanimously."[65]
- The Spring Meeting was held at the Oakville Club on April 13th, 1953.
- Mrs. Deacon suggested "that the section of the Constitution which reads 'no one shall hold the same office for more than two consecutive years' be amended as follows:- 'No one shall hold the same office for more than two consecutive years,

---

[61] The A.C.W.A. minutes, May 8th, 1952.
[62] The A.C.W.A. minutes, October 31st, 1952.
[63] The A.C.W.A. minutes, February 10th, 1953
[64] Ibid.
[65] The A.C.W.A. minutes, March 17th, 1953

August 10,1953.

Herein is a summary of the events surrounding the recent visit of the School Chapel Choir, accompanied by the Headmaster, Dr.Bell and Mrs.Bell,to Great Britain under the aegis of the Commonwealth Youth Movement.

At the outset, I should say that I am both pleased and proud to tell you that, on every occasion, the boys justified everyone's faith and confidence in them. Letters from prominent people in the United Kingdom attest to the fact that they were excellent ambassadors for their country. Furthermore, they were a great credit to their School and to their respective families. Their singing was always of the highest standard and their work evoked high praise from several eminent musicians and critics; their smart appearance and general deportment won them many friends everywhere.

On the eastbound Atlantic crossing, the boys sang two concerts and one Sunday Service. They made a similar contribution on the ship which returned them to Canada.

Nineteen full concerts were given during the six weeks in Great Britain. In addition to this, the boys sang Services in nine Parish Churches, performed in five Public Schools and made two appearances on the B.B.C.

Apart from singing in the Cathedrals of Winchester, Chichester, St.Mary's (Edinburgh), Yorkminster and St.Albans Abbey, the boys were invited to sing at two special Services of Dedication for Commonwealth Youth - at St.George's Chapel, Windsor, on June 1st, and in Westminster Abbey, in the Coronation setting, on the Sunday following the Crowning of the Queen. The latter Service was recorded.

To this summary of the full programme of engagements can be added visits to the Castles of Winchester, Arundel, Warwick and Edinburgh; a tour of the Tower of London, and of Madame Tussaud's famous waxworks; expeditions to the Port of London Docks, the Goldsmith's Hall, Hampton Court, the University Towns of Oxford and Cambridge, and an evening performance in the Royal Festival Hall. Further, the boys were entertained by the Mayors of Winchester, St.Albans, Cambridge, Appleby and York; by the Secretary of the M.C.C. at Lord's during the first match against the Australian Cricket Eleven. Noteworthy visits were those to the Wedgwood Potteries and The Hudson's Bay Company,Beaver Hall. At the former place, each boy was presented with a Coronation souvenir piece in the shape of a pottery tankard, while at the latter, each boy was given a spoon commemorating the great occasion. The Governors of the Shakespeare Memorial Theatre entertained at tea following a matinee performance of "The Taming of the Shrew".

Account of the Choir Visit to England, 1953 - First Page
On the Occasion of the Coronation of Queen Elizabeth II
(Continued on Page 62)

<u>unless</u> the number of officers retiring leaves less than three of the previous Executive ."[66] This was passed.

- In commemoration of Coronation year "It was finally decided to plant a tree with a plaque of explanation. The tree was to be planted by Mrs. Deacon and dedicated by the Headmaster before the departure of the Choir for England."[67]
- Dr. Bell announced the death of Mr. Guest (the co-founder, and first Headmaster of Appleby) and also the passing of Dr. Horan (a friend of the school).
- Mr. Bott, the Choirmaster, displayed an exhibit of photographs, clippings and billings of the Coronation Tour at the October meeting which was held in the gymnasium. A gift of appreciation was presented to Mr. Bott.
- There was talk of a clothing exchange but it was felt it would be too difficult to take on at that time.

1953-1954
President   **Mrs. T. R. Deacon**

- $20.00 was given to purchase games for the little boys living in Colley House.
- Lady Baillie spoke of Life Membership.
- Dr. Bell spoke of the Coronation Tour "The singing of the boys was of the highest standard and their behaviour a credit to the School and their respective families."[68]
- A combination record player (voted on in 1951) was given to the school.
- New Colours were dedicated and presented at the Annual Inspection of the Corps.
- A Bursary of $300.00 was given to the school, the cheque was presented to the Headmaster. This was the first Bursary, a fund that the parents support to this day.
- One dozen records were donated.

1954-1955
President   **Mrs. J. P. Curran**

- The project for the year would be redecorating the infirmary sitting room.
- Needed volunteers to help with decorations for the Christmas Dance.
- Mrs. T. R. Deacon presented the Association with a silver tea urn.
- Mr. Blenkhome, an architect friend of Mrs. Curran, would give professional advice on the infirmary sitting room. It was suggested that wood paneling be used on the walls. Mrs. Scarlett would donate curtains.
- $250.00 would be given to begin renovations.
- *Of interest-The Headmaster said "that the Board of Governors are (sic) determined to keep the School a small one, as originally planned. Day boys are not to exceed 60 in number and no day boy is accepted over 15 years of age. Plans are underway for the building of a new gymnasium complete with changing rooms, lockers, etc."[69]*

---

[66] The A.C.W.A. minutes, April 13th, 1953.
[67] Ibid
[68] The A.C.W.A. minutes, October 30th, 1953.
[69] The A.C.W.A. minutes, October 29th, 1954.

On June 2nd, we saw the Coronation processions from the first stand on the north side of the Mall, opposite Buckingham Palace. Three days later we were invited into the forecourt of the Palace to witness the Changing of the Guard on the morning the Canadian Regiments took over.

One of our boys was chosen from all the Canadians to represent Canada on a Commonwealth Television programme of the B.B.C., which was televised on the day after the Coronation. Eight children of the Commonwealth were interviewed on their respective impressions of the events of Coronation Day. We were highly pleased to have had an Appleby boy selected. As Canada's High Commissioner and his wife were entertaining us at tea at Canada House we had no opportunity of seeing the broadcast.

In Edinburgh we were assigned a special spot on the route of procession, from which we saw the arrival of the Queen and the Duke of Edinburgh. Later, in the Trossachs, we saw Queen Salote of Tonga who, when she alighted from her car, spoke to the boys and posed for photographs.

With the utmost in co-operation from every boy in the group, the trip proved to be a worthwhile outing - an adventurous experience that will leave treasured memories to last a lifetime.

I should be most remiss if I did not mention the excellent work of the two older boys; Rapley Bunting and Peter Schlesinger. Each in his own way made a worthwhile contribution to the success of the enterprise, while together, they were a tower of strength in maintaining morale on a sufficiently high level to keep us moving contentedly and happily together.

E. Leslie Bott

Account of the Choir Visit to England, 1953 - Page Two
On the Occasion of the Coronation of Queen Elizabeth II
(Continued from Page 60)

- Four new Life Members.
- Mr. Dewar (in Dr. Bell's absence) addressed the Women's Association. "Mr. Dewar spoke of the aims of the school in regard to the boys:
    1. To learn to live with others.
    2. Cultivate good personal habits – neatness and cleanliness.
    3. Development of proper study habits, the most important being to do the work on the day it is set. If this is done, study for exams is practically eliminated."[70]
- Dr. Bell was persuaded to donate a painting (his own art work) as a raffle prize for the AGM.

1955-1956
President   **Mrs. J. P. Curran**

- Bursary of $300.00 given.
- Flowers were sent on notice of the death of Past President Mrs. R. R. Hart.
- $250.00 given toward the purchase of silver bugles.
- Spring Meeting held in the new gymnasium.
- "Lady Baillie congratulated the Executive on the state of the Treasury saying that it was the original purpose of the organization that funds were to be used in full each year so that the boys presently attending school were benefited by the current mothers' Association."[71]
- It was moved that "Mrs. Curran and all future presidents be invited to become an ex-officio member of the Committee for a period of one year following their retirement."[72]
- *Of interest-Dr. Bell reported that "the official dedication of the new buildings will be held on Cadet Day May 1. The reported $156,000.00 of the necessary $200,000.00 for the building fund has been collected."*[73]

1956-1957
President   **Mrs. R. G. Wace**

- Intermediate Trophy for Cross Country Run was donated to the school. The cost of the trophy was $40.00.
- $300.00 Bursary donated to the school to be used for a student, at the Headmaster's discretion.
- Mr. Shorney (a parent) donated equipment and helped set up a dark room (for photography) in Powell's House.

---

[70] The A.C.W.A. minutes, October 29th, 1954.
[71] The A.C.W.A. minutes, April 9th, 1956.
[72] Ibid
[73] The A.C.W.A. minutes, April 9th, 1956.

JUN · 56 ·

Appleby College Gates
June, 1956

1957-1958
President   **Mrs. R. G. Wace**

- The project for the year would be the purchase of two chairs for the entrance hall of the office and class room building. The seats and backs of the chairs to be done in hand worked needlepoint coverings of the Appleby crest.
- Also 6 or 8 bedside tables would be purchased for the hospital (infirmary).
- The $300.00 Bursary was ongoing. Canon Bell said "…the bursary was most appreciated. It meant that some child could attend Appleby, who otherwise would not be there."[74]
- Donation of costumes for the Appleby Costume Wardrobe given by Moulton College.
- *Of interest-Canon Bell reported that "The school is full with 134 boarders and 65 day boys. Four or five boys had to be refused for grade five because it is full. There are 22 sons of old boys. The boys are a fairly diversified group; 109 from Ontario, 3 from Quebec, 2 from B.C., 2 from Alta., 1 from Man., 8 from U.S.A., 6 from South America, 1 from Central America, 3 from the West Indies. Last year there were 13 seniors. This year there are 8. From last year's class 3 are at Toronto University, 1 at McGill, 1 at McMaster, 3 at Waterloo, 1 at Assumption, 2 are working, 1 completing his Matriculation elsewhere. A student must now attain 60% before going on to grade 13. … the universities may not be able to go on demanding senior matriculation. At present three in Ontario require Senior Matric. Before long more universities may take pupils from grade 12. There will probably be more students going to University in the future, as at present at the U.S.A. This is why work is being stiffened for grades 11 and 12; to enable a boy to do better at University. For a University graduate opportunities will be greater, as they get the first chance."[75]*
- Mr. Wm. Grant[’29], father of Ian[’60], donated a pew to the Chapel in memory of Mrs. Grant.
- A slide projector, purchased wholesale for $127.00, was donated to the school.
- A white Wedgewood vase was donated by Mr. C. F. W. Cooper and was raffled at the Spring Meeting.
- $10.00 for new games for the infirmary, some paint by number sets were bought.

1958-1959
President   **Mrs. E. L. Taylor**

- Two tennis courts had been resurfaced thanks to Messrs. Quigley and Wace.
- One sample table was purchased for the hospital. It was expensive at $44.00 and could not be returned. The other tables were given new arbourite tops at a cost of $90.00.
- The old tray tables were fixed for $15.00.
- $200.00 to be donated toward the $1400.00 cost of netting for the tennis courts.
- A cart was purchased for the hospital.

---

[74] The A.C.W.A. minutes, November 1st, 1957.
[75] Ibid.

JUN · 56 ·

Colley House
June, 1956

- Bursary $300.00.
- For the foyer chairs – "Mrs. Stanton is now in London, and has found a pair of chairs of 1680 period; and these are on their way here. These chairs have been purchased for the school by Mrs. Taylor and Mrs. Stanton."[76]
- Miss Niblett (the nurse at Appleby for 27 years) passed away and a letter of sympathy was sent to her friend Miss James.
- Flowers were given for the Carol Service in the Chapel.
- Mr. C. F. W. Cooper had Wedgewood ash trays made with a design of the School Building and the School crest, these were sold by the Women's Association.
- Card tables were bought second hand at a cost of $3.95 each rather than $8.95 new. Ten tables were donated and ten purchased by the Association.
- Black Watch plaid curtains were made for the hospital.
- Mrs. Elizabeth Wilkes Hoey did the design for the seats and backs of the chairs that had been donated for the foyer. She also did the design for the library curtains. The Royal School of Needlework put the design on canvas and the seats and backs were covered beautifully with the help of many including Association members.
- Mrs. Wace was named convenor for ash tray sales (the ash trays made by Wedgewood and donated by Mr. C. F. W. Cooper).

1959-1960
President   **Mrs. E. L. Taylor**

- Although Mrs. Taylor's sons had graduated and gone on to university the women on the Executive felt that Mrs. Taylor had the best interests of Appleby at heart and asked her to please finish her term of office. She agreed. A motion to allow this was passed and to cover any future situation similar to this.
- $300.00 Bursary.
- Purchased prizes for the formal.
- 300 Wedgewood ash trays (now called plates) had been sold.
- An additional Bursary of $150.00 (from the sale of Wedgewood plates) to be given to the school.
- Flowers were again given and arranged for the Chapel Carol Services.
- New table cloths were made for the Christmas dance.
- In Dr. Bell's absence Mr. Merritt addressed the meeting. "Mr. Merritt explained the set up of the new Junior School, its aims and what he hopes to accomplish with the help of the parents. He spoke of team spirit, the importance of always demanding the best of the boys and never to be satisfied with less than the best. He spoke of the monitor system he was using, giving boys certain duties thus a sense of responsibility and accomplishment."[77]

---

[76] The A.C.W.A. minutes, October 31st, 1958.
[77] The A.C.W.A. minutes, April 20th, 1960.
*Daughter-in-law of the first Headmaster and co-founder of Appleby School.

Lady Baillie and Family, 1961

1960-1961

President **Mrs. D. G. Guest***

- Publicity – it was decided that students should report the sports. Mike Hutchins[61] would write the reports and Michael DesRoches [62] would phone them into the newspapers.
- $500.00 given to the Bursary.
- $25.00 given to the hospital for canes, games cards and books.
- $10.00 given to the Dance Committee for candy, paper cups etc. for the formal.
- Wedgewood plates were donated as prizes for the formal.
- Decorated a tree by the Chapel with Christmas lights.
- The Association sold Zippo lighters with the School crest, large for $5.00 and the small ladies lighter for $6.00.
- A dining hall was to be built that would accommodate 250 boys. The Board of Governors offered to give half of the $525,000.00 needed for this project.
- *Also of interest-Dr. Bell "spoke briefly of the aims of Appleby-To produce purposeful mature adults by*
    1. *Teaching good habits of conduct, manners, and study and most important Worship and Devotion. Dr. Bell said 'A feeling of God is good. It gives them confidence and calmness.'*
    2. *Discipline-learning to live together and*
    3. *By teaching them to accept responsibility, to try it out and helping them along the way."*[78]
- Heads of the Women's Associations of Ridley, U.C.C., T.C.S., Hillfield, Lakefield and Ashbury were invited to the Spring Meeting.
- Sherry was served, at the Headmaster's house, before the meeting.
- The Association would loan tablecloths out to schools or Church groups as a goodwill gesture.
- Key rings, cuff-links and tie clips with the School crest were purchased to be sold at a profit to raise money.
- To date $100.00 had been made on the sale of book matches.
- Portable T.V. and radio ($43.00 wholesale for the radio) were purchased for the hospital.
- Dr. Bell showed those assembled for the Spring Meeting blue prints and sketches for the proposed dining hall. "The Association was looking forward to Appleby's 50th anniversary and the opening of the new dining hall and the new dorm [named New House, currently Walker House]."[79] The dining hall was to be ready for September opening.
- Dr. Bell's dream of having the 50th Anniversary Dinner in the new dining hall would become a reality.

1961-1962

President **Mrs. D. G. Guest**

---

[78] The A.C.W.A. minutes, October 28th, 1960.
[79] The Argus, Volume 69, June 1961.

THE GAVEL PRESENTED TO THE APPLEBY

COLLEGE WOMEN'S ASSOCIATION BY THE

BOYS WAS MADE IN THE CRAFT SHOP BY

T. R. MERRITT, AGE 11, Grade 7.

File Card accompanying Gavel, 1962
*There is no photo record of the gavel because it
has been misplaced over the years.*

- Amendments were made to the Constitution; "The Past President shall attend all meetings of the Executive for one year after terminating her term of office. The Nominating Committee Chairman is to be appointed annually by the President from the membership of the Association and may not be a member of the Executive. She shall appoint two members, one of whom shall be a member of the Executive to act on her committee."[80] And "The Executive shall consist of six officers. Five to be elected at the Annual Meeting, and the sixth to be appointed in the fall to represent the Mothers of New Boys."[81]
- $20.00 given to the School formal and $10.00 to the Sixth Form* dance.
- Book matches increased in price to $1.25 a box. These were taxed.
- Mrs. Curran donated subscriptions to <u>The National Geographic</u> and <u>Popular Mechanics</u> to the library.
- Dr. Bell spoke of his trip out West where he had attended The Canadian Conference of Headmasters, seventeen schools from across Canada were represented. He also spoke of a forum on "Education and Business" that he attended in Montreal. "A wonderful opportunity to compare notes and exchange ideas with other teachers and men of learning."[82]

1962-1963
President   **Mrs. B. H. Collins, Jr.**

- $500.00 Bursary.
- Presented a handbag to Mrs. Sampson. (Mrs. Sampson worked in the school office and did a great deal for the Women's Association.)
- New job descriptions – 1st Vice-President: Committee of Arrangements, complete charge of general meetings and luncheons.

2nd Vice-President: All publicity.

Secretary: To keep the minutes, copies of the new Constitution and prepare lists of the Executive members complete with addresses and telephone numbers. Printing, posting and sending out notices etc.

The Treasurer: To keep the books and to appoint a person or persons to be responsible for the Wedgewood plates, the matches, lighters, cuff-links, etc.

The Dancing Classes: To arrange for partners.

A Magazine Committee: To replace the Hospital Committee.

A Cultural Committee: To investigate what worthwhile entertainment was coming to Toronto. To form a plan to visit art galleries, factories, theatres, anything that might interest and benefit the boys.

- A pair of paintings of the Chapel, by Mr. Weykamp, was purchased and given to Dr. Bell, on the occasion of the 50th anniversary of the school, for the foyer.

---

[80] The A.C.W.A. minutes, June 2nd, 1961.
[81] The A.C.W.A. minutes, April 19th, 1962.
* Grades 11, 12 & 13.
[82] The A.C.W.A. minutes, April 19th, 1962

APPLEBY COLLEGE WOMEN'S ASSOCIATION

OAKVILLE, ONTARIO

October 23, 1965.

Dear Mrs. Wilder :

The Appleby College Women's Association appointed a Committee last Spring, to arrange for a suitable memorial in honour of your Mother, who, as you well know, was the Founder, and for many years Honorary President of this Association.

This has been carried through, with the help of Dr. Bell, and I am happy to tell you that a pair of sterling silver candelabra will be presented to the School, inscribed in memory of Lady Baillie, from the Women's Association, at our Fall Luncheon on Friday, November the fifth.

It would be an honour for us to have Lady Baillie's daughters and daughters-in-law seated at the Head Table on this special occasion, and we hope that you will find it possible to attend. The Luncheon will take place at half-past one, in the John Guest Hall.

If you would care to attend the meeting which precedes the luncheon in the Gymnasium at eleven forty-five, you would, of course, be more than welcome.

In any case, I look forward to meeting you in the foyer of the Dining Hall a few minutes before one-thirty.

Sincerely,

Lloy Winchell

President.

Mrs. J. R. Winchell,
11 Kingscourt Drive,
Toronto 18, Ontario.

Letter to Mrs. Wilder regarding Lady Baillie Memorial, October 23, 1965

- A billiard table was purchased at a cost of $500.00, the W.A. paid $300.00 and the school $200.00.
- Dr. Bell wrote a prayer for the Women's Association to be said before meetings.
- The School Shop built display cases to show the jewellery that the Association had for sale. (cuff links, tie clips, key chains etc.)
- School pennants were purchased for sale at meetings.
- First talk of field trips – "All of this is a very new venture and it was felt we should underwrite it until it has proved itself and the school is willing to take it over. We hope for at least one Tour per term."[83] In November 1962 grade 9 class visited the Nelson Crushed Stone Co. and the grade 10 class visited the Dominion Foundries in Hamilton. In March 38 grade 10 boys went to the Goodyear Plant. "He (Dr. Bell) thanked us for 'field trips' which have proved both exciting and educational for the boys."[84]
- A new gavel, made in the School workshop by Tommy Merritt[69] was presented to the Association.
- Scrabble games and paint sets had been purchased for the hospital.
- An air foam pillow and colouring books had also been bought for the hospital.
- The Executive was given discretionary spending of $50.00 without the need of general membership approval. That would be $25.00 for infirmary expenses and $25.00 for unforseen expenses.
- *Of interest-Dr. Bell spoke to the assembled women and thanked them. He noted that there were 123 boarders and 2 day boys in the Senior School and 52 boarders and 77 day boys in the Junior School for a total of 256 boys enrolled in Appleby. Full time staff of 21, 3 part time teachers, a full time librarian and a chaplain. The Librarian and Chaplain had come to the school in 1962.*
- Mr. Hardwick spoke briefly on the Appleby College Foundation. "Its aim to provide three open scholarships and one bursary every year to be held for five years, if the high standard of work is maintained. In fact he won us over so completely, it was moved by Mrs. J. R. Winchell that we give $200.00 to the Appleby College Foundation. Seconded by Mrs. P. Redgrave and passed."[85]

1963-1964
President   **Mrs. B. H. Collins, Jr.**

- $500.00 Bursary.
- School charms and bracelets in silver for sale.
- The Association had looked into the cost of an artificial ice rink but learned that it would cost $36,000.00, out of the question.
- $15.00 to be donated annually for flowers in the Chapel.
- $15.00 given for prizes for the Christmas dance.
- $25.00 donated for books for dormitories.
- $1,000.00 to be spent on the common room in Powell's House.

---

[83] The A.C.W.A. minutes, October 12th, 1962.
[84] The Argus, Volume 71, June 1963.
[85] The A.C.W.A. minutes, April 11, 1963.

CANDELABRA PRESENTED IN MEMORY OF FOUNDER
Dr. J. A. M. Bell, headmaster, aid Mrs. J. R. Winchell, WA president.

Headmaster Gives Lunch For New Appleby Mothers

OAKVILLE — More than 100 members of Appleby College Woman's Auxiliary met yesterday afternoon for the annual Fall meeting.

Mothers of new boys were introduced to school life. Headmaster Dr. J. A. M. Bell spoke on the school curriculum and the ways in which parents could help their sons adjust to the changing conditions of the world today.

Following the business rpogram, members adjourned to the John Guest Hall where they were luncheon guests of Dr. and Mrs. Bell.

Preceeding the lunch, a presentation was made by the WA of a pair of silver candelabra in memory of the late Ladie Baillie, founder and honorary president of the Appleby WA.

BAILLIES PRESENT

The presentation was made by Mrs. J. R. Winchell, president. Special guests at the head table included Ladie Baillie's two daughters, Mrs. T. G. Wilder and Mrs. C. M. Serson, and her two daughters-in-law, Mrs F. W. Baillie and Mrs. J. F. Baillie. A third daughter-in-law, Mrs. Aubrey Baillie, was unable to attend.

The choice of a memorial gift was made by a special committee under the convenership of Mrs. Douglas Watson. In presenting the candelabra, Mrs. Winchell said the WA hoped they would "light many functions for several generations of yet unborn Baillies."

Lady Baillie's three sons, and three grandsons all attended Appleby.

The first great-grandson will be attending in the near future.

Dr. Bell, who received the candelabra on behalf of the school, performed a candle-lighting ceremony to mark the end of the presentation.

Newspaper Article, November 6, 1965
A pair of silver candelabra, in memory of Lady Baillie, was presented to the school.

74

1964-1965
President   **Mrs. J. R. Winchell**

- "When Lady Baillie died on March 14, 1965, the School lost one of its earliest and best friends. Space does not permit us to record all her kind and generous acts, there were just too many! It was not, however, materially only that the School benefited from her generosity: she sustained us at all times, through years of prosperity or adversity, by her interest, her moral support and her confidence in the ideals of Appleby tradition, which she and her family helped to create. Ever since Aubrey was enrolled in 1918, right up to the present day, there have always been members of her family in the School. Here is the record: three sons – Aubrey, Frank and Jim; nine grandsons – Brem and Donald Green (sons of Marion); Frank Jr. (son of Aubrey); Donald and Bill Benson (sons of Edith); Aubrey and John (sons of Frank); Rusty and Peter (sons of Jim); one great grandson – George Hagey (son of Betsy). We confidently expect to see on the Campus in the near future many more of her great grandsons, who will certainly carry out the Appleby tradition – a tradition so closely knit to the Baillie family. In earlier times, Appleby boys did not enjoy the amenities to the extent that they do today. This condition was appreciated by Lady Baillie, who determined to improve the situation. In 1928 she inaugurated the Appleby College Women's Association, established its policy and became its first President. The primary function of this Association was – and still is today – to provide amenities for the comfort of Appleby boys. In later years, Lady Baillie became the permanent Honorary President of the A.C.W.A. ..."[86]
- A suitable memorial would be undertaken in Lady Baillie's honour.
- 90 members were present at the Spring Meeting.
- $500.00 to the Bursary.
- $25.00 to school dance.
- *Of interest-the boys produced a School newspaper called* <u>Double Blue</u>, *copies cost 5 cents. First Term Editor – Tim Finch, Second Term – John Bell and Last Term – Sandy Lind.*
- Dr. Bell spoke on Modern Education. He talked of university entrance requirements and had a question and answer period at the end of his talk.

1965-1966
President   **Mrs. J. R. Winchell**

- As a memorial for Lady Baillie, a pair of candelabra was purchased and inscribed 'In Memory of Lady Baillie', to be used on the Head Table. On the occasion of the presentation of the candelabra members of Lady Baillie's family sat at the Head Table.
- $500.00 for the Bursary.
- New drums and a new mace for the Cadet Corps.
- $25.00 was given towards decorations for the Annual Dance.

---

[86] <u>The Argus</u>, Volume 73, June 1965.

Dr. and Mrs. Bell

Marion Baillie (Frank '31)*, Dr. MacArthur, Mary Wace*

- Of the $1,000. intended for the redecoration of the Powell's House Common Room, only $500.00 had been paid. It was moved, seconded, voted on and carried that the additional $500.00 not be paid. "Dr. Bell felt that we had instigated the improvement to this room by our first $500.00 and since it was now all paid for by the school we should spend our money on necessities as they are required."[87]
- Two pairs of silver, crested sugar tongs had been purchased and were to be used at all functions where coffee and tea were served.
- Position of 2nd Vice-President was eliminated.

1966-1967
President   Mrs. D. W. Newlands

- $500.00 for the Bursary.
- Prizes and $25.00 were given for the Annual Christmas Dance.
- New cover provided for the billiard table in New House.
- Dr. Bell was unable to attend the Spring Meeting but Mr. Dewar came in his place and paid a great tribute to Dr. Bell "and all he has accomplished in nearly forty years at Appleby."[88]

1967-1968
President   Mrs. D. W. Newlands

- *Of interest – a copy of the first newsletter to parents was included with the minutes. This newsletter was issued by the College not the Women's Association but had much of interest. "Twelve boys wrote their complete Ontario Grade XIII examinations. ... The Optimates Club – Est. 1951, This Club consists of boys in Forms 6C, 6B and 6A, who have First Class Honours Standing in their examinations. Each member must maintain an average of 75% *...There are twenty-three full-time and two part-time members on the Staff, as well as the Headmaster...Work on the extension to the Chapel is progressing favourably. The stone facing on the exterior has been completed, as has the work on the roof. When the interior is finished, it is hoped that we may again begin worshipping there, possibly by mid-November. Meanwhile, Morning Prayers and Sunday Evening Services are being held in the Gymnasium."[89]*
- A letter was sent to all parents on behalf of the A.C.W.A. "The Women's Association intended to present a gift to Dr. Bell, the retiring Headmaster, as a token of the outstanding guidance he has given to our boys for the last 39 years....We are not soliciting a large donation: any amount from one to five dollars will be appreciated...."[90]

---

[87] The A.C.W.A. minutes, November 5th, 1965.
[88] The A.C.W.A. minutes, April 15th, 1967.
* Optimates is now 85%
[89] Appleby College Newsletter, September 30th, 1967.
[90] Letter of February 12th, 1968, written by Lloy (Winchell) Greenhough (Mrs. G. H. Greenhough)

Ned & Marion Larsen, June Bramall (Gurth '41),
Miss Chamberlain, Fran Waters, Betty Newlands

Dr. J. A. M. Bell, retiring head master of Appleby College, examines a scroll presented to him by the College's Women's Association. Mrs. David W. Newlands, retiring president of the Association, holds the scroll, Mrs. Bell (left), and Mrs. George L. Waters, associate president, look on. Dr. Bell was also given a $1,000 bill to buy a color television.

1968 Newspaper Clipping
Presentation of Scroll to Dr. Bell, retiring Headmaster, by Mrs. David Newlands,
with Mrs. Bell and Mrs. George Waters looking on.

- $1,000.00 had been raised as a gift of appreciation for Dr. Bell. Mrs. Newlands presented him with a cheque on behalf of the Women's Association. Over 300 women had responded to the letter requesting funds.
- $500.00 Bursary paid.
- $225.00 spent on furnishing for the Common Room in New (Walker) House. A three seater couch, three chairs and new draperies were chosen and installed.
- Prizes and $25.00 for the Annual Christmas Dance.
- Sherry and lunch were served.

1968-1969　　　　　　　　*Headmaster – Ned Larsen 1968-1980*
President　　　　　　　　　　**Mrs. G. L. Waters**

- It was decided to charge $1.50 on lunch so that Association monies could be spent on the boys not on lunch.
- $500.00 Bursary.
- The billiard table in New House was leveled and got new pockets.
- 'Friends of the Library' Committee formed.
- The furnishings for New House common room were completed.
- Mr. Larsen, the new Headmaster, addressed the meeting.
- Rather than a sit down lunch in the John Guest Hall, the ladies were served sherry and a snack lunch in the gymnasium. "This seemed to be appreciated by busy Mothers and busy Masters who were able to attend."[91]

1969-1970
President　　　　　　　　　　**Mrs. G. L. Waters**

- *Of interest – A $150.00 re-registration fee was charged for the first time. This would reserve a spot for your son. It must be paid by July 1st. "To this date we have had one hundred and sixty-eight applications to join Appleby's Teaching Staff in September,...I must request specifically...that the boys do not return with elephant pants, or coats without lapels, or in fact with any of the mod fashions..."[92]*
- Mrs. D. M. (Skin) Dewar was made an Honorary Life Member of the Women's Association.
- $500.00 Bursary.
- Voted to purchase an ultra short wave machine for the infirmary.
- The gift of a gold maple leaf pin with the School crest on it was presented to Miss Chamberlain (dear teacher of the 'little boys') on her retirement. She had been at the school since 1947.

1970-1971
President　　　　　　　　　　**Mrs. G. Bramall (Gurth[41])**

---

[91] The A.C.W.A. minutes, March 26th, 1969.
[92] A letter to the parents written by the Headmaster, E. R. Larsen, July 18th, 1969.

THE REV. CANON J.A.M.BELL, B.A.,D.D.
HEADMASTER

Appleby College

Oakville, Ontario

April 4, 1968

Mrs. G. L. Waters,
P. O. Box 11,
Dundas, Ontario.

Dear Mrs. Waters,

      Peg and I are now enjoying a new colour
television set which was put in the house on Monday. It
is a Zenith and a dandy.

      I am sure that we will enjoy a great
many programmes which are much more interesting in colour
than in black and white.

      I am going to write to Betty and to Lloy,
but I should like to thank you and all the other members
of the Appleby College Women's Association for a wonderful
luncheon and a very generous and thoughtful gift to Peg
and myself.

Yours sincerely,

John Bell

1968 Letter of Appreciation from Dr. Bell

- $300.00 Bursary given.
- Dancing Classes were discontinued.
- *Of interest - it was suggested that "the wearing of the school tie be obligatory."[93]*
- $2.00 charge for lunch, i.e. $1.00 to the kitchen and $1.00 for sherry. Any 'sherry surplus money' would also go towards the cost of lunch.
- $20.00 to Mr. Bott for magazine subscriptions.
- Mrs. Lloy Winchell Greenhough, Past President, 1964-1966, passed away and it was agreed that a memorial donation should be made. A sterling silver rose bowl was purchased and would belong to the Women's Association but could be used by the school. Contributions were sent to the Cerebral Palsy Association in Mrs. Greenhough's name. Mrs. D. Snowden, also passed away, and donations were made to the Cancer Society.
- Both Mr. Larsen and the new Director of Art, Mr. McConnell addressed the assembly. Mr. McConnell spoke on the future of Art at Appleby, "He mentioned in particular the need for expansion and greater facilities than the present ones which limited the number of boys who could participate. He said that the school planned visits by professional craftsmen, the rental of exhibits and the introduction of screen printing, silversmithing and welding, with a display area for the boys' work. He closed by saying that art was an essential form of self expression which was inherent in every child."[94]
- Raffled a School blazer from Jack Fraser's.
- At this time there were 280 Members of the Association, 5 of those being Honorary and 85 Life Members.
- *Of interest – "The Board of Governors of Appleby College has asked me to advise all Parents that with great regret they have had to raise fees to take effect this coming September. ...Boarders from Grade IX to XIII - $3,000.00.*
  Boarders below Grade IX - $2,850.00.
  Day Boys - $1,400.00.
  "These increases are due to the continued rise in the general cost of operation, to an increased variety of activities at our School, and particularly to the substantial increase in Teachers' salaries throughout the Province. ...In fact the new fee scale set out above will put Appleby in the middle, from a fee standpoint, of the main eight Ontario Independent Schools for boy. ..."[95]

1971-1972
President   **Mrs. G. Bramall (Gurth[41])**

- $500.00 Bursary.
- Mr. Allison was no longer able to provide the Association with jewellery. Ostrander's took over in supplying jewellery to the Association.
- Library was in need of books – it was suggested that a book be given in your son's name on his birthday.

---

[93] The A.C.W.A. minutes, September 22nd, 1970.
[94] The A.C.W.A. minutes, November 4th, 1970
[95] A letter written by the Headmaster, Mr. E. R. Larsen, March 20th, 1970.

- A stereo record player purchased for the school.
- Help needed driving the Choir Boys and help with their robes.
- Mrs. Burn was to set up a clothing depot (used uniforms) at the school. But it was decided that it would not be practical. The May Court Club of Oakville offered to place a rack for Appleby boys' used clothing in their Shop.
- A book fair was held in the library.
- A Bell and Howell film strip projector was purchased for the school.
- The rose bowl was presented in Mrs. Loy Winchell Greenhough's name.
- Mr. Michael Nightingale* was the guest speaker. "Mr. Nightingale touched briefly on his life as a schoolboy, stating that his ideal Junior School was based on three things. A choir school, high academic standards and outdoor activities. Boys get much enjoyment out of attempting difficult tasks. They should use all of their time in a useful way. The act of living together is the most important team sport. Boys have to learn to live together and work together. It is also important that boys be encouraged to enter into non-academic activities. In a school that is loyal to certain principles, it is essential for the boys to learn to live, work and play together in harmony and trust. Each boy must attain the highest academic standard of which he is capable. The whole intellectual atmosphere of the school must be stimulating. Boys should be exposed to all kinds of activities to which they wouldn't expect to be exposed at home. Art, music, choral work. There must be a vigorous and varied athletic programme in the School. ..."[96]
- There was a raffle for a $25.00 gift certificate from Jack Fraser's.
- *Of interest - "Last year the School had a formal closing ball, which was attended by the graduating class and their parents. If planning to come to this year's, reserve early."[97]*
- *Of interest – Mr. Larsen spoke... "The bursaries have been given to worthy sons on the basis of entrance exams. Next year there will be a Grade 4 class, because of the tremendous demand, and there will be day boys in Grade 9. A forum was held for Grades 11, 12 and 13, to bring forward suggestions re: greater freedom and a relaxing of the hair rules. ... The rule is: hair must be clear of the face and it must be neat and clean at all times. It may not grow over the bottom of the ears, nor side-burns over the bottom of the ears. Hair may not hang over the eyebrows and may not hang over the bottom of the collar. For cadets and Church parades, it will be cut as now. ...He then spoke of the building of the new Science and resource centre, which will include a resource centre or library, fully equipped with all the audio-visual materials needed these days for teaching. There will also be three full-size and fully equipped science labs, and in addition, there will be separate smaller labs for boys to work on special projects. This will give the opportunity to encourage the boys for independent study."[98]*

---

* Michael Nightingale was Head of the Junior School, greatly respected by his peers, parents and students.
[96] The A.C.W.A. minutes, October 8th, 1971.
[97] The A.C.W.A. minutes, March 16th, 1972.
[98] Ibid.

1972-1973
President   **Mrs. I. Jamieson**
- At the A.G.M. the School Prayer was printed on the top of the Agenda page.
- $500.00 Bursary.
- $190.00 for a screen and projection table.
- The Clothing Exchange (Turnover) was started. Clothes to be dry cleaned with the cost added to the price of the clothing. The clothing would be donated to the Women's Association. The mothers could purchase clean, used clothing from the Association. Mrs. Larsen with the help of staff wives looked after this. At the end of the school year the boys were to leave anything they had outgrown. This would be taken as a donation.
- "Some of the women at Appleby would like to have some type of fund raising. The Executive and Mr. Larsen are very enthusiastic. Many ideas were discussed: a rather elaborate cocktail party; raffle; Monte Carlo night; gourmet dinner, to feature members' specialty dishes; fashion show put on by Mrs. Keil. The general feeling of the meeting was that the event should be held at the School."[99]
- A guided tour of the new Resource and Science Centre was given to those attending the Fall Meeting.
- Parents help in the library.
- Heraldic Shields were purchased for $7.65 to be sold for $10.00.
- "Mrs. Bramall then presented a gift to show her appreciation of having worked on the Executive for the past nine years. Calling Mr. Larsen and Mrs. Jamieson to the lectern, she gave them a gavel and striking plate, which she had made from the wood of one of the large red oak trees that were cut down to make way for the erection of the new science and resource building. ..."[100]
- A cricket score board was purchased.
- The first fund raising event was a Champagne and Strawberries party. Tickets were $25.00 per couple. The money raised, $1,930.59, was to be used for the infirmary.

1973-1974
President   **Mrs. I. Jamieson**
- $500.00 for the Bursary.
- $600.00 given toward the cost of a trampoline. An additional $400.00 was to be given the following year.
- Name tags were provided for all mothers and masters to be worn for the luncheon.
- Heraldic Shields were purchased for $9.75 plus postage and were to be sold for $15.00 each. Sixty were purchased and would arrive in three months time. Matches were still available but were sold at the reduced rate of $ .50.
- A motion was made that an inscription be put on the gavel, to read: "Carved from Appleby Oak Tree" "Presented by Mrs. G. Bramall, 1973"[101].

---

[99] The A.C.W.A. minutes, September 11th, 1972.
[100] The A.C.W.A. minutes, May 18th, 1973.
[101] The A.C.W.A. minutes, September 11th, 1973.

The Appleby College Women's Association

cordially invite you to attend

The Annual Fall Meeting & Luncheon

to be held in the School Gymnasium &

John Guest Dining Hall

Friday, October 10th, 1975.

Guest Speaker: The Lieutenant-Governor of Ontario,

The Honourable Pauline M. McGibbon

Meeting &	*10:15 a.m.*	*Sherry will be served in the*
Registration	*$5:00*	*Gymnasium at 12:15.*

Luncheon 1:00 in the John Guest Dining Hall - $3.00   *R.S.V.P.*

Invitation to Fall Meeting & Luncheon, 1975

- Mothers were encouraged to volunteer in the library.
- $1,300.00 given to the infirmary for 4 cold-water vaporizers, 1 coloured T.V. set, 1 eye chart, and 1 odometer. This totaled $965.65, the remainder would be used on future purchases for the infirmary.
- $500.00 given to the boys toward the purchase of a hockey clock. The boys had earned $1,400.00 and were $500.00 shy of their goal.
- *Of interest – "Mr. Larsen spoke of another exciting dimension of Appleby education – the northern campus – which will be integrated with Appleby for prolonged periods for part of the Appleby programme. 20 boys will spend one month with two masters, alternating camp craft, bush rescue, etc. This will encourage the boys in self-reliance, discipline and comradeship. This programme is unique on the continent, largely due to a far-seeing Board who supports this idea in principle..."[102]*
- 170 members in the Association.
- Jewellery sales totaled $868.33, $300.00 more than the last year.
- It was suggested that sports equipment be included in the clothing exchange.
- Notice of $5.00 membership fee mailed to all mothers who had not paid.
- Wright Cleaners donated two white table cloths to be used for the meetings.
- Halpern's, on Yonge Street in Toronto, would handle uniforms for the boys.

1974-1975
President   **Mrs. J. E. Thomson**

- $500.00 Bursary.
- Pewter tankards and individual ash trays were priced as were silver coffee spoons, all bearing the Appleby crest.
- $500.00 given toward the purchase of choir gowns.
- A profit of $1,000.00 had been realized on the sale of jewellery.
- Decision to hold a Country Fair in the fall of 1975 was approved. The Historical Society would provide a lemonade stand. Candy bags and popcorn would be sold from the same stand. Warren Beasley[50] (parent and owner of games and what not on Centre Island) would run gambling games and the boys would oversee other games such as beanbag toss, coconut shot, horseshoes, bottle toss etc. There would be an exhibition of art and pottery. Food items would be in the gymnasium and would include cheeses from the Mennonite Market in Elmira. Many plans were made and much work took place over the summer months.

1975-1976
President   **Mrs. J. E. Thomson**

- $500.00 Bursary.
- Used clothing sale brought in $500.00. The Clothing Exchange was to operate on a 40%/60% basis, 40% to the W.A. and 60% to the seller. (Used clothing, clothing exchange were synonymous with Turnover.)

---

[102] The A.C.W.A. minutes, October 5th, 1973.

Auction Sale Poster, 1977

- $400.00 to complete the balance on the choir gowns.
- Needlepoint kits produced by Oakville House, which depicted the Appleby crest, and were suitable for cushions or wall hangings were purchased and sold.
- It was decided to save Dominion Store tapes to purchase articles for the school.
- Silver crested coffee spoons were now for sale.
- The profit from the Fair was $5,167.00. "Mrs. Thomson read a letter from Mr. Larsen expressing his wishes for the allocation of our funds, which included $3,500.00 for improvements to the residential houses, and $600.00 for trophy cases."[103]
- Mr. Larsen said, "He felt that at the present time, the academics at Appleby were well provided for, and that good teachers were more important than sophisticated teaching aids we would purchase. He said the accommodation at Appleby was adequate, and it was good for the boys to co-operate and make do where necessary. However, the cost of necessary repairs to the buildings far exceeds the funds available. Our money would be used to provide mattresses and painting in Walker House, mattresses, desks and bureaus in Powell's, bathroom facilities, ventilating fans, plastering, etc. in Colley House. While it would appear our resources were being used only for boarders, Mr. Larsen said that the present day boys would benefit in future from what we did today."[104]
- Mr. Ellery donated material for new curtains in the infirmary and Mr. Schmidt had donated paint. Volunteers would sew the curtains.
- *Of interest -* "*At a meeting of the Public Works Committee on Oct. 14 at 8:30 p.m., Appleby would present a petition to the town regarding the speed limit on Lakeshore Road, and the necessity of a crossing guard. Our support was requested by attending the meeting and signing the petition.*"[105]
- Guest speaker for the Fall Meeting was The Lieutenant Governor of Ontario, The Honourable Pauline M. McGibbon. She spoke on 'The Emerging Woman'. It was International Women's Year. "She said that this was a year for all women, irrespective of their marital status, and that the theme of this year encompassed three words, equality, development, and peace. She said the year had focused on the examination of existing laws, and attitudes towards women, making people aware of inequalities, and where necessary effecting change. She urged us not to try to promote the ideals of this year, equality, development and peace, without first living up to them."[106]
- *Of interest –* "*Mr. Larsen made two important announcements regarding next year. In the Junior School there would be a full academic programme on Wednesday, with no classes on Saturday, thus encouraging the boys to work on special projects, hobby activities, and individual accomplishments. Detentions and defaulters will be served on Saturdays, and school matches will be played. This will enable the younger boys to enjoy family activities, and will be for the Junior School only.*

---

[103] The A.C.W.A. minutes, October 10th, 1975.
[104] Ibid.
[105] The A.C.W.A. minutes, October 10th, 1975.
[106] Ibid.

Saturday, September 20,1975
Appleby College Grounds
Oakville — Ontario
2 p.m. — 6 p.m.
Tickets on Sale at Gate or phone 278-9669

APPLEBY COUNTRY FAIR

"WIN
A
$50.00
T.D. BANK
ACCOUNT
"BINOCULARS"
"CAMERAS"
"WATCHES"

"WIN"
A COMPLETE
DINNER FOR TWO
ROYAL YORK
HOTEL

Bake Table — Preserves
Cheeses — Antique Auction
Arts & Crafts — Door Prizes
Fair Games — Win Assorted Prizes
Admission — $2.00 per person
Includes — Hot Dog, Hamburger, Corn

This Flyer compliments of Graphic Arts Press Inc.

Appleby Country Fair Flyer, 1975

> *"An extension will be built on Walker House, providing accommodations for eleven boys, thus relieving overcrowding in other areas. The extension will consist of five double rooms, and one single."*[107]

- $1,100. of jewellery items were sold at this meeting.

1976-1977
President   **Mrs. K. M. Gibson**

- $500.00 Bursary.
- $1,000.00 given for the purchase of folding chairs.
- Clothing Exchange to be a 50 – 50 split.
- A fall picnic was held, $2,000.00 was raised. This money was given toward the cost of dining room drapes. The drapes cost $2,794.75 plus $181.77 sales tax. Hilda Chattaway[108] very generously donated the balance of the funds needed for the drapes. The W.A. thanked her with the presentation of a needlepoint (Appleby crested) cushion.
- A filing cabinet was provided for Mrs. Ford, the school dietician.
- Jewellery was sold on Mondays in the foyer of the Classroom Building.
- $375.00 worth of Dominion Store tapes was equal to $1.00 for the Association.
- Mr. Walter Pitman, President of Ryerson Polytechnical Institute spoke at the Fall Meeting. Mr. Pitman spoke on the school curriculum and the need for continuing education for adults.
- Preparations were made all year for the Country Fair of September 1977.
- For a number of years there was a Father and Son Night at the school. Marion Larsen (the Headmaster's wife) hosted an informal supper party (as she had done for a number of previous years) for mothers. The Executive members prepared the dinner. A $2.00 donation could be made by the mothers.
- The first newsletter with Executive members contributing was issued.
- The first Appleby Cookbook was published. That would mean recipes submitted, tasted and tested, compiled, edited and printed. A major undertaking. The book was called <u>Bon Appetit Appleby</u>. Angela Platt and Mary Tarbett steered this project.
- Water leaked into the room where the Clothing Exchange was housed. Another area was outfitted for the Exchange at a cost of $365.00. Shirley Jamieson's husband gave $50.00 toward this. At this time not only were boys' clothes sold but also men's clothing.
- Mr. M. Nightingale was the guest speaker but there are no notes as to the content of his speech. It was mentioned in the minutes that mothers would prefer to hear about the school than to have an outside speaker.

1977-1978

---

[107] The A.C.W.A. minutes, May 21, 1976.
[108] Hilda was the cook. She came to the school in 1928. Mrs. Dewar said that Hilda was much loved by all.

The Appleby College Women's Association presents

Monte Carlo Night

dinner and dance

at Appleby College Oakville

April 22nd. 1978 at 6.30pm dinner at 7.30pm

catered prime roast dinner

**Dancing 8.30-12.30 to the
The Wright Brothers Band**

proceeds to the Appleby Development Fund
$15 per person

door prizes ★ blackjack ★ roulette ★ crown and anchor
over and under seven

BRING YOUR FRIENDS

Join us for a complimentary first drink

- -

Please detach and return before March 15th to:
Mrs F.V.Jelinek, 1158 Lakeshore Road East, Oakville, Ont. L6J 1L2
Please send me .... tickets at $15.00 per person. Enclosed is my cheque
for $...... made payable to Appleby College Women's Association.
Name ....
Address ....
Telephone ....

Monte Carlo Night Flyer, 1978

92

President   **Mrs. D. G. Dorion**

- Two $500.00 Bursaries were given.
- Audio visual equipment for the library was purchased with Dominion Store tapes.
- Cuisinart for the kitchen at a cost of $130.00.
- $6,000.00 given to resurface a tennis court.
- $1,000.00 for 100 chairs.
- $650.00 for a trophy case.
- $200.00 for a microphone.
- $1,000.00 for the music programme.
- $500.00 for a rug for the staff room.
- The Fall Fair generated a profit of $8,110.00.
- "As most of you know, Appleby is embarking on a major fund drive, covering the corporate sector, Old Boys, and Parents. We have been asked if we as the Women's Association would contribute whatever resources were possible, and I have accepted that challenge on your behalf. For most of us, this means the gift of our time and talents, precious resources in themselves, but capable of great things. We are proud of this school that we have entrusted our sons to, and would like its high standards to be maintained. Therefore I know we can count on your support. To that end we are planning other events to take place during the year. These will be more social in nature, but still capable of generating funds...."[109]Further to this "The target of the Parents' Division is $200,000.00 spread over 5 years made up of donations and pledges, tax deductible in the year of donation. ..."[110]
- The cookbook, <u>Bon Appetit Appleby,</u> was launched. Mr. McConnell illustrated the book. Hilda Chattaway, Marg Ford and Sheila Peck were given complimentary copies as was Mr. McConnell. The books sold for $4.50 each. They were available for sale at: the Appleby front office, St. Mildred's-Lightbourn School, St. Jude's, Harbour Books and the Appleby meetings. It was advertised for sale in <u>The Appleby Quarterly</u>.
- Jennifer's Kitchen catered the lunch for the Fall Meeting. (The dining hall staff had a much deserved rest.)
- Ms. Betty Gibb, the Librarian, was the guest speaker. She spoke of the importance of the library, its present and its future.
- The Clothing Exchange was now called Appleby Turnover. It would no longer take men's clothing or other items, only uniforms, sportswear and equipment.
- The Women's Association sold a little of everything at this point; zinc paper weights (donated by Bill Moffatt), key chains, silver spoons, mugs, steins, rings, cuff links, pennants, shields, pillows, rear window decals, redicals (peel off crests), coasters, porcelain dishes, sterling mini charms, sterling chains and earrings, sweater coats in School colours, sweat shirts, playing cards, plates with pictures of the Houses on them, 20 booster cables (had been donated) and would sell for $4.00 each. There were probably other items.

---

[109] Letter from Connie Dorion, August 1977.
[110] Letter from John W. Hueton, Board Member and Chair of the Development Committee, October 20th, 1977.

Appleby College Needlepoint, 1976
Top: Needlepoint Kit
Bottom: Finished Pillow

94

- The W.A. initiated and organized the taking of school photographs by a photographer. They also assisted on the day of photographing.
- The Spring Fling fashion show was held at the Oakville Club. Lily Keil of Lily's generously put on the event. Appleby mothers modeled and Cindy LeBrocq did the commentary. $625.00 was raised and given to the Bursary.
- An informal supper was held at the home of Marion Larsen for the mothers whose husbands were attending the Father and Son Dinner. The Executive prepared the meal for the mothers.
- Considered the name 'Bluer's Retail' for the Jewellery Shop.
- At this time a change was made to the By Laws: "Life Membership shall be granted to those members whose last sons or wards are leaving or graduating, and may be purchased for $25.00 during the final year. All proceeds will be applied to the Bursary Fund."[111]
- A Monte Carlo Night was held. The amount raised is uncertain as there are conflicting figures.

1978-1979
President   **Mrs. D. G. Dorion**

- $1,000.00 Bursary.
- 16mm projector for $714.00 for the school.
- Appleby picnic held in the fall. $875.00 from this event was given to the Development Fund, plus an additional $1,900.00.
- Photographs of students - $1,371.50.
- $500.00 for library books.
- $200.00 for four cassette players.
- Soup tureens at a cost of $360.16.
- A projector for $959.95.
- $175.00 given to the library from Dominion Store tapes of $66,000.00.
- Resusi-Annie, at a cost of $1,185.25, was purchased as an aid to teach the boys artificial respiration.
- "Gail Bascombe had a suggestion for raising funds to finance the restoration of the barn. Scenes of Appleby could be attractively frames as a special edition of prints by our Art Director, Mr. McConnell. The limited number of signed prints could be sold…"[112] *This came to fruition but the funds went to the Art Department, it had been hoped to house the Art Department in the barn. (The cost of renovating the barn was prohibitive. It was decided that it was beyond the capabilities of the W.A.).*
- Turnover to be open all year, not just June and September.
- Appleby hosted a meeting of independent boys' schools. This was called the Interschool Guild Meeting. Twenty representatives from other schools met at Connie Dorion's. They had coffee and discussed fund raising, constitutions, recruiting committee volunteers, etcetera. They were treated to lunch thanks to

---

[111] A letter to parents from Connie Dorion, April 12th, 1978.
[112] The A.C.W.A. minutes, May 29th, 1978.

Appleby Fall Fair, circa 1975

Connie and her Executive Committee. It was such a successful meeting that a future meeting was planned for the spring at St. George's to discuss fund raising.

- Once again Jennifer's Kitchen catered the Fall Meeting lunch in the gymnasium.
- Additional items for sale: crested coffee mugs, sports bags, lead pencils, pens, navy leather book marks, rings with a blue stone, lapel pins and enamel ski hat pins. To date the Shop did not have a name. Some suggestions were Apple Core, Core Store, Golden Apple and once again Bluer's Retail.
- A bingo night was held for parents and their sons. $835.00 was made.
- Marion Larsen, once again, had an informal supper (prepared by the Executive members) for mothers whose husbands were attending the Father and Son Dinner.
- Marion Larsen and a few staff wives regularly cleaned the Chapel. It was suggested that the W.A. might take this on. Gloria Anderson was in charge of the newly formed Chapel Guild.
- The Citizenship Cup, given by the W.A., bore no record of past recipients. This was rectified and also a replica cup was provided so that winners would have a keepsake.
- *Of Interest – Michael DesRoches*[62] *set up an Old Boys registry. (He assigned a class year to each Old Boy.)*
- Appleby Turnover on a need basis only. Rosalind Nightingale or Ann Mann was available to be called if one wanted to shop at Turnover.
- The Executive Committee was enlarged to include: corresponding secretary, assistant treasurer, membership secretary, new mother liaison, social convenor and telephone committee chair. Thus the by laws were changed to reflect these additions and it was written under finances "The Executive Committee shall authorize all expenditures deemed necessary to carry on the work of the Women's Association."[113]
- Root Kits were purchased from the Kidney Foundation of Canada. Each kit had an attractive wooden stand that held glass tubes for rooting plant cuttings. The kits were sold and monies collected, half given to the Women's Association and the other half given to the Kidney Foundation.
- "Mrs. Dorion paid tribute to Hilda [Chattaway] who has served the school with great devotion for fifty years. Her cooking has been enjoyed by countless boys, countless masters and all four headmasters. Hilda has received messages from all over the world this year. The Appleby College Women's Association presented Hilda with a mini-crested pen as a small token of our appreciation."[114]
- Mrs. Maxwell, the school nurse for the past 8 years, retired and was given a silver charm and Life Membership to the W.A. She was praised and thanked for looking after the boys so well. She moved to Vancouver.
- As well as all the ongoing projects the women spent much of the year preparing for the September 1979 Fall Fair.
- At the Spring Meeting the Reverend Ian Stuart, assisted by Paul Bundschuh[80], gave a full demonstration in the use of Resusi-Annie.

---

[113] The A.C.W.A. minutes, April 26th, 1979.
[114] The A.C.W.A. minutes, May 3rd, 1979.

ATTIC TREASURES AUCTION AND SALE

N.B. Saturday, September 24, 1977 at the APPLEBY COLLEGE FAIR
ACT NOW, CLEAN UP, CLEAR OUT AND HELP OUT!

Dear Appleby Family and Friends:
Attic Treasures — How can you help?

1)   Start collecting from now until September. We would
     be pleased to pick up your donations immediately.

2)   What to collect — Articles that you and your friends might
     have finished using — grown tired of — lack space for or
     just want to get rid of!
     These would be some other buyer's treasures.

     The articles you collect could be an old rocking chair, a
     flower vase, a tin cup, an iron or toaster or a dish, bed,
     a plastic flower — the range is far and wide.

3)   What to do with your collection:

     Deposit with May Dickens
     Home on the Campus   — 844-1015

          OR

     Janet Manbert
     543 Lakeshore Rd. W.
     (Opposite the College)   — 845-3753

     For pick-up or answers to any questions, please call upon
     the Committee Members:

     Mrs. Don Skinner (Barbara)   274-4232

     Mrs. L. Cooper (Barbara)   823-2978

     Mrs. M.R. Rogers (Sylvia)   822-1146

     Mrs. T. Husebye (Orse)   822-8125

Request for Auction Items, 1977

- Mr. Anthony Royse, Director of Music at Appleby, addressed the members at the Spring Meeting. He spoke of the importance of music, both listening and playing. Jonathan Haldane[82] and Philip Thompson[82] gave a short musical recital after Mr. Royce's words.

1979-1980
President   Mrs. D. J. DalBianco

- Bursary Fund $1,000.00.
- Donwoods Program[*] $5,000.00.
- Development Fund $3,500.00.
- The Houses $2,000.00.
- 100 Folding Chairs $1,400.00.
- Computer printer $ 700.00.
- Colour Analyser $ 500.00.
- Dining Room jugs $ 730.00.
- Toward piano $ 375.00.
- *The Donwood Institute gave a comprehensive course of study on drugs and alcohol. It included grades 12 and 13 and also seminars for parents. The total cost of the program was $6,750.00.
- The Fall Fair took place with great raffle prizes. "As most of you know this most generous donation was made by three Appleby fathers. One ticket consists of two chances to win two return airfares to Jamaica, use of a four bedroom oceanfront home and the choice of one week between January 10th and March 10th, 1980."[115] The second raffle prizes were wonderful too! Over $4,000.00 was made on raffles. A profit of $15,900.22 was realized overall.
- The Fall Meeting was held at the Credit Valley Golf Club. The guest speaker was Mike McManus, Producer of TV Ontario, he spoke on 'Today's Family'. "He told his audience that it was predicted that by 1990 in the United States 25% of wives would be working. He stressed that love and discipline in a family cannot be delegated. He felt children needed a close relationship with the central figure of a family. In his opinion family life must give a child his start, and that the bond of the family must be strong."[116]
- A donation was made to the Development Fund in memory of Charlie Berriman, son of Diana and John, who died in an accident. "The Berrimans are planting a tree in Charlie's memory. The Development Fund received $450.00 in his memory from various individuals. A plaque is to be put in the Junior School stating that a donation to the Colley House building was made in his memory."[117]
- The minutes had always been read at the Spring and Fall Meetings. From this time on the minutes would be circulated and adopted as such.

---

[*]   The Donwood Institute gave a comprehensive study on drugs and alcohol. It included grade 12 and 13 and also parents.
[115]   Letter to parents from Libby DalBianco, August 1979.
[116]   The A.C.W.A. minutes, October 3rd, 1979.
[117]   The A.C.W.A. minutes, November 27th, 1979.

Appleby College Principal Ned Larsen watches while Ontario Lieutenant-Governor Pauline McGibbon cuts the ribbon to officially open the newly renovated, 68-year-old Colley House. It was the first building of Appleby College.

Colley House at Appleby College rejuvenated after 68 years

By KATHY YANCHUS
OJR Staff Writer

Colley House, the 68-year-old residence at Appleby College, was officially opened Friday after a $1.2 million renovation program. Lieutenant - Governor of Ontario Pauline McGibbon was on hand to perform the ribbon cutting ceremony as school officials, parents, former and current Appleby students watched.

Colley House, built in 1911 through the generosity of Appleby's founder Sir Edmund Walker, was the first building on the college grounds. Named after Thomas Colley, a classics teacher who died in 1940, Colley House was the residential quarters, dining room, kitchen and classroom, all in one, for the college's first 20 students.

In a six-month renovation program started last June, part of a massive expansion and renovation project the college is undertaking, Colley House was gutted leaving only the floors and walls standing.

Although the exterior of the building has not been altered, its new modern interior includes carpeted bedrooms, for 60

boys, a common room, locker rooms and painted cement walls as opposed to wood and plaster interior walls for a quieter effect.

In her brief address to the assembled group, Lt.-Governor McGibbon said she thought it was important to retain the Colley House exterior.

"I think it means so much to boys who have lived in Colley House. Maybe they can't find their bedrooms and bathrooms as they were in 1911," she joked "but I think with schools it's very important to retain the memories."

Appleby's headmaster Ned Larsen said he looked upon the re-opening of the renovated Colley House "as part of the overall work in developing for our country a truly great Canadian school."

The remaining projects in the vast developmental program at the college include a new infirmary at a cost of $200,-000 and the establishment of a endowments and bursaries to the tune of $1 million through donations from corporations, former students, parents, foundations and friends.

Colley House

Colley House Article
Oakville Journal-Record, January 9, 1980

100

- On February 2nd the Father and Son Dinner took place as did the mothers informal dinner. The mothers' dinner was held at the Larsen's home. About 50 women generally attended.
- School pictures were taken.
- A dinner/art auction was planned for the fall of 1980 – it was called 'An Evening of Art'. The Development Fund gave the W.A. the original McConnell drawings to be raffled. Prints were sold and other artists donated works. Mary Gilbert of the York Fine Art Gallery, Aurora, helped organize the Art Auction.
- Sports Day picnic was organized by the W.A.
- Mr. Larsen addressed the women at the Spring Meeting. He spoke about the great number of applicants and the importance of keeping a family atmosphere at the school. Members of the Association wished Mr. Larsen well – he was going abroad for a year.
- *Of interest - John Latimer, owner and director of Kilcoo Camp for boys spoke to the assembly. "He finds children of today no longer respect a person just because of title. Respect has to be earned. He pointed out that parents must learn to adjust to the times but not give in to them completely. He took away some restrictions at this camp and found campers were not happy. He is worried about the "so-so" society. The number of suicides is increasing in the age range of 12-24. The children are no longer feeling wanted. He feels the children of today are watchers, are more sophisticated and more experienced, more open and more likely to be hurt and disappointed. He asked that we support these children and love them for what they are."[118]*

1980-1981   ***Acting Headmaster – Jack Dickens 1980-1981***
President   **Mrs. L. C. Leach**

- $ 1,000.00 Bursary.
- Grade Parties were started. These were either coffee or sherry parties.
- Fall luncheon meeting was held at the Oakville Golf Club.
- Mr. Dickens, acting Headmaster spoke to the women. He asked a number of questions and asked for input regarding the dress of students, the pros and cons of cadets and the situation of day boys. "He stated there will be no major changes this year but wants the conclusions of many of these matters to be there next year for the new Head Master."[119]
- The guest speaker was Reverend Cam Taylor from Knox Presbyterian Church. He said "The 'throw-away' society that crept into our lives in the 70's is now being changed and the attitude of the young people in the 80's is now swinging back to a more supportive and solid family life. Rev. Taylor stressed that God's will cannot be avoided and the young people today really are going in the right direction."[120]

---

[118] The A.C.W.A. minutes, May 6, 1980.
[119] The A.C.W.A. minutes, October 2nd, 1980.
[120] Ibid.

President's Pin, 1981 - 82

- It was decided that Life Memberships should be followed up with a post card after five years asking if the member wished to continue on the mailing list.
- A Fall Family Picnic was held. Mixed soccer, softball and tennis games were held. There was a senior football game in the afternoon.
- Anne Mann built shelving herself for the Turnover room.
- In order for the dance tickets for the Art Auction and Dance to be tax deductible the Women's Association books were audited. This was the beginning of the W.A. audit.
- The Art Auction/Dinner Dance was held at The Bristol Place Hotel, on Friday, November 14th, 1980. This event launched the series of limited prints by John McConnell, Appleby's Art Director. A profit of $8,111.94 was made. This money was put into an Art Development Fund which at some future date would contribute to an improved art facility at Appleby.
- $3,000.00 from the W.A and $1,000.00 from two private Executive members was donated to maintain the Donwoods Program from January through September 1981. "Joan Milburn moved that the W.A. would like to recommend to the Board that in the future, the cost for the Donwoods program be included in the budget and be incorporated in the fee structure. The motion was seconded by Lynn Batty and was carried unanimously."[121]
- Chapel Guild needed mothers to keep the choir gowns in good repair.
- Preparations for the 1981 Fall Fair had begun.
- Dominion Store tapes were collected. They wanted to purchase an electric typewriter for the library. This meant collecting $264,000.00 worth of tapes. As of October they had $75,000.00 and by May $249.898.00. Almost there.
- Supper party was held at Mrs. Dickens' home for the mothers while the Fathers and Sons had their dinner.
- The Association purchased 10 sleeping bags for Northern Campus. These were to be rented out to students.
- There was sadness over the sudden death of Frank W. Baillie[57*]. It was decided to provide a new trophy case in memory of Frank W. Baillie[57]. A brass plaque in his name was placed on the trophy case.
- $1,200.00 made available to Mr. Nightingale for traveling expenses if needed on the Choir Tour to England.
- National School Photos took the school photographs.
- Mr. Dickens addressed the Spring Meeting. He said "that one of his great pleasures was to see first hand what the Women's Association does around the school and to realize how important the Women's Association really is."[122]
- Mr. Wally Gabler, Vice-President and Chief of Toronto Retail Sales for Nesbitt Thomson was the guest speaker at the Spring Meeting. "Mr. Gabler stated that today women are a dominant force in the work field and are becoming more so. Women are beginning to accumulate dollars and need investment assistance.

---

[121] The A.C.W.A. minutes, November 21st, 1980.
[*] Frank W. Baillie[57] was Chairman of the Board from 1975-1980.
[122] The A.C.W.A. minutes, May 6th, 1981.

Headmaster - Alexis Troubetzkoy, 1981 - 1987

Women who are interested in investing should take a course and then find a good broker....."[123]

- Jennifer's Kitchen made submarine sandwiches for Sports Day.

1981-1982   *Headmaster – Alexis Troubetzkoy 1981-1987*
President   **Mrs. C. E. J. Davidson**

- $1,000.00 Bursary.
- New choir gowns for fifty boys were purchased.
- A light for outside of the Chapel was installed.
- A second trophy case and light fixture in the foyer were given.
- A set of weights was donated.
- Headphones for Mr. Boyd's class were provided.
- A loan to the first cricket team to purchase twenty blazers was made.
- Assistance in the purchase of three computers given to the school. ($2,409.00)
- $5,000.00 was given to the Art Development Fund.
- An electric typewriter was purchased for the library with the Dominion Store tapes.
- The Fall Fair was a great success. $13,392.58 was raised.
- Grade Parties were held.
- Dr. Bell passed away in the fall. $1,000.00 was given to the Bursary Fund in Dr. Bell's name.
- Jewellery was sold on the first Wednesday of each month in the foyer. Added to the inventory were glass crested mugs, paper weights, a blue pot holder with the Appleby crest, sports bags, toques, gold and sterling charms, football shirts and silver pen knives.
- A bar with a charm would be given to the outgoing President each year
- The Jewellery room got much needed shelves.
- The Fall Meeting was held at Glen Abbey Golf Club. Mr. A. Troubetzkoy, the new Headmaster was the guest speaker. He said "that this is the fifth independent school he has worked at and he is very surprised at the enthusiasm at Appleby displayed by the organizing of the class parties, the Fall Fair, billeting of out-of-town boys, etc. He had a special thank you for the mothers who helped with the cooking program. Mr. Troubetzkoy thanked us for our patience and forbearance while he attends to the idiosyncrasies of Appleby and remarked that his family is now happily settled. He asked the question: 'How are things going?' His own impression is that there is a happy spirit about the School. He remarked that we have at Appleby a most beautiful and well-equipped School with a warm, pleasant student body and selfless teaching staff. He feels there is no reason why Appleby cannot become a great School, a beacon for other schools. Mr. Troubetzkoy indicated that his approach to the job was to get to know the teachers and boys, to determine what goes on during the week and to find out the faults and strengths. He wants to evolve a plan of action to implement programs and to achieve the purposes of the School. He stated that there must be a close association between

---

[123] The A.C.W.A. minutes, May 6th, 1981.

AMMENDMENTS TO THE BY-LAWS OF THE REVISED CONSTITUTION 1976

NOMINATING COMMITTEE BY-LAW

1. The Chairman of the Nominating Committee shall be appointed by the Executive Committee. The Committee shall be chosen by the Chairman, and consist of one member of the Executive, and one member at large.

AMMENDMENT: The Chairman of the Nominating Committee shall be appointed by the Executive Committee. The Committee shall be chosen by the Chairman, and consist of at least one member of the Executive, and one member at large.

EXECUTIVE COMMITTEE BY-LAW

1. The Executive Committee shall consist of six officers, and up to four members at large. Officers are to be elected at the Annual Meeting, and a New Mother representative is to be appointed in the Fall, remaining in that office for one year.

AMMENDMENT: The Executive Committee shall consist of seven officers, and as many members at large as are deemed necessary.

OFFICERS BY-LAW

1. Officers of the Association shall be composed of the Past President, President, 1st Vice President, 2nd Vice President, Secretary and Treasurer.

AMMENDMENT: Officers of the Association shall be composed of the Past President, President, 1st Vice President, 2nd Vice President, Recording Secretary, Corresponding Secretary, and Treasurer.

DUTIES OF OFFICERS BY-LAW

AMMENDMENT: The Corresponding Secretary shall send to the membership all notices and letters, and shall conduct the correspondance of the Association except as otherwise provided.

RETIRING OFFICERS BY-LAW

2. Unless a Committee member assumes an office, she shall retire at the end of two years.
3. No office shall exceed a two year term.

AMMENDMENT: The term of office for each Executive member shall be one year. Re-election is permissible.

FINANCES BY-LAW

1. The Executive Committee shall be authorized to withdraw money for administrative needs only, at its discretion. All other expenditures shall require the authorization of a majority of the membership at a general meeting.

AMMENDMENT: The Executive Committee shall authorize all expenditures.

Revised Constitution, 1976

the parents and the School in the training of our boys, and because it is a partnership he is interested in what goes on at home as well as at School. He invited parents not to hold back, but to speak to him about both the good and bad things happening with their boys."[124]

- Purchased new Women's Association letterhead.
- Trudy Davidson suggested a fee lottery. It was put off until the next year.
- McConnell prints sold very well this year.
- A supper was held for mothers at the Troubetzkoy's on the night of the Father and Son Dinner.
- Spring Fling was held April 22nd at the Toronto Golf Club. $6,433.50 was raised.
- School photos taken.
- A trip to the Shaw Festival was made available thanks to Audrey Johnston who had a son at Appleby and worked for Royal Travel. Tickets were $30.00 each which would pay for bus, lunch at the Oban Inn and theatre. There were 40 tickets available, they sold quickly. It was a great outing.
- Cindy Lebrocq was the guest speaker. She "entertained us with a delightful and humorous speech on volunteering."[125]

1982-1983
President   Mrs. J. A. Milburn

- $1,000.00 Bursary.
- $500.00 for video games.
- $1,000.00 given to John McConnell to purchase work benches and silver smith tools.
- $600.00 given to Mr. Boyd toward the purchase of a video tape recorder.
- $500.00 to each house, a portion to be spent on recovering their billiard tables.
- A 2nd Art Auction/Dinner Dance was held. A Jack Reid watercolour was raffled. $1,839.00 was realized by the raffle. The cost of the event was $100.00 per couple. A profit of $7,708.28 was made.
- Half page ad taken in the Argus for $80.00.
- Grade Parties took place once again.
- The Fall Meeting took place at Toronto Golf Club on October 27th. The guest speaker was Honour de Pencier of the R.O.M. Honour was with the Sigmund Samuel Canadiana Gallery. She spoke of the Gallery and the Canadian Treasures stored there. She also showed slides.
- Gail Bascombe wrote a history of the start of the Art Development Fund. (It was not found in the archives.)
- The Father Son Banquet was held in January and likewise the mothers dined at Mrs. Troubetzkoy's. (In this case, the out-of-town mothers.)
- "The School's Administrator, Ian MacMillan has suggested that the W.A. take on the 'College Shop' as a new venture. It has been suggested that once a week would be sufficient to have the Shop open (possibly Wednesday after school).

---

[124] The A.C.W.A. minutes, October 27th, 1981.
[125] The A.C.W.A. minutes, May 18th, 1982.

SPRING FEUER AUCTION
APPLEBY DINING HALL - APRIL 27/84 - 8 p.m.

Flyer for 'Spring Fever' Auction, 1984

After late August and September, it could be that once a month would work nicely as long as everyone (students and Moms) knew the dates."[126] Katie Way and Bonnie Wace looked in this proposal, spoke with Mr. MacMillan and it was decided to take over the Tuck Shop after Easter, 1983.

- "It has been suggested by Peter Cameron['48], the Chairman of the Board of Governors that the W.A. consider a two-year term for the President (and therefore for the Past Pres.). This way one person would serve on the Board of Governors for four years, two on the larger Board, and two on the Management Committee. He feels this would enable the W.A. to be better integrated with the Board...."[127] ♣

- Additions to the Shop were manicure sets, address books and wallets.
- Preparations were underway for the 5th Fall Fair.
- School photographs taken by Colortron.
- The Art Fund was now $30,649.96.
- $6,000.00 was allocated to decorate and improve the reading area in the library.
- *Of interest – "This year we had such a good group of suggested workers it was difficult to choose. I hope no one feels left out as a result but the way the system works is that the Old Exec. because of their work throughout the year get to choose to move to another position before new people are considered. This year half the Executive is retiring in favour of new faces and the Nominating Committee has done a super job of filling the places. ..."[128]*
- April 30th Open House, jewellery was on sale.
- At the May meeting changes were made to the By Laws:
    1. "Officers of the Association shall consist of the Past President, ... the change being 'consist of' rather than 'be composed of'.
    2. The term of office for each Executive member shall be one year. Re-election is permissible.
    3. No office shall exceed a two year term. Re-instatement of No. 3 which had been deleted with last revision. It reflects what actually happens by tradition."[129]
- *Of interest - "A curriculum committee is working on courses for next year and how to effectively teach them and is planning for the elimination of Grade 13."[130]*
- Susie Loewen of the Toronto Garden Club was the guest speaker at the Spring Meeting. She spoke of growing herbs in your garden.
- Once again a picnic lunch was provided for Sports Day.

1983-1984
President   **Mrs. J. A. Milburn**

---

[126] A letter from Joan Milburn, January 5th, 1983.
[127] Ibid.
♣ For a number of years both President and Past President sat on the Board of Governors, today only the President does.
[128] A letter from Joan Milburn, April 1983.
[129] Ibid
[130] The A.C.W.A. minutes, May 17th, 1983.

- $1,000.00 Bursary.
- The W.A. Endowment Fund was started with an initial deposit of $10,000.00
- Purchased 6 Commodore 66 computers with disc drives and a printer.
- Donated a PA system - $1,500.00.
- Respirator for the infirmary - $650.00.
- Leatherette folders for the choir - $500.00.
- Gave more choir gowns - $600.00.
- Spent funds on refurbishing and upgrading the infirmary - $3.500.00.
- Provided metal rolling mills for the Art Department - $300.00.
- An additional $578.80 was paid to the library for the reading area.
- Katie Way and Bonnie Wace were the first convenors of the College Shop. The Shop was open Wednesdays from 12:00 – 2:00.
- W.A. membership fees were automatically included in the school fees in the Fall Term.
- The Grade Parties which had been coffee or sherry parties now became wine and cheese parties.
- More volunteers were needed in the library. Isabel Hodge, the Librarian, new to the school 1982-1983 school year, encouraged mothers to help out in the library.
- Another successful Fall Fair was held with a profit of $11,261.42.
- The Fall Meeting was held at the Burlington Golf Club followed by a fashion show by Faubourg St. Honore, Kettle Creek and Sabina. As well as the fashion show there was a guest speaker, Mrs. Nancy O'Connor, a director of the Sir Edmund Hilary Foundation. Mrs. O'Connor spoke of Sir Edmund's work among the Sherpa people and of his provision of schools and a hospital for them.
- Jewellery was still sold in the foyer of the school on the first Wednesday of each month 11:00 a.m. to 1:00 p.m. Valerie Burke ordered 50 garment bags and 5 dozen bath sheets with the Appleby crest. She also brought in for sale 5 dozen oven gloves, pot holders and tea towels all imprinted with "Kiss the Cook" in navy blue. (It was suggested that all clothing and jewellery be purchased by the College Shop.)
- Spring Auction Evening held on April 27th, 1984 in the dining room. In conjunction with this there were tickets available for a Tour of the McMichael Gallery and a Progressive Dinner to be held on May 26th. The Auction raised about $5,800.00. Together with the McMichael evening and the Hagood Hardy evening about $10,140.00 was raised.
- A book fair was held and netted $3,500.00
- Dinner for mothers once again at Mrs. Troubetzkoy's while the Father/Son Banquet was on.
- School photos taken and mothers on hand to make sure the boys were presentable.
- Two delegates went to the Interguild Meeting at Bishop Strachan School.
- Donna Piasecki arranged for volunteers for the Fulford Cup Debating Competition that took place at Appleby.
- The College Shop earned more than $5,000.00 in its first year of operation. The W.A. was offered the weight room to house the College Shop and possibly the

Jewellery. Mr. Troubetzkoy "suggested the W.A. assume stationery sales here as well (generating $9,000.00 in sales)..."[131]

- The Annual General Meeting was held on May 12th in the Raymond Massey Library. Mr. Troubetzkoy spoke briefly on the plans for the new art and music wing to be completed by January 1985. David Singer[70], spoke on the study skills guide he compiled and finally Stewart Large, head of Guidance, spoke on counseling the students prior to university entrance.

1984-1985
President   **Mrs. R. B. Humeniuk**

- $1,000.00 Bursary. "The Bursary Fund (which is the interest received from the Endowment Fund) may fall short of $1,000.00. Joan Milburn moved that should this happen, the W.A. will make up the shortfall. Seconded by Jane Moore."[132]
- $10,000.00 donated to the Endowment Fund.
- $41,000.00 was spent on furnishings and equipment for the new Art Facility.
- On October 11th to the 14th Appleby hosted a booth at the Exhibition Grounds in Toronto. The booth was called 'Time for Children'. Parents with knowledge of the school manned the booth in the day and faculty members did so in the evening.
- Presentations were given to prospective parents in the homes of current parents, in Burlington, Oakville and Mississauga.
- Paul Moore was asked to review the W.A. Constitution with a view to making it more relevant.
- Grade Parties were a great success. In future up to $100.00 would be given to parent hosts.
- The College Shop now sold clothing, stationery, and jewellery. The turnover was also housed with the Shop. The College Shop opened on Thursdays over the lunch recess as well as Wednesdays.
- A successful book fair was held. A profit of $5,015.00 was made. $700.00 was spent on the library, $250.00 to the cost of an author to teach editing, $140.00 for two authors to discuss their books and the remainder on pocket books and a printer. An additional $400.00 was given to purchase a dual disc drive.
- The Fall Meeting was held at the Glen Abbey Golf Club. The guest speaker was Mr. William Kent, Director of Admissions at the University of Toronto and Chairman of the Peel Board of Education. Mr. Kent spoke on how the new high school credit system would align itself with university entrance requirements.
- The mothers once again were welcomed to the Troubetzkoy's to dinner on the night of the Father/Son Banquet.
- A flea market was held on May 3rd in the arena. Sue Verdon organized this event. Total sales were $5,180.82.
- A Jubilee Ball (Appleby College, 75 years old) would be held in November 1985. Tickets $150.00 per couple.

---

[131] The A.C.W.A. minutes, May 7th, 1984.
[132] Ibid.

Appleby College Women's Association

Presents

The Bursary Ball

Saturday, April 16, 1988

1988 Bursary Ball Program Cover

- School photos were taken.
- Invitations were received by a number of independent schools. This was a reciprocal arrangement. It was voted that the Association pay for a ticket. In this way the invited person did not have to attend the luncheon alone.
- A full page advertisement was taken in the Argus.
- The Annual General Meeting was held in the John Guest Hall. Mr. David Boyd gave a brief history of the Black Magic Mime Troupe. The group performed to an enthusiastic audience. $200.00 was given to the group to help with expenses. Tours of the new buildings were given. (Nicholas Arts Centre.)
- *Of interest – BSS (Bishop Strachan School) wants all school W.A. Executives to draw policy and guide lines regarding teenage parties, to be implemented by all parents. A suggested outline was circulated. This will be discussed at the next Interguild meeting and all independent school parents should be advised on the policies determined."*[133]
- Held a ring day in April.
- White sweaters with blue trim were purchased to be sold to prefects.
- Coffee, pop and donuts served on Sports Day. Parents were encouraged to bring a picnic lunch.
- Parent information evenings were held to discuss alcohol. Judy Rowntree, Head Nurse of the Infirmary, chaired these evenings.

1985-1986
President　　　　　　　　　　　　**Mrs. R. S. Maich**

- $1,000.00 Bursary.
- $10,000.00 to the Endowment Fund.
- $1,500.00 was given to The Jubilee Quarterly.
- $500.00 was donated in Hilda Chattaway's memory to the Appleby College Foundation.
- After having given $41,000.00 to the new Art Facility, $3,814.32 remained from recent sales of McConnell Prints. This money too was directed to the Art Facility.
- $500.00 spent on improvements to the College Shop and Turnover premises.
- $10,000.00 spent on refurbishing Powell's House Common Room. Information evenings were held on drug and alcohol abuse. Students were encouraged to attend.
- Photographs were taken earlier this year. Europa Photographers from Kerr Street did the photos.
- The Grade Parties were barbecues. It was felt that these were special celebrations for the 75th anniversary. The format was left up to the hostesses. $100.00 was given but did not seem adequate.
- Turnover moved away from the College Shop to a separate locale.
- The English Department organized a book fair and the W.A. provided the volunteers to operate it. It raised $4,000.00.

---

[133] The A.C.W.A. minutes, April 3rd, 1985.

The Appleby College Bursary Ball has been organized to raise monies to strengthen the Appleby College Endowment Fund. Established in 1959, the Fund provides essential financial aid for deserving and promising students who require it. Truly, a healthy Endowment Fund is a vital component of a vibrant School.

1988 Bursary Ball Program, Inside Cover Note

- The new facility (Nicholas Arts Centre) was opened with a celebration. The Right Honorable the Countess Mountbatten of Burma was in attendance, not only to open Nicholas Arts Centre but also to review the Cadet Corps. Susan and Issa Nicholas were the principal donors of this project. They had three sons in the school. Susan remembers that the journalist for the local newspaper felt that only Lady Mountbatten was properly attired for the day. (It was a miserable, blustery day.) Susan said that in looking back she would agree with the reporter. Regardless of the weather it was a festive and wonderful day. "After cutting a ribbon to declare Nicholas Court officially open, Lady Mountbatten toured the new facility in the company of Mr. Troubetzkoy, new Board chairman Pearce Bunting[47], and Mr. and Mrs. Issa Nicholas. She then attended a luncheon given by the Women's Association."[134] The school provided the wine and the W.A. the luncheon. *Of interest – the Nicholas Arts Centre would become an extremely busy and productive centre. "The Nicholas Arts Centre has been a hub of activity this year with the debut of its first Concert Series; a private lesson programme encompassing art, music and drama; and a summer Centre for the Arts run for both the Appleby and Oakville communities."[135]*
- School photos were taken with an 8" x 10" being taken of the classes.
- The Jubilee Ball was a great success, with 400 in attendance. Four Victorian Benches were purchased for Nicholas Court from the proceeds of the evening. The 48 prints by Betty Goodfellow that were left over were sold in the Shop for $10.00 each.
- Canadian Tire money was collected by the Junior School. This money was used to purchase a vacuum for the Chapel Guild for cleaning.
- $100.00 was spent by the Chapel Guild on Christmas decorations. These would be used in years to come and were considered an investment.
- Mr. Peter Cameron[48]* (Mr. Cameron sent a thank you letter to the W.A. thanking them for all the support they had given him and all that they had done for the school) stepped down as Chairman of the Board and Mr. Pearce Bunting[47] took on this role.
- A flea market was held in the Arena in May. Details of profits were not available.
- The mothers' dinner which had been held in conjunction with the Father/Son Banquet was discontinued.
- The Annual General Meeting was held at the Glen Abbey Golf Club. Mr. Troubetzkoy thanked the women for all that they had done over the past year and for the endowment funds. The guest speaker, Mr. Jack Batten, author of <u>The Appleby Story</u>, answered questions from the floor.

1986-1987
President   **Mrs. R. S. Maich**

---

[134] <u>The Appleby Quarterly,</u> December 1985, Volume 10 Number 1
[135] <u>The Appleby Quarterly,</u> July 1993, Volume 15 Number 1.
* Peter Cameron[48] was Chairman of the Board of Appleby College from 1980-1985.

Headmaster - Guy McLean, 1987 - Present - with wife Joanne

- $10,000.00 to the Endowment Fund.
- Photographs were taken once again by Europa Photography.
- The Grade Parties were held. Each hostess chose the type of affair – a coffee party, wine and cheese, a dinner (pot luck) or whatever.
- The College Shop flourished.
- Turnover did well.
- The Chapel Guild carried on with their good work.
- The W.A. hosted Interguild. The delegates were given tours of the school by the boys. Meetings were held both morning and afternoon. The guests were treated to a delicious and elegant lunch prepared and served by Executive members and volunteers from the Association. Sharon Maich recalled cooking pots and pots of asparagus and making hollandaise sauce to serve on it. The lunch was served in Hardwick Hall. It was a most successful, productive and fun day.
- The Walker House Common Room was refurbished.
- There would not be another Fall Fair. The women felt that for the amount of work entailed and the monies generated it was not worth all the labour. There were other ways of raising funds. In lieu of the Fall Fair a Pot Luck Luncheon was held for the mothers – this generated good will and camaraderie. One of the greatest by-products of the Association was the friendships that were formed.
- The Annual General Meeting took place at the Glen Abbey Golf Club. Mr. Troubetzkoy was the guest speaker and spoke on education.
- The Canadian Tire Money Blitz took place. Clocks were purchased for the classrooms with the funds that were collected.
- Plans for the Bursary Ball were devised during this spring.
- The W.A. assisted with Sports Day and sold Shop items as was their usual.
- Mr. Troubetzkoy left Appleby to go to the Toronto French School.

1987-1988   *Headmaster – Guy McLean 1987-*
President   **Mrs. B. G. Coleman**

- $57,500.00 given to the Endowment Fund.
- The College Shop and Turnover thrived.
- Mothers continued to volunteer in the library.
- Chapel Guild carried on cleaning but also decorating for Carol Services and other functions.
- Canadian Tire Blitz was held.
- Grade Parties were ongoing and held in private homes.
- Pot Luck Luncheon was held in Hardwick Hall.
- The Bursary Ball was held April 16th, 1988. It was a great success allowing the W.A. to enrich the Endowment Fund by $57,500.00. There was a silent auction, dinner and dancing. It was also the precursor of the Board sponsored auction which is held today at the school and has been held since 1990.
- School photos were taken.
- The Annual General Meeting was held at the Glen Abbey Golf Club. Mr. Guy McLean, the new Headmaster, addressed the assembled group.

Past Presidents of Women's Association Honoured with Plaque at AGM - May, 1989

Standing: Connie Dorion, Barbara Gibson, Joan Milburn, Trudy Davidson, Past President Mary Coleman,
President Maggie Larock, Sharon Maich, Judy Leach, Barb Humeniuk, Libby DalBianco, Brenda Bisiker

Seated: Shirley Jamieson, Frances Waters, Isabel Collins, Mary Wace, Betty Newlands, June Bramall (Gurth'41)

- The W.A. provided refreshments for Sports Day.

1988-1989
President   **Mrs. B. G. Coleman**

- $10,000.00 to the Endowment Fund.
- $10,000.00 spent on refurbishing Colley House.
- The first <u>Parents' Handbook</u> was laid out and edited by this Executive Committee, in particular, Maggie Larock.
- Grade Parties were held once again in the homes of parents.
- School photographs were taken.
- The Canadian Tire Money Blitz continued. Items were purchased for the infirmary.
- The first Tuition Lottery was held. Sharon Campbell, Jeanette Cooke and Doreen Weston looked after this project.
- *Of interest – "Blue suits are being phased out as the Senior School boys' No. 1 kit, and Saturday morning classes have been done away with.*
    "The blue suit will be replaced by a navy blazer with a bullion (wire) pocket badge. Grey flannels, white shirt and school tie complete the Senior School's official ensemble.
    "In explaining the change, Headmaster Guy McLean cited ease of recognition and considerations of expense in the break with tradition."[136]
- The Annual General Meeting was held at the Glen Abbey Golf Club. There was great excitement at this meeting. All Past Presidents had been invited for the presentation of a plaque which named all the Past Presidents and the year or years they served. Brenda Bisiker had "conceived and spearheaded the creation of the record board".[137] Mrs. R. G. Wace, President 1956-1958 unveiled the plaque. Mr. McLean addressed the meeting and thanked the women for their hard work and the cheque for the Endowment Fund. Sally Armstrong, the guest speaker, spoke to the women encouraging them to reach their full potential. (Sally, an Oakville girl, was at that time the Editor of <u>Homemaker's Magazine</u>). There were 189 persons present for this luncheon.
- The W.A. new fund raising initiative was to build a new Student Health Centre.
- As usual the W.A. helped with Sports Day.

1989-1990
President   **Mrs. J. B. Larock**

- $10,000.00 to the Endowment Fund.
- $40,000.00 to the Student Health Centre.
- There was a Friday the 13th barbecue, "to foster Appleby family spirit as well as raise awareness of W.A.'s Student Health Centre Project".[138]

---

[136] <u>The Appleby Quarterly</u>, December 1989, Vol. 12-No. 2.
[137] Ibid.
[138] The A.C.W.A. minutes, June 6th, 1989.

Maggie Larock, Teena McDiarmid and Michael Nightingale

- Purchased ¼ page space in the <u>Argus</u> for the photograph of the Past Presidents and Present President.
- $2,242.04 for printing of the <u>Parent Handbook</u>.
- Grade Parties were held. Appleby dishes were used in homes. Midge DesRoches (Michael[62]) organized the first Grade Parties held in the Headmaster's home.
- *Of interest – In regard to the first Board auction "Maggie discussed with the Executive the importance of understanding that this is a Board event and not a W.A. function. Although we support the Board as much as possible, and will volunteer to help out to our utmost, the usual W.A. activities are our first priority."[139]*
- There was a contest for a logo for the Student Health Centre – Jeremy Hurst[94] won $25.00 for his design. Betty Goodfellow and Helen Barnes helped with the logo.
- The Friday the 13th Barbecue raised almost $4,000.00 for the Health Centre.
- Canadian Tire Money Blitz was held.
- Drama Costume Committee was set up to have everything catalogued and cleaned.
- Pot Luck Luncheon was held once again. Art teachers, Betty Goodfellow and Chris Finn displayed art work in Hardwick Hall.
- Turnover moved to the basement of the Development Office, now called Alumni House, once the home of Bert Hardwick and his wife and at a later date, among others, home to Sue and Fran Richardson and Rosalind and Michael Nightingale.
- *Of interest – Bert Hardwick was an English and French master. He wrote English help books such as <u>Words Are Important</u>. He also directed and produced many of the plays that were performed at Appleby during the 50's and 60's.*
- Christmas Shopping Days saw the College Shop open a couple of days for parent shopping.
- Once again Appleby hosted the Fulford Cup Debates. Parents helped with the event, 75 judges were needed. Approximately 96 students from grade 8 to senior year and 25 coaches attended.
- The W.A. helped with Open House for the Junior School, the ladies served refreshments.
- The College Shop generated a profit of $33,588.65.
- The Bookstore was opened in the fall. A great deal of thanks to Maggie Goh for her initiatives and support during the inception of this undertaking. She not only got the project off the ground but served as the first Bookstore convenor. The Association made 20% on each book.
- Permanent name tags were purchased for Executive members and College Shop volunteers.
- A new photographer looked after school photos. Mr. Nightingale requested that class pictures be taken as well as individual.
- A Plant Committee was established to look after plants in the library.

---

[139] The A.C.W.A. minutes, October 3rd, 1989.

Pot Luck, 1993 - Jackie Haroun and Libby Heisey

- The second Tuition Lottery was held. Association members sold tickets all during the year. The final draw was held at the Board auction on June 1st. *Of interest – "There will be 4 preliminary draws for $500.00 on May 4, 11, 18 and 25 with the major draw of $10,500. on June 1 at the Auction. 1,000 tickets will be printed and can be purchased by cheque or charged to school account. They will sell for $25.00 each or 5 for $100.00. Parents will be reminded that it is not necessary to attend the auction to be eligible to win."[140]* The profit was $5,845.48 and was given to the Health Centre. The Mostad family of Campbellville won the tuition.

- Shirley Kent, School Secretary retired and was presented with a silver tray and staff party in her honour. The W.A. gave her an atlas and letter of thanks from the Association.

- "Mary [Coleman], Maggie [Larock] and Joan Milburn have reviewed the Constitution and everyone will receive the revised version shortly. The major change is the name: to the Appleby College Parent's Association, reflecting the involvement of the fathers in so many activities of the School and W.A.".[141] The name change was made because co-education was imminent.

- The Annual General Meeting was held at Glen Abbey Golf Club. "Mr. McLean thanked the Women's Association for all their efforts on behalf of the School, and for the two donations to the Endowment Fund and the Student Health Centre.

    Mr. McLean then described the efforts of the School to help the students become more socially aware of the world outside the School gates through community service and the Student newspaper. He also described the benefits that he has seen with Saturday School no longer a part of the Curriculum (better physical and mental health on the part of the students and teachers). Mr. McLean also reported on the Coeducation Steering Committee and the various focus groups in place to study all aspects of implementation of coeducation in 1991."[142]

- Both a Junior and Senior Sports Day were held. The W.A. sold hot dogs again this year and the usual Shop merchandise was available.

- *Of interest – The fees for 1990-1991 were: boarders $17,900. plus a $600.00 personal service fee, Upper I and Upper II $11,000. plus a personal service fee of $500.00, and grades 4 through 8 $9,850. plus a personal service fee of $400.*

1990-1991
President   **Maggie Larock**

- $15,000.00 to the Endowment Fund.
- $100.00 given to the Chapel.
- $4,212.25 for Chapel vestments
- $200.00 for ad in the Argus.
- $10,000.00 for furnishings for new Common Room in the Student Health Centre.
- $500.00 to the Drama Costume Committee to be used as they saw fit.

---

[140] The A.C.W.A. minutes, March 6th, 1990.
[141] The A.C.W.A. minutes, April 10th, 1990.
[142] The A.C.W.A. minutes, May 2nd, 1990.

House Tour, 1992
Guest at left, Nancy Baillie (Jim '37), Pam Ostrom

- A mural in the gymnasium, on the wall behind the bleachers was painted at a cost of $700.00 which the P.A. (Parents' Association) covered. The mural was designed and painted by Appleby students under the supervision of Art teacher Chris Finn.
- $100.00 donation was made to the Chapel in memory of the Nicholsons' daughter.
- The first and only male to date, Jim Valade, served as Treasurer on the Executive Committee.
- The Jewellery section of the College Shop sold watches. Ring day for graduates was held.
- The Bookstore had a profit of about $10,000.00 in its first year of operation. The Bookstore inventory was input into a computer by Laurel Lavalle. This helped tremendously.
- The College Shop or the Bookstore carried $115.00 calculators for the students at the request of the math department. Some students lost them early in the year – the women began to record the serial number on the calculator in order to be able to track them if misplaced.
- It was recommended that the Turnover be open once a month next year rather than weekly.
- Grade Parties were held. It was decided that a thorough explanation of how Grade Parties operate should go into the August Newsletter. At this point in time each parent was expected to bring wine or food, but some did not realize. It was also decided that Hostesses should receive greater reimbursement. Grade 5 hostess to receive $100.00, grades 6, 7 and 8 $150.00 and Senior School $200.00. The classes got larger each year thus the increase in funds.
- Pot Luck Luncheon was held as usual in Hardwick Hall and was most successful. There were 100 persons served, 25 to 30 of them being staff members.
- Sue Wu, convenor of the Chapel Guild looked into the cost of refurbishing the Chapel. Mr. McLean felt that this was a cost to be borne by the College, replacement of rugs and window cleaning. *Of interest – "Some parents have expressed concern to Sue [Wu] about the fire hazards of the many candles burning in the Chapel during the Christmas services. Suggestions to allay their concerns are: to have fire extinguishers visible and handy; and to increase the number of Chapel wardens who monitor the burning candles and perhaps snuff them out sooner rather than later. Sue is going to try freezing the candles, in the hopes that they will burn more slowly."[143]*
- Another Tuition Lottery was held. The grand prize was $10,000.00 toward tuition with four $500.00 early bird draws. Deb Schnarr looked after this project. The draw was held on Junior Sports Day. A $1,500.00 profit was made.
- A periodical called Parent Association Line (PAL) was subscribed to. True to its title it talks of parent issues and is still available today.
- "Marg [Shorey] contacted John McConnell about signing the remainder of his school prints. He has agreed to do this, but has requested that some of the proceeds be returned to him. Marg Shorey made this MOTION: that 15% of the

---

[143] The A.C.P.A. minutes, November 6th, 1990.

First House Tour - Some Volunteers

Standing, Back Row - L to R: Margrit Ross, Jeannie Osmak, --, Elaine Mahoney
Standing, Middle Row - L to R: Isabel Hodge, Christine Apted, Lynn Brown, Jill Mark,
Colleen Balders, Isabel Fox, Jana Gray, Margaret Bennett
Kneeling, Front Row - L to R: Marjorie Alliston, Maggie Goh with son, Yang-Yi, Diane Boston, Lille Amm,
Lorraine Shrigley, Stefa Williams (Co-Chair with Lorraine Chapman)

proceeds of the sale of the McConnell prints be returned to John McConnell, and that these funds be paid to him annually. Seconded by Libby Heisey. Carried."[144]

- A United Way walkathon was held. Many parents volunteered as crossing guards, manned food and beverage depots and helped in any way they could.
- G.S.T. was discussed with Ian MacMillan.
- Senior Grade party was held at the Headmaster's home.
- Turnover was open every Monday from 3:30 to 4:30. Turnover sale was held on Sports Day.
- There was discussion of the purchase of computers for the College Shop and Bookstore. It was decided that this was premature until the College decided what direction it would take.
- Student photos were taken in front of the classroom building. It was suggested that next year photos should be taken with the Chapel as a backdrop as had been done in the past.
- Executive job descriptions were updated and each Executive member was given one.
- Development Office took over the publication of the <u>Parent Handbook</u> with the P.A. liaising.
- Deanna Laws ran the Canadian Tire Money Blitz which generated $651.02.
- *Of interest – "It is becoming apparent that the Development Office will be doing the major fundraising for the School through capital campaigns and the annual fund. But the fact remains that both the Art facility and The Student Health Centre received their start from the Women's Association. Perhaps the role of the A.C.P.A. is now more one of 'moral suasion', encouraging new projects at a preliminary level. In this respect a new Student Centre is an excellent focus as a new project of the Parent's Association."[145]*
- The Annual General Meeting was held at Glen Abbey Golf Club. *Of interest- Mr. McLean reviewed the progress of the Art and Music programs in the past ten years. He outlined a new structure for the Arts program for next year: with two departments, Visual and Performing. A short term goal for the Arts Department is a small theatre and other arts facilities (e.g. photography) in a new Student Centre."[146]*

Appleby parent and child psychiatrist, Dr. Alan Brown, gave a warm and sometimes funny talk on teenagers. He was very well received.

1991-1992
President   **Maggie Goh**
- $15,000.00 to the Bursary (endowment) Fund
- $20,000.00 for dining hall curtains.
- $5,000. 00 for the initial drawings for the Student Centre.
- $20,000.00 to the student newspaper over a two year period.

---

[144] The A.C.P.A. minutes, December 4th, 1990.
[145] The A.C.P.A. minutes, April 2, 1991.
[146] The A.C.P.A. minutes, May 1st, 1991.

Bookstore Sale

Vicki Kennan seated, Vicki Lydall standing, unidentified student.

Bookstore Volunteers

Sally Ng and Eve Willis

- Girls began to attend the College. As Maggie stated in her August Newsletter she had a daughter entering the school in September.
- Maggie Goh (editor and owner of Rubicon publishing) improved the A.C.P.A. Newsletters. With the advent of computers and people who knew how to operate them, great publications were possible. Maggie added a new dimension to the P.A. Newsletter.
- The parents worked hard, under the guidance of Elaine Mahoney and Anne Sinclair, in hand with David Paul, to billet 225 for the Under 13 National Soccer Tournament. Appleby hosted this event and very successfully.
- A $50.00 fee was levied by Interguild for all participating schools.
- Grade Parties were successfully held. The school was growing and it was getting harder to find hosts who could house so many guests. It was decided that the evenings be wine and cheese parties held at the school.
- The College Shop added grey dress socks for boys, navy tights and knee socks for girls, dress shirts for boys – on a pre-order basis, and navy knit vests for boys and girls. They also added items for team uniforms. They advertised in order to appeal to families that there was no G.S.T. (Goods and Services Tax), better prices than retail and profits went directly to the school. (this is still true today)
- Once again a successful Potluck Luncheon was held in Hardwick Hall. About 98 were in attendance.
- Maggie Levy started an evening Bridge Club. They are still playing today.
- Marg Shorey undertook the project of producing a new cookbook. $20,000.00 was put up to fund the printing of the Cookbook. The Art Department took on the task of preparing a cover and sketches for the book. Parents and other Appleby family members submitted recipes. Marg and her committee cooked and tasted and wrote and cooked and tasted and wrote. They laughed a lot too!
- School photos were taken and overseen by the P.A. as always.
- Once again there was talk of a cross walk or stop light to be installed in front of the school.
- Stefa Williams reported "The College Shop sales for September were $45,000. more than all of last year. This is thought to be due to the new gym uniform and the buying habits of the female students."[147] Jackets without a crest in navy nylon were purchased for the Shop.
- Shop hours to be Mondays, Tuesdays and Thursday from noon to 2:00 p.m.
- 39 grad rings were ordered. There was some question over whether red hair bands were allowed.
- Turnover was open only the first Monday of the month or special arrangement was to be made with Gerry Walters.
- The Chapel Guild was given $200.00 for flowers for the Carol Services. The services were earlier – last week in November or first week in December.
- School photos were taken. In order that graduate pictures were the same from year to year the P.A. purchased two black graduation gowns and graduation colours for use in the senior school photos.

---

[147] The A.C.P.A. minutes, October 1st, 1991.

Bookstore Line up - A September Ritual

Some of the Bookstore Convenors, 1998 - 99
Colleen Balders, Maggie Levy, Hilary Selby, Jana Gray, Amber Ing
at Glen Abbey for the Annual General Meeting.

- Margaret Bennett (Mark[64]), Jackie Haroun, Hilary Maile and Ann Sinclair ran the Tuition Lottery.
- The Canadian Tire Money Blitz was once again organized and run by Deanna Laws. A T.V. and V.C.R. were purchased for the Health Centre.
- Jim Valade built a barrel and basketball net contraption for pennies. It was felt that much could be raised by collecting pennies. The pennies from the Penny Blitz needed to be counted, there was a 4% charge at the bank to use their counting machine.
- Plans for a House Tour in December 1992 were made. Lorraine Chapman and Stefa Williams chaired this event. Being the first it was quite an undertaking, just like the first Fall Fair or first anything. Once this was completed Lorraine and Stefa passed on an outline for future tours making it easier for those who would follow in their footsteps.
- There was talk of work being done on the archives. (The archives are still waiting. They amount to two boxes of papers. Sad to say few photos, far too few mementos, all the minutes with the exception of 1928-1932 and sadly 1986-1989 [but there is still hope they may turn up]. Perhaps Michael DesRoches[62] as Appleby Archivist will take this project on and see that we preserve our history to the best that we are able.)
- Life Membership fees were raised from $30.00 to $40.00 per year.
- The Parents' Association decided to have composite pictures made up each year of all the graduating students, thus depicting the class as one. A small (about 8½" x 11") composite would be presented to each student and a large composite would be hung in the foyer of the Classroom Building. This is still being done in 2003.
- The Annual General Meeting was held at Glen Abbey Golf Club. Erica Smith had some moments of question while Glen Abbey decided whether they would be renovating or operating. Fortunately they were open. Chairman of the Board, Aubrey Baillie[63], addressed the Parent's Association as did Headmaster Guy McLean. The guest speaker was Phil Johnson who spoke on "Time Out: Low-Tech Wisdom for High Stress Lives".[148] This talk was based on a book that he had written.

    At this meeting Guy presented each outgoing Executive member with a book, presented in her name, and for use in the library. This is an ongoing practice.

1992-1993
President   Maggie Goh
- $15,000.00 to the Bursary Fund.
- $2,110.00 for the Bursary Fund from profits from the Tuition Lottery. This was set up as the start of a separate Loan Fund, a branch of Bursary.
- $14,627.27 for the CD-Rom for the Raymond Massey Library.
- $24,500.00 for a computer lab.
- $1,482.39 for composite grad. pictures.

---

[148] The A.C.P.A. minutes, March 3rd, 1992.

The Chapel decorated for Carol Services and Christmas

- $2,500.00 for soil testing for a proposed Student Centre.
- $191.34 for the waterfront project.[*]
- $300.00 for an ad in the Argus.
- $5,000.00 was donated for a conference. This would be done again for the next two years. Guy McLean would arrange for the speakers for the student body.
- The grade 8 and Senior Year parties were held at Guy McLean's home. The other grades were hosted at individual homes.
- Barbara Lennox chaired the Canadian Tire Money Blitz.
- Pot Luck was held as usual in Hardwick Hall. It was laborious carrying plates from the kitchen and rental tables up the stairs. For a number of years the women had done this labour with much help from the kitchen staff.
- Eve Willis arranged for a silver tea service to be donated to the Parent's Association from Oneida. This service complimented the one tea service the association already had and enabled two women to pour and serve approximately 1500 guests on House Tour day. The original tea service was donated to the W.A. by Mr. and Mrs. R. Rumsey of Winnipeg. It has been treated with loving care and has been used countless times.
- The first House Tour was held and to great acclaim. It was a most successful financial venture, $30,000.00 was generated. It was also a tremendous vehicle for great public relations for Appleby. The ticket itself was beautifully designed by Mariella Holmes and it became a keepsake for many. The House Tour generated a great deal of goodwill. Not only were the homes gorgeous but so too were the Chapel and the John Guest Hall. Marjorie Alliston convened the bake sale and Margaret Bennett (Mark['64]) the tea. Bake Sale and tea were held in the dining hall as well as a raffle that Gerry Walters organized. It seemed that the dining hall was the heart of the tour. Lorraine Chapman, Stefa Williams and the other volunteers set quite a standard to be followed.
- A fitness day was held on April 17th. A number of parents took part.
- Chapel Guild convenor, Anne Sinclair had a friend recover the kneelers for bride and groom in the Chapel. She arranged for maintenance to build a cupboard for Reverend Lennox to hang his vestments in and also an advent wreath stand.
- The Interguild Meeting was held at Trafalgar Castle School in Whitby. A number of delegates from Appleby attended.
- The P.A. suggested that parent interviews be held twice yearly. As of 2003 they are held twice a year, fall and spring.
- The Annual General Meeting was held at Glen Abbey Golf Club. Maggie Goh welcomed 11 Past Presidents (11 of the 18 living presidents) of the Association and parents of the first graduating class that included girls.

The new Cookbook, A Taste of Appleby, was launched. There was great excitement – at the luncheon many books were sold as were aprons (these were made up to be sold along with the cookbooks) and complimentary book marks

---

[*] It had been hoped that the waterfront might be developed with docks and on the shore house a Biology Centre. With this in mind, Robert Bateman donated a print which was raffled in 1994. To date nothing has been done with the waterfront because there have been so many other more pressing needs. One day a research centre and heaven knows what else may be on Appleby's shores. Sailing?

1994 - Drunk Driving Talk
Students listening attentively, (in fact riveted) to a guest speaker who had been severely affected by his drunk driving where his best friend had been killed in the accident.

Afternoon Bridge Group
*Sally Ng, Ann Ferguson at left
Dede Hacking, Angela Lukowski at right*

(thanks to Jackie Haroun) were given with 'A Taste of Appleby' written on them. The aprons were given to each committee member, sponsors and kitchen staff. The books sold for $16.00 each. They were sold in the College Shop, at Bookers, Quest Booksellers and as Marg Shorey said 'from the trunk of the car'.

Michael Nightingale, the guest speaker, spoke of his travels with his wife Rosalind. Michael had taken a sabbatical year and traveled with Rosalind "to France, Thailand, India, Hong Kong, China, Russia, Hungary, Czechoslovakia and Austria knowing that, somewhere along the way, they would be robbed."[149] Indeed they were. Rosalind said "It was a good lesson, actually. We learned to travel light very early on in the journey …".[150] The talk of their adventures was received with enthusiasm and a number of questions that reflected the great interest of the listeners. (It was so well received that Michael gave a chat, with slides and Rosalind's insights in the dining hall one evening as well.)

1993-1994

President   **Marg Shorey**[*]

- $15,000.00 for the Bursary Fund.
- $20,000.00 for the Baillie House Common Room.
- $2,000.00 given for fitness equipment.
- $10,000.00 for a sound system for the John Guest Hall.
- $10,000.00 given to the Art Department for a print making studio.
- At this time there were 160 Life Members.
- Eve Willis ran the Tuition Lottery for this year. It was frustrating because parents were no longer able to bill the school for such extras. It made for a harder sell. Nonetheless Eve did a terrific job.
- Pot Luck was held in Hardwick Hall. Once again laboriously setting up. Everything hauled up the stairs. It was successful and generated some of that Appleby family warmth. The women enjoyed themselves, even the set up and clean up.
- *Of interest - By this time grades 4, 5 and 6 had been phased out. This allowed for more students in the upper school.*
- Dede Hacking started an afternoon bridge group which has now become another Appleby evening bridge group. Initially they met in the dining hall on Thursday afternoons. Both groups, the one started by Maggie Levy and the other by Dede still play in 2003.
- The Bookstore was thriving. It was particularly busy at the beginning and end of term which would be a natural. Many volunteers were employed here especially in September with students needing books and in June with book returns.
- Once again there was talk of getting the archival material in order. This did not take place.

---

[149] The Appleby Quarterly, April 1993, Vol. 14 No 4.
[150] The Appleby Quarterly, April 1993, Vol. 14, No. 4.
[*] Marg Shorey was always called Mags by husband Roger and a few dear friends. She began to sign her Newsletters Mags and from then on it has been Mags, not Marg.

Some of Appleby's Kitchen Staff - Always so helpful!

- The Chapel was done up beautifully for Carol Services. All the Chapel Guilds over the years had done a marvelous job decorating and cleaning the Chapel. Not only did they do this for Carol Services but also for Confirmation, Graduation and any other special event that arose.
- There was an Interguild Shop Meeting held at York School. Wendy Smith attended and felt this was a step forward for the Shops in that collectively the buying power would be great.
- Stationery, jewellery and Turnover were all prospering. The jewellery section of the College Shop added leather belts, cake tins and car mugs to their inventory.
- Grade Parties were held successfully with two at the Headmaster's, Senior and Upper One. Next year three would be held at the McLean's – the Middle One as well.
- *Of interest – Baillie House (girls' residence) was officially opened. "Forty members of the Baillie family were on hand for the opening, including Board Chairman Aubrey Baillie[63]. A plaque, also designed by Gren Weis[69], commemorates the names of all 28 family members who have studied at Appleby, and features a portrait of Lady Baillie. Unveiled by Jim Baillie[37] and his granddaughter Nancy Unsworth[99], an inscription on the plaque reads: "Baillie House is named in honour of the Baillie Family and acknowledges the gratitude of Appleby College to Lady Baillie, whose abiding faith in the School set an example of leadership and support which has been sustained by succeeding generations of her family."[151]*
- The DARE program (The Drug Abuse Resistance Education Program) was presented in the school. In conjunction with this Libby Heisey made arrangements for a presentation to the whole school "by a lawyer, Mr. Miller, and a young man whose life has been severely affected by his drunk driving, including the death and injury of his closest friends. Libby has met with Guy to ensure that there is follow up discussion with students by appropriate staff. She is also meeting with Jennifer Neal to ensure media coverage. Reuben Levy[94] will introduce the speaker."[152] The young fellow came and spoke to a stunned but attentive audience. What an impact his speech had on students, faculty and parents. To this day people have a clear remembrance of that young man's presentation. It was sad and extremely emotional but went to the hearts and minds of all present.
- On a happier note. Maggie Goh and Pat Chiang organized a Chinese New Year dinner. It was held in Mississauga at a Chinese restaurant. Bill Coleman spoke on Chinese culture. People had a marvelous time and learned a little of how the Chinese celebrate their New Year. Sadly Maggie was called away home to Singapore shortly before the event and missed all the fun.
- The Canadian Tire Money Blitz was held again. It was not as successful as in previous years. The student body no longer had the young students who were so enthusiastic competing with each other to bring in the most money. This had been a very successful fund raiser thanks not only to our volunteers and parent body

---

[151] The Appleby Quarterly, December 1993, Vol. 15, No. 2.
[152] The A.C.P.A. minutes, January 11th, 1994.

The Appleby College Parents' Association
cordially invites you to attend the

ANNUAL MEETING and LUNCHEON
Wednesday, May 17, 1995

APPLEBY COLLEGE
Special Guest
J. PEARCE BUNTING
"Changing Traditions"

	The Gym
10:30	Arrival & Coffee
* 11:00	O.S.T. Preview
11:30	Meeting
12:30	Speaker Reception
1:30	Lunch in The John Guest Dining Hall

R.s.v.p. by May 3
Margaret Bennett
849-5594

Invitation to AGM & Luncheon, 1995

1995 AGM Luncheon

L to R: Stephanie Bunting, Maggie Goh, Pearce Bunting '47, Marg Bowes, Mags Shorey,
Les and Stefa Williams, Fran Richardson, Brian O'Leary

but particularly to Don Butorac, a former parent, and Canadian Tire owner. Don was extremely generous with the Association, allowing it triple the amount we collected and also allowing parents a discount when they shopped in his store.

- Each spring the Headmaster would visit the Executive Committee wherever they met, at this time in the Library Conference Room and present his 'wish list'. The Executive Committee would deliberate, discuss and decide where monies would be spent, based on the wish list and any strong suasion from within. This happened in Lady Baillie's time as it does today in Jane Minkhorst's. It seemed that the wish list became more elaborate as the years went by but indeed so too did the monies increase and everything else about the school.

    Guy McLean did not just present this list. He came and chatted with the Executive Committee about the future of the school. He would outline the plans and leave it to the Committee to decide where monies would be spent.

- To date the cookbook had raised $22,000.00 and the Committee expected at least $25,000.00 from the College Shop and Bookstore.
- Interguild held its Annual General Meeting at Havergal. A number of Appleby representatives went.
- The Telephone Committee had operated for years – they would call on storm days or for other reasons. It was decided that the students were older now that there was no longer a Junior School only a Middle and Upper School, thus the Telephone Committee ceased to exist. However, the school set up an information line. Parents could phone the school number 845-4681 and extension 540 (the school address). Should there be a storm, closing would be announced on this line and other information was given in the same manner.
- Plans were underway for the second House Tour. Patti Hnatiw and Jill Mark chaired this event. The tour would be held December 10th, 1994.
- It was decided to hold the Annual General Meeting and luncheon at the school as in earlier years. This was done in that A.C.P.A. would host Interguild the next year and it would be nicer to entertain them at home, Appleby, rather than at a golf club. This gave the Association the opportunity to test it out. It worked beautifully – the meeting was held in the gymnasium and luncheon in the dining hall. The students were treated to box lunches. The guest speaker was Priscilla DeVilliers of CAVEAT (Canadians Against Violence Everywhere Advocating its Termination). Her speech, of course, touched everyone's hearts. Her daughter had been abducted and murdered. She started CAVEAT to try to stop such an occurrence from happening again. The Bateman raffle took place. There is no record of the winner. The raffle raised $1,947.00.

1994-1995
President   **Marg (Mags) Shorey**
- $25,000.00 to Bursary Loan Fund.
- $5,554.00 to Bursary Fund. (proceeds from the Tuition Lottery)
- $5,640.00 for a CD-Rom.
- $378.00 for a printer for the Computer Lab.
- $5,000.00 for a conference organized by the school.

Pot Luck Cake, 1995

Pat and her father, Archie Izzat
Our dear and delightful bartenders

- $1,081.00 for Physical-Education software.
- $18,400.00 for a grand piano for the music department.
- $2,284.00 for composite grad. pictures.
- Eve Willis acquired a pair of silver crested sugar tongs from Oneida. These are used whenever the Association hosts a tea.
- $2,739.50 was realized by the sale of older items from the College Shop.
- Eve Willis organized Community Service driving for last year and once again this year. She also ran the Tuition Lottery. Eve and Anne Sinclair ran the raffle for the House Tour as well.
- The Grade Parties were hosted on the campus. M1, U1 and senior year at the Headmaster's house. Joanne and Guy McLean kindly opened their home for three dinners and many parents and faculty members. The other grades were treated to wine and cheese in the dining hall.
- A drop box was started for lost books. Provided students had put their names in their books at the beginning of the year a lost book could and would be returned.
- The College Shop and Bookstore had a combined income of $45,000.00 over the past year. A supplier provided suede bottomed back packs for the Shop.
- Over 25 parents volunteered in the Bookstore this year.
- Pot Luck Luncheon had the excitement of a fashion show staged by the College Shop's Isabel Fox, Barb Lewis and Wendy Smith with student models. It was a great success. On the same day Lorraine Shrigley chaired the Book Fair with books from Quest and School Book Fairs. A profit of $1,584.28 was attained. The Book Fair was held in Hardwick Hall and the Pot Luck in the gymnasium - no stairs to get the plates, glasses, tables, chairs, and other paraphernalia up.
- The House Tour was a resounding success. Patti Hnatiw and Jill Mark reported a net profit of $28,500.00. Ten percent of the profit went to Oaklands Regional Centre. Once again the house tour generated wonderful good will for the school as well as funds for the P.A. Joanne and Guy McLean kindly opened their home for the tour and many a guest was delighted not only to view the Headmaster's house but also the beautifully decorated Chapel. Many visited the dining hall for Tea and to purchase baked goods. Patti and Jill added another dimension to the House Tour by having live music in homes and in the dining hall. Students played piano or other instruments, choirs sang and there was much music on the tour.
- A wine tasting evening was held at the Mississaugua Golf Club. It was a truly enjoyable event. There was great warmth and camaraderie and much laughter. A number of faculty members were present as well as parents.
- A Robbie Burns night was held in the dining hall on January 25th. The music was wonderful, a great time was had by all and $2, 077.was made and donated to the Music Department.
- Anne Sinclair organized a fund raising fashion show at the Oakville Club. The funds raised helped to offset the cost of the Rugby Teams' trip to Australia and New Zealand. The fashion show was a sell out with rave reviews.
- A drug-awareness night was held. Glen Ricketts[81] of ADAPT (Alcohol and Drug Assessment Prevention and Treatment Services) was the speaker.

Reception & Dinner prior to 'The Compleat Macbeth'

Bruce Jenkins, Les Williams and Roger Shorey

Hugh Balders, Roy and Daphne Collins

- The Interguild Annual General Meeting was held at Appleby on April 19th. Tours of the school were given by students. The meetings were held in the gymnasium. The speakers and their respective topics were: Guy McLean, The Full Service School-Intellect and Character, and Michael Pierce, University Selection-Where do Parents Fit In? The delegates were treated to a sumptuous lunch à l' Appleby. Appleby shone. Delegates left feeling that they had received the 'royal treatment' and indeed they had.

- David Boyd[*] asked the Parent's Association to host the opening night of his Macbeth production. Mary Catherine Acheson chaired this gala event in the Studio Theatre at the Oakville Centre. Jennifer's Kitchen catered a delicious fare, finger foods which were easily eaten while standing at chest high tables. Guests sat for the production, of course, and it made for an interesting and enjoyable dinner to stand and chat. It was a delightful and dramatic evening. A profit of $4,709.09 was realized and given to the English Department.

- A chocolate mould in the form of the Appleby crest (for after dinner chocolate mints) was purchased jointly by the Parents' Association and Appleby College.

- The Annual General Meeting had been so successful in its return to the school that it was decided future general meetings would be held on campus. Thus the A.G.M. took place at the school. The Parent's Association had commissioned a painting by an Appleby student, Jackie Lu['95]. This was done in memory of Valerie Burke, a marvelous and exemplary volunteer who had died in the past year. She loved gardening and the picture depicts lilacs. Mary Coleman, past president and fellow volunteer with Valerie, presented and dedicated the painting in Valerie's memory. Mary spoke warmly of Valerie and her devotion to the school. The painting hangs in the library.

  In Guy McLean's absence, Fran Richardson, Assistant Headmaster, presented the retiring Executive with books that would go to the library in their names. In turn Mags gifted the retiring faculty members, Brian O'Leary and Fran Richardson, with books. These books would be placed in the library with an inscription.

  The guest speaker was "Mr. Pearce Bunting['47♥], who has devoted over forty years of time, dedication and wisdom to Appleby delivered a speech entitled, 'Changing Traditions'"[153]. His reminiscences were historical, humorous and upbeat.

1995-1996
President   **Stefa Williams**

- $15,000.00 to the Bursary Loan Fund.
- $20,000.00 to Student Services Facilities, i.e. the Guidance Office.[♦]
- $30,000.00 for the Sports Bubble.

---

[*] David Boyd is an English and Multi-Media teacher, he is also the In-house author, a novelist.
[♥] Pearce Bunting['47] was the ninth Chairman of the Board of Appleby College from 1985-1989.
[153] The A.C.P.A. minutes, May 15th, 1995.
[♦] This money had been ear marked for the Student Centre, however, it was decided that Student Services would be a good use of the money. A Student Centre is not on the drawing board for now.

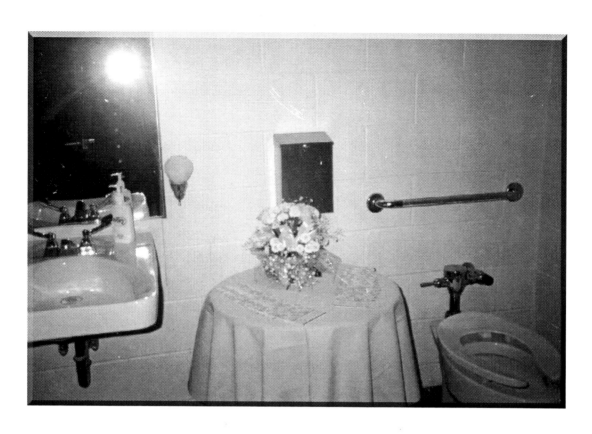

1994 AGM
Transformation of a washroom into a Powder Room!

- $40,000.00 for multi-media equipment in the dining hall and the gymnasium.
- $2,485.86 for composite grad. photos.
- $2,000.00 from the McConnell prints to a visiting Inuit printmaker.
- $5,000.00 conference money was used for Multi-Cultural and Science Fair Weeks.
- Grade Parties were held at the school once again.
- Eve Willis ably ran the Bursary Lottery (formerly Tuition Lottery) once again. Half the income would go to the winner of the draw and the other half to the Bursary. The Bursary received an additional $8,000.00 thanks to the lottery.
- Sue Baillie (Rusty[66]) and Mags Shorey in accompaniment with Sandy McDonald (Havergal College) compiled and edited the Interguild publication Guildlines.
- A poinsettia sale was held. Sue Ksiazkiewicz chaired this sale. At the same time the first Gift Wrap sale took place. Ann Hepburn chaired this fund raiser. A combined profit of just over $4,000.00 was made.
- Debbie Cunningham chaired the Book Fair. Author Ken Dryden, former NHL player and recently coach, lawyer as well, had written In School, Our Kids, Our Teachers, Our Classrooms and promoted his book at the Pot Luck Luncheon. He gave an amusing and most interesting talk on school day. The Book Fair and Pot Luck Luncheon were held in the gymnasium. The Book Fair generated $1,484.87. In the past a fee had been charged to parents to offset the cost of rentals for the Pot Luck, this was done away with. "Stefa [Williams] stated that the Parents' Association received $25.00 in fees from each family … "[154]
- Turnover operated on Mondays after school. Vicki Lydall requested that the cadets be encouraged to offer clothing they no longer needed.
- Photographs were taken and were overseen by parents.
- An additional $4,526.92 was needed to complete the multi-media requirements. The Association had given $40,000.00 and now gave the addition forty five hundred and change.
- Once again the Board sponsored the auction that was operated and run by parent volunteers. In fact Mags Shorey and Eve Willis chaired this years' event. Although it is a Board initiative the parent involvement in so great that the Auction Committees have been listed in the appendix of this history.
- Appleby hosted the Fulford Cup Debating and needed 80 volunteers. The Association filled this need handily.
- Sue Baillie (Rusty[66]), Isabel Fox and Barbara Lennox, the Shop convenors, "packed and delivered eight boxes of written off clothing to the Anglican church which they will send to the Arctic. The tundra sweaters were delivered to Halton Women's Shelter.[155]
- *Of interest – the school had always generously allowed the parents access to the kitchen. They provided coffee breaks and at times lunches. As of 1995 all groups were to make a written request for coffee or any thing from the kitchen. This made sense and helped keep track of kitchen expenditures.*

---

[154] The A.C.P.A. minutes, October 3rd, 1995.
[155] The A.C.P.A. minutes, November 7th, 1995.

Turnover
Vicki Lydall

Turnover, 1996
Vicki Lydall with students

- It was announced that Chatelaine had three photos of the A.C.P.A. House Tour (1994) in its December 1995 issue.
- Plans were begun for the 1996 House Tour that was chaired by Hilary Maile and Judi Vincent.
- Interguild held workshops on fund raising, communications and the Shop. Delegates from the A.C.P.A. attended these.
- Another May Walkathon was held to raise funds for Round Square and other Appleby charities. The Association recruited parent volunteers.
- *Of interest – Guy McLean was interviewed for the Appleby Quarterly and it was reported that "Planning for next year includes the introduction of Mandarin in Middle One and Upper One, a full dance programme as both an academic and extracurricular pursuit, figure skating as a sport, and residential don/intern teacher positions in each residence to assist the Housemasters and assistant Housemasters. We are also working towards being able to build the new Powell's House, additional faculty housing and a regulation size hockey field on Walker Field that would be partially covered by a bubble in the winter to provide the space equivalent of a triple gymnasium."[156]*
- The price of Life Membership was raised to $50.00.
- *Of interest – Vicki Lydall reported that Turnover income was up. "The large sale [of clothing] was made to a film company for an episode of the television series Due South."[157]*
  Vicki also donated small size sweaters, pants and shirts to Canadian Food for Children. She sold $176.00 of cadet items to the Surplus Store on Speers Road. As had been done in recent years a major sale was held in Hardwick Hall on the Monday after Closing Ceremonies.
- The Interguild AGM was held at Bayview Glen followed by lunch at the Donalda Club.
- Volunteers worked in the measles clinic – student had to be re-vaccinated. The nurses need help with organizing students and checking names off.
- The A.G.M. was held at the school. The lunch was served in the dining hall.
  Willie Canham, David Jenner, Jennifer Neal and Michael Nightingale all retired. Each of these faculty members had been at the school for a good many years and was held in high regard by all. Stefa presented them with books with their names inscribed and which would be placed in the library.
  Stefa also recognized Guy McLean who had been at the school for 25 years, first as a young teacher and beginning in September 1987 as Headmaster. Rosa Skrotzki, who had arrived at the school at the same time Guy did, was also honoured. Rosa was like a mother to many a student and such a dear to the parents.
  A drama and music presentation was made by the students.

---

[156] The Appleby Quarterly, April 1996, Volume 18/Number 1.
[157] The A.C.P.A. minutes, March 5th, 1996.

Pot Luck Luncheon, 1996
Author Stuart McLean, Jana Gray, Colleen Balders, Judith Nestmann

1996-1997
President   **Margaret Bennett (Mark[64])**

- $15,000.00 to the Loan Fund.
- $40.000.00 to Powell's House (the first installment of a pledge of $100,000.00).
- $15,000.00 for renovations to the dining hall.
- $10,607.60 for computer equipment.
- $2,433.40 for the composite grad. pictures.
- $3,002.39 to Arts Week. (additional monies from last year went to this as well)
- $2,650.00 for a piano for Hardwick Hall.
- Sue Baillie (Rusty[66]) worked with David Boyd to produce a three fold brochure to advertise Shop items.
- Puma windsuits were the big selling item in the Shop this year.
- A display case was installed in the foyer of Nicholas Arts Centre it was to be the P.A. bulletin board. The Executive Committee was listed there and any upcoming events or whatever needed to be conveyed to the parents on a day to day basis. The other form of communication was the newsletter which came out three to four times a year depending.
- Community Service driving continued under the care of Eve Willis. Denis Desrosiers and Norm Landry ran the Community Service programme.
- Pot Luck was held in the gymnasium along with the Book Fair. It was most successful and brought in $6,100.00. A good deal of credit went to Debbie Cunningham, who chaired the event and Lorraine Shrigley, who operated the Book Fair in Debbie's absence, and to author, Stuart McLean. Stuart McLean spoke and even read from his book <u>The Vinyl Café</u>. Everyone was enthralled and many of his books (other titles as well) sold. House Tour tickets were available at the Pot Luck Luncheon.
- Ann Ferguson, the treasurer at that time, presented a chart that had been prepared by the business office. It showed how sales had climbed over the years. In 1991-1992 the Bookstore and College Shop generated a profit of $38,000.00 and in 1995-1996 a profit of $52,000.00; the Bookstore brought in $39,000.00 and the College Shop $13,000.00. Not only did the Shop and Bookstore make good money but the spirit and sharing in these two locales was amazing. So many friendships were formed while working at Appleby. Another note on the Shop the annual ring sale sold forty five graduation rings.
- Ann Hepburn chaired the Gift Wrap sales. This enterprise brought in $3,600.00.
- Grade Parties were held once again. Convenor, Patti Hnatiw reported that a record number of parents and faculty members attended.
- Eve Willis and Diane Treharne looked after the Bursary Lottery for this year. "Diane will be specifically handling the proactive sale of tickets with the help of a committee. Eve will continue the soft sell approach through the use of Appleby mailings."[158] They also had the help of Karen Bergen, Lauren Leduc and Jane Muddiman. They made over $8,000.00.
- School photographs were taken and ready for Christmas.

---

[158] The A.C.P.A. minutes, October 1st, 1996.

AGM Luncheon, 1997
David and Bev Paul, Jane Rahan, Rose Copeling

Pot Luck & Book Fair, 1996-97
Lorraine Shrigley, David Boyd (In-House Author), Ruth Adler (Bookers)

- Susan Mactaggart, Chapel Guild convenor, made a beautiful crèche for the Chapel. It is still in use today.
- Another extremely successful House Tour was held under the capable leadership of Hilary Maile and Judi Vincent (Judi had moved down East that summer. Much of the organizing was left to Hilary but Judi was there for the actual House Tour and in the early days of preparation). <u>City-TV</u> filmed the Headmaster's house, which had been so beautifully decorated, for airing on <u>Cityline.</u> As an added delight, Simply Chocolate made beautiful scenes of chocolate – not only did the guests ooh and ah over the gorgeous homes but also over these culinary creations. People streamed through the Chapel and dining hall as well. Tea was served in the dining hall and cider at a couple of stops along the way. The House Tour brought in $32,106.96, ten percent of this was given to Halton Women's Place for a computer programme.
- Hilary Selby, Bookstore convenor, began to stock David Boyd's novels. Thirty six volunteers helped in the Bookstore with the September onslaught, half of these were new volunteers. The Canadian Book Exchange was the supplier.
- The Oakville Independent Schools, as a joint venture, hosted a fundraising fashion show. Some members of the Parents' Association were reluctant to hold such an event and raise funds for anyone other than the P.A. Thus "After much discussion Dede Hacking moved that the Executive Board vote whether the fashion show be under the auspices of Appleby College or the Parents' Association, seconded by Vicki Lydall. A ballot vote was requested and the outcome was 12-6 in favour of Appleby College."[159] The Appleby parents did partake in this event but through the school. "Spring was definitely in the air for the 450 people who attended the Oakville Independent School's Dinner and Fashion Show at the St. Volodymyr Cultural Centre on April 17. Appleby parents Margaret Bennett (Mark[64]) and Dede Hacking were the co-chairs for this year's event, which helped raise more than $20,000.00 for the Halton Branch of the VON Hospice Programme.

    "The show featured the latest sports and casual fashions from Sporting Life's Sherway Gardens location."[160]
- On February 13th a social was held in the dining hall. A wonderful and entertaining evening was had by all. Faculty entertained and they were marvelous. David Boyd, Cissy Goodridge, one of Cissy's brothers, Heather Grant and other talented faculty members outdid themselves. What terrific talent the school has. There were 118 parents in attendance, $350.00 was raised and was given to the Music Department to purchase sheet music.
- Appleby held a 20k walkathon. Parents volunteered as was the norm. "The proceeds of the Walkathon will be distributed as follows:
    - one third to the United Way
    - one third to the Round Square Project
    - one third to charities determined by the student committee."[161]

---

[159] The A.C.P.A. minutes, September 19th, 1996.
[160] <u>The Appleby Quarterly,</u> July 1997 – Volume 19, Number 2.
[161] The A.C.P.A. minutes, February 4th, 1997.

United Way Week, 1996-97

Wendy Derrick, about to order from Headmaster Guy McLean
...raising funds for a good cause

United Way Walkathon, 1996

Patti Hnatiw, Guy McLean, Jill Mark, Eve Willis, Wendy Smith, Ann Ferguson, Sue Baillie (Rusty '66)

- "After much discussion, the Executive agreed to add Grade Party Coordinator to the responsibilities of Social convenor, to add a second person to the Executive as an additional Bookstore convenor. It was also agreed that the Executive would like to continue with the Bursary Fund-raiser and that the person running it should sit on the Executive."[162] As well as this Stefa Williams "pointed to the desirability of establishing a committee system, as recommended in the minutes (November 7, 1995) to foster more depth and to provide a future pool from which to draw new Executive Committee members."[163]

- *Of interest –* "*Mr. McLean presented the plans for the proposed Powell's House building. He pointed out the advantages every student receives because Appleby has a boarding component. If funding is available, construction is to start April 19, 1997, with occupancy scheduled for January '98. The total cost is estimated at approximately $4,000,000.00. We need $3,100,000.00 in pledges by April 19; we currently have $2,500,000.00. He is requesting $100,000.00 pledge from the P.A. over five years.*"[164] This was part of the Headmaster's wish list for '96-'97. The Executive did vote in favour of the $100,000.00 pledge and it was looked after in the five year time slot. The A.G.M. was held on May 7th. There were 128 people in attendance. Mary Catherine Acheson, the Social convenor, had arranged for the lunch and speaker. "Chris Shannon and several students who have attended conferences in Kenya and India will speak. The video that was shown in Kenya will also be run. The ticket price will be $30. with any profits going to Round Square."[165]. The meeting was in the gymnasium, lunch in the dining hall. Guy McLean thanked the retiring Executive and presented each with a book which will be used in the library. Margaret Bennett (Mark'64) did the same with retiring faculty members: Dr. Howie had taught at Appleby for 16 years, Madame Taylor after 17 years and David Smith'53 who had been with Appleby for 40 years. Margaret and the Executive felt that Barb Smith had also contributed greatly to the Appleby family over the past 40 years and presented her with a bouquet of long stemmed roses.

1997-1998

President   **Dede Hacking**

- $15,000.00 Bursary Loan Fund.
- $34,392.40 for computer equipment.
- $10,000.00 to Powell's House pledge.
- $17,818.09 for the climbing wall.
- $2,484.00 for composite grad. photos.
- $900.00 for an advertisement in the Argus.
- $1,453.30 for Women's Health Day.
- $2,869.50 CD-Rom for library.

---

[162] The A.C.P.A. minutes, March 4th 1997.
[163] Ibid.
[164] The A.C.P.A. minutes, March 4th, 1997.
[165] Ibid.

House Tour Tea - Kitchen Help!
Marsha Baillie (Aubrey '63), and Nancy Baillie (Jim '37)

- $150.94 for Inuit artists.
- Finally a computer was installed in the Bookstore.
- The College Shop was upgraded by the convenors, Heather Armstrong, Sue Baillie (Rusty '66) and Lynn Brown. An expenditure of $2,642.45 was made to this end. Under stationery the Shop was now selling Bell Calling Cards in denominations of $5.00, $10.00 and $20.00. Karin Schulte and David Boyd got the Shop's website up and running. Last year the Bookstore and College Shop earned combined commissions of $43,499.20. New to the Shop were polar fleece tops, at Christmas, secret Santa gifts and of course treats at Valentine's. Heather Armstrong, a parent and local retailer (The Wool Bin) shared her wealth of experience.
- Eve Willis was organizing drivers for Community Service.
- Judy Mills chaired the Bursary Raffle. It had been a tough sell but $7,470.00 was earned in profit.
- Dr. Sampson gave the Parents' Association Executive Committee a workshop on the school computer system. This was the precursor to introductory computer courses being offered to the parent body.
- The Bookstore had become a hive of activity every spring and fall. Jana Gray, Bookstore convenor, "commented on the very busy summer and start of the school year. On average 40 students an hour passed through the Bookstore during the pre-school week."[166]
- Grade Parties were held at the Headmaster's and in private homes once again.
- Mina's Portraits was doing the school photos and had done so for several years.
- Another hugely successful Pot Luck Luncheon and Book Fair were held in the gymnasium. Jane Raham arranged for author, Lawrence Hill to speak about self discovery, the realization that writing was his future and he also spoke of his book. He wrote Any Known Blood, "Lawrence's latest novel, is a family saga that spans 170 years and traces the lives of five generations of ancestors. The novel moves between the U.S. and Canada as its characters escape slavery in the 19th century, travel across Lake Ontario and eventually settle in Oakville."[167] He was very well received but there was much chatter about his brother, Dan (Daniel) Hill, the singer, who sang 'Sometimes when we touch the honesty's too much'…. and so on. Several English classes attended the talk by Lawrence Hill.

    Prior to the lunch the senior girls put on a wonderful dance demonstration to help promote the OAC dance programme.
- Dr. Nora Curran-Blaney had a wonderful idea that the Parents' Association should hold a health day for the women. Judy Mills worked with Nora to arrange for a speaker and health related exhibits. This event was held in the Chapel, its narthex and undercroft, with refreshments from Appleby's dining hall. Rather than give an honorarium to the speaker and contributors, a donation was made in their names to the Breast Cancer Association. There was a mammo-check which many booked appointments for. Dr. Lawrence Komer spoke on menopause. Dr. Otto Weiglein had a display dealing with plastic surgery, laser, and the like. He

---

[166] The A.C.P.A. minutes, September 9th, 1997.
[167] The Appleby Quarterly, December 1997, Volume 19 Number 3.

'The Bluebird' by Robert Bateman
Waterfront Raffle

also had a representative to answer any questions. Dr. John Sanford had a presentation on snoring, Dr. Kahn on osteoporosis, Maggie Levy on therapeutic touch, Liz Beecker on birth control, and Brad Gibb on ortho-kinetics. It was a most informative and interesting day.

- Gift Wrap was once more a successful venture. To save funds Mary Anne Sarne gave out the order forms on the pre-school Shop and Bookstore days. This undertaking brought in $4,327.50. People anticipate this sale because the paper is of such good quality. This project is on-going.

- A new lost and found system was instituted. Rather than several spots for lost items there would be one central location. This would be monitored by a parent and open at set times.

- The Turnover Shop was operating quietly and successfully as it had done for years. A number of pairs of skates had been donated but were not a seller and were donated instead to the OMHA skate exchange.

- Interguild continued to offer workshops and generally every year Appleby sent delegates.

- The Chapel Guild was comprised of 21 volunteers this year. They were needed to keep all in order and particularly to prepare the Chapel for the dedication of the Little Memorial Window. The window reflects the A. J. Little['31*] family history. As well as the dedication there was once again a royal visit. His Royal Highness the Duke of York visited the school. One of the duties he performed while at Appleby was "to attend a special chapel service and to unveil a plaque commemorating the new stained glass window in the Chapel."[168] "Mr. McLean reported on the VISIT OF PRINCE ANDREW, the object of which was to raise the profile of the Round Square Conference in the community. He noted that the visit had been extremely successful. The Prince had spoken casually and at length with groups of students as well as participating in the more formal occasions. He also attended the service for the dedication of the new stained glass window in the Chapel."[169]

- Aubrey Baillie['63+] was honoured by the Board of Governors on November 4th for his years of dedication and service to the school. The Parents' Association presented him with an engraved pewter stein.

- The job of Grade Party and Social convenor once again became two, not one, positions. "Consideration was given to the fact that Executive positions should not be too onerous, and that the Social convenor's job was already very demanding. Either position may be easier to fill if it was split."[172]

- There was talk of a giant book sale as a possible fund raiser. The logistics of such an event were great. Where would the books be stored prior to the sale? How would they be transported and on and on. Much discussion took place and finally it was decided that in the spring of 1999 a giant book sale would take place.

---

[*] Arthur John (Pete) Little was a former Chairman of the Board of Governors of Appleby College.
[168] The Appleby Quarterly, December 1997, Volume 19, Number 3
[169] The A.C.P.A. minutes, November 4th, 1997.
[+] Aubrey Baillie['63] Chairman of the Board of Appleby College, 1989-1997, and grandson of Lady Baillie.
[171] The A.C.P.A. minutes, January 13th, 1998.

AGM, 1998
Peter Willis (Chairman of the Board) accepting P.A. donation from Dede Hacking
(outgoing President of the Parents' Association)

AGM, 1998
Mary Catherine Acheson (incoming President
of the Parents' Association) and Colleen Balders

- *Of interest – Appleby was moving into a new phase – laptop computers were to be introduced. Guy McLean spoke to the members of the Executive Committee "The faculty and staff now have their computers; 73 in total. Mr. Steve Poplar has joined Appleby to help with the training of the staff. Individual departments will develop their own plans and additional curriculum will be added over the year. The intention is that all students will be technologically literate, and that the computer becomes an essential tool in their lives. The questions of insurance, security, network strength, leasing arrangements, portability, accessibility and the ethical use of computers continue to be assessed. Final decisions on the networking capability of the students' computers have not yet been made. Work is still being done on the classrooms to prepare them for the arrival of the students' laptops.*

  " Mr. McLean is in contact with other schools and universities who are moving towards greater technology in the classrooms. No Canadian schools are on line at the moment, though a few have their faculty fully equipped."[173]

- The chairs for the 1998 House Tour were named. Pat Hetherington-Keys and Barbara Lennox would chair the tour. Much work would be done between November of 1997 and December 5, 1998. Just as the Fall Fairs took much time, talent and dedication so too did the House Tours. Nothing just happens at Appleby it is with tender loving care that events are executed.

- "Dede indicated that several people had suggested a history be written of the Parents' Association. She suggested that Margaret Bennett [Mark[64]] might take on this project if it was acceptable to the Committee. Margaret added that Isabel Hodge had suggested such an undertaking to her. At present there is no such document, and the Committee felt that it would be a valuable asset to the school and the Association….Perhaps it might be completed by the Association's 75th year."[174]

- In February there was a social for parents and faculty members. Barb Barone and Olga Harper organized an English pub night that was held in the dining hall. Tosh MacFarlane entertained playing his guitar and singing. Great fun was had by all.

- Another auction took place with much parent support and in fact chaired by two parents, Patti Hnatiw and Charlotte Riddell. Another resounding success. In fact monies from this auction went to Powell's House and there is a plaque commemorating Patti and Charlotte in Powell's. In chairing an event such as the auction you generally give at least a year of your precious time. At the '96 auction the Parents' Association gave a basket of wine – each member purchased a bottle. In '98 funds were collected and wine was purchased collectively on the P.A.'s behalf by Peter Willis.

- Parent, Barbara Crary assisted Carol Bysouth of the English Department by enlisting the help of 33 parents to help with public speaking competitions.

- Susan Martin and Judy Mills helped Don Stewart with volunteers for the Walkathon.

---

[173] The A.C.P.A. minutes, November 4, 1997.
[174] The A.C.P.A. minutes, January 13th, 1998.

Fall Pot Luck, 1997

Sandy White, Guy McLean, Jane Raham, Lawrence Hill, author

Womens' Health Day, January, 1998

Pat Hetherington Keys, Nicole Formanek, Eve Willis, Eveline Dear, Wendy Smith, Jill Mark, Sharon Timmerman, Sue Baillie (Rusty'66), Bev Peat, Judi Pangman, Susan Forsey, Ann Veel

- Mary Catherine Acheson and Diana Finucane worked out plans for Appleby Christmas cards. The designs were chosen from submissions of Appleby students. This would be a new fund raiser.
- The A.G.M. was held in the gymnasium and the luncheon in the dining hall. Dede Hacking opened the meeting with the School prayer, a welcome to one and all and she recalled "seventy years ago Lady Baillie had founded the organization 'to further the welfare of the school and to add to the comfort of the Masters and boys'. Dede felt that it was a fitting tribute to Lady Baillie that so many Life Members, current parents, new parents and guests were present at the meeting, and that so many people continue to volunteer their time and talents to Appleby."[175]

Peter Willis, Chairman of the Board, thanked and gifted with the library books the retiring Executive members. Dede Hacking, in turn, thanked and presented books to Paul Bentley, Cindy Galway[*], Kathleen Manneke, Anita and Norm Landry, Wesley Peel, Sheldon Rose, and Hank Tebrake[+].

There was a special presentation given by the school on Tomorrow's Classroom. Parents were seated in "a prototype of the classrooms planned for the fall of 1998. The layout and furnishings have been designed to complement **e.school.** The tour will include the opportunity to try an IBM Think Pad for yourself."[176]You must remember that parents may not even have seen a laptop let alone handled one. This was the height of high tech at that time. People were in awe. What an innovation? Our children will learn like that! Wow!

1998-1999
President   **Mary Catherine Acheson**

- $15,000.00 to Bursary Loan Fund.
- $20,000.00 to the Powell's House Pledge.
- $40,000.00 for a Fitness Centre.
- $15,000.00 computer – College Shop and Bookstore.
- $5,000.00 for benches around the campus.
- $2,019.40 composite grad. pictures.
- $900.00 for Argus ad.
- *Of interest - The school year began "with the rollout of the laptop computers to all students in Upper One to Junior Year now complete, Appleby has taken a major step forward in the integration of technology into its curriculum....Renovations to classrooms took place over the summer to accommodate the use of the laptops. This included the reconfiguring of desks and the addition of electrical outlets and modem ports to allow each student to plug in*

---

[175] The A.C.P.A. minutes, May 6th, 1998.

[*] Cindy Galway is the daughter of Dr. J. A. M. Bell, long time Headmaster. She was also an Appleby parent and worked in the office in various capacities over the years.

[+] Hank was known to everyone by his Christian name. He was a very helpful maintenance man and gardener extraordinaire.

[176] Quote was taken from a handout from the meeting; prepared by Jane Hamilton, Appleby's Director of Marketing and Communications.

Giant Book Fair in the Arena
Ola Dunin-Bell
All for Appleby!

and connect to the school's local area network. In addition to its collaboration with IBM Canada (which manufactures the laptop computers), Appleby has also worked with a number of suppliers to outfit the classrooms with several technological teaching aids to complement the use of the laptops. Recent additions include the installation of special electronic whiteboards and video projectors in the classroom that enable teachers to present their lessons using an array of sources which students access for later use."[177]

- The Grade Parties were held with the senior year first in the hope that parents from overseas would still be in town and be able to attend. All the parties were well attended by both parents and faculty members. At the Headmaster's house a marquee was installed and added greatly to the success of the evening. It was as if a room had been added. The terrace became an extension of the living room.

- Tear away pants and wind suits were the best sellers in the College Shop. Key ribbons, to be worn around a student's neck, were also popular. In the stationery section Art kits were available. The Shop finally got on line and purchased a computer "Mr. McLean suggested it was time for the Executive Committee to spend money on itself. He noted that, since computers are now fully integrated into the curriculum and the Business Office will be totally computerized by February 2000, perhaps it would be appropriate for the BOOKSTORE and COLLEGE SHOP to have their own COMPUTERS. The Shops could then bill their sales electronically to the Business Office."[178]

- In the Bookstore pre-school days, 181 students were served on one day alone. The Bookstore now carried CD-Roms for Middle One and Upper One as requested by the Math Department. Twenty three boxes of unsold books were sent to Kenya to the Round Square project.

- In the treasury department – Bev Peat registered the Association as a 'Charitable Organization' with the TD Bank thereby saving on bank charges.

- Photographs were taken early once again to allow for pre-Christmas delivery.

- "Eve Willis has resigned as Community Service convenor as a result of the major changes in the programme. The school has incorporated the programme into the curriculum and will involve all the students. Ms. Paula Schutz and Ms. Andrea Jelinek have been hired to run the programme. Mr. McLean has noted though, that parent involvement will still be necessary."[179]

- Powell's House had its official opening on Homecoming weekend. A plaque was hung in the House in recognition of the $100,000.00 pledge from the P.A.
A number of plaques throughout the house recognize the many donors.

- A parent-teacher walk took place in support of United Way week.

- Pot Luck was held on October 30th. The décor was wonderful, Halloween! Barb Barone did the decorating.

    A book fair was not held because a Used Book Sale (the giant book sale) would be held in May.

---

[177] The Appleby Quarterly, April 1999, Volume 21, Number 1.
[178] The A.C.P.A. minutes, March 2nd, 1999.
[179] The A.C.P.A. minutes, September 15th, 1998.

Appleby College Shop

Giant Book Sale - Children's Area
John Berriman and Liz Blunt, Janet Suchanek (David'78) and Emily

Transformation of Arena to Bookstore

House Tour tickets were on sale. Orders were taken for Gingerbread Houses and Christmas cards.

- Valerie Dolegowski chaired the Gift Wrap fund raiser. The week prior to school Val gave out 280 gift wrap packages and mailed the remainder. Even with the cost of postage a profit of $4,069.47 was made.

- The Christmas card project was off to a great start. The cards were sold in the Shop and also in the dining hall on the day of the House Tour.

- The House Tour was a tremendous success. Prior to the House Tour Guy and Joanne McLean hosted a dinner for the home owners. It was a gracious way to thank them for their generosity in opening their houses to the public for a tour. Ten percent of the proceeds went to Cedarbrook Home (renamed Rose Cherry's House, in memory of Don Cherry's wife), a hospice for children. $38,688.91 was made. Every tour the profits were greater. Each tour became more polished and professional in every way. The first tour was everything you could want it to be but somehow each year it gets better. At the cider stop this year 800 cookies, baked by Liz Goddard, were happily consumed.

- A February social was held in the dining hall. Cissy Goodridge, Paul McCulloch, Julia Olson and Leslie Stewart entertained. Another great evening was had.

- Heather Armstrong chaired the Used Book Fair. Books had come in all during the summer, fall and spring. They were initially stored in Guy McLean's garage and eventually moved to the house on the lake (formerly the Campbell MacKay, Norm Landry, Ian Stewart and Harry 'Sarge' Bailey house). There were books everywhere. Every type you could imagine – gorgeous children's books, remember those little readers 'See Jane, See Spot', sets of books, gorgeous old volumes, leather bounds, you name it they had it. Rusty Baillie[66] and Mark Bennett[63] generously installed bookshelves in the arena. Not only were they practical but they transformed the arena, not quite to a library but indeed a very different site than one was accustomed to see. The children's section was inviting and comfortable thanks to the creativity of Heather Christiansen. The labour involved was incredible. Those books were heavy, thank heaven for maintenance, some students (primarily the children of the volunteers) and the volunteers themselves. The volunteers worked hard but as always had a great deal of fun. Unfortunately the sale did not do as well as expected. It did earn about $7,305.56 which is good in anybody's books. The Oakville Literacy Council was sent ten percent of this money. And children overseas benefited. Books were shipped here, there and everywhere thanks to the resourcefulness of the volunteers. Maggie Levy knew someone, Rosemary Hawkrigg knew so and so and on and on. The books had to be out of that arena and it was a mad and weighty dash to accomplish the task. That was friend raising at its best, over 100 volunteers worked over the weekend.

- A garage sale for the Rugby Tour was held the same weekend as the book sale. It did very well. Sue Baillie (Rusty[66]) and Judy McKnight organized the sale.

- The position of New Parent Liaison was added to the Executive Committee. A number of parents would form a committee to welcome new parents and keep them informed on all the happenings in the Appleby Community. Each

Pot Luck Luncheon, 1999
Paula Carson-Wood, Karen Wilson (facing at back), Ann Veel, Mary Anne Sarne (front-right)

committee member would have several families to take under her wing so to speak for the year.

- Judy McKnight coordinated the volunteers for the Public Speaking and Debating
- There was a walkathon in May. Pat LeBlanc and Sue Martin organized the many volunteers needed for that day.
- The Oakville Independent Schools held a fund raiser at Bookers Bookstore.
- The A.G.M. was held at Glen Abbey Golf Club. Guy McLean presented and thanked the retiring Executive members with books with their names inscribed within and which were placed in the library. The departing faculty members, Colleen and Jim Mackay, Carol Nesbitt, David Paul, Sue and Fran Richardson[*], and Chris Shannon, were also given books and thanked by Mary Catherine on behalf of the parents.

   "Mr. McLean remarked on the phenomenal level of volunteerism at Appleby. He is constantly made aware of this involvement as he talks to Headmasters and faculty at other independent schools. Using the College Shop as an example, he noted that having so many extremely competent volunteers saves the school significant amounts of money."[180]
- The guest speaker was Carol Bertuzzi Luciani. She spoke on going into the millennium.

1999-2000
President   **Judy Mills**

- $15,000.00 to Bursary Loan Fund.
- $10,000.00 to the Powell's House pledge.
- $50,000.00 pledge made for the Chapel courtyard.
- Preparations were begun in June of 1999 for the Fall 2000 Round Square Conference which was hosted by Appleby College. Approximately 350-400 delegates plus about 50 Appleby students would attend. There was much planning to be done, guests to be billeted, not only menus to be drawn up but the logistics of where all these people would be fed, where the meetings would be held – Appleby faced a great challenge but would rise to the occasion. Don Stewart spoke to the Executive members of the P.A. "The theme is 'The Power of One – Building Community Through Individual Initiative'. He highlighted some of the plans for speakers, workshops, excursions, activities and theme dinners. Mr. Stewart asked for the support of the Parents' Association and help with the many aspects of the conference. He would also like to have parents as hosts and hostesses to help make the visitors feel welcome."[181]The Appleby Community acts and has acted as a family supporting each other no matter what the event. The auction is a great example of that and even in the year of the Conference, first there would be an auction in May and the arrival of delegates at the end of September. The P.A. and the school had an incredibly busy year ahead.

---

[*] Honorary Old Boy, Assistant Head Master.
[180] The A.C.P.A. minutes, May 6th, 1999.
[181] The A.C.P.A. minutes, June 8th, 1999.

AGM 2000 - Terry Guest
Speaking about Round Square

**Opening of Round Square Conference,
September 2000**

Don Stewart, Mounted Police and unidentified student

Marilyn Freeman chaired a sub-committee for the P.A. to liaise with the school. Patti Hnatiw and Eve Willis organized the food service and the closing dinner. The P.A. would be responsible for the closing Thanksgiving dinner. Plans began in earnest.

The P.A. was asked to operate a Tuck Shop with crested Appleby items, snack foods and sundry items.

More details are listed at the time of the event – September 29 – October 5, 2000.

- David Boyd set up a web page for the P.A. It included a logo he designed for the P.A., a brief history, details pertaining to Bookstore, College Shop and the Turnover such as hours of operation and items carried. David Boyd also enumerated volunteer opportunities, fund raising events, lost and found items and Executive listings.

- The New Parent Liaison Committee had a most successful orientation day with new parents. The parents received extremely good care because the Development Office also set out a team to welcome the new families. This was the Appleby family at work double time.

- Middle One and Middle Two students were outfitted with laptops.

- The College Shop added to its inventory a School crest, pop-up calculator, pen letter opener and a small stuffed bear wearing an Appleby shirt. The bears sold quickly. Golf balls with the Appleby logo were also brought in. Pre-Christmas candy canes were a hot seller. Sue Martin became the volunteer coordinator for the Shop.

- The Turnover Shop has had its second flood, there had been one last year. Many items were damaged and thus discarded. A new location needed to be found. The Headmaster was consulted. Temporarily things were housed with the lost and found.

- Turnover held a year end sale in the gymnasium. Beatties came for pre-orders. Beatties would now donate 1% of all Appleby purchases to the P.A. at the request of the P.A.

- *Of interest – Hardwick Hall could no longer be used for events. It now has a sprung hard wood dance floor for OAC dance, ballet and other related activities.*

- Amber Ing, the Bookstore, recommended that all old books be donated to the Canadian Book Exchange for use in other countries. The Bookstore generated $46,218.60 in profits.

- Grade Parties were a great success. Convenor Heather Hogarth felt that it was thanks to all the phone calls her committee members made.

- The opening days of school for the College Shop and Turnover were held in Hardwick Hall. It was wonderfully convenient for the parents who shopped but labour intensive for the volunteers who carried everything to Hardwick Hall. By year end the College Shop had earned $17,495.97. Turnover also did very well.

- The computers were installed in the Bookstore and College Shop. Rohani Agnew and Diane Treharne trained the volunteers in their respective areas.

- Jane Muddiman chaired the Gift Wrap fund raiser. She and her committee hand delivered the order forms. The profit reflected the labour of the committee

Christmas Chapel

House Tour
Dining Hall
Mags Shorey & Aubrey Baillie '63

$8,906.46 was banked. The P.A. pays the school $1,000.00 computer maintenance fee annually.

- "Last fall Mags Shorey hosted the first 'annual' luncheon for Life Members. On Wed. Oct. 6th a Life Members' Luncheon will be held at the school, with tours of the school and possibly a chapel service."[182] The October 6th lunch was called the 'Parent Emeritus Lunch'.

- A 5k parent-teacher walk took place on October 20th.

- On the same day Barbara Coloroso came to speak about her new book Parenting With Wit and Wisdom in Times of Chaos and Loss. Wendy Osmar did all the planning for the event. This evening was billed as a Bursary fund raiser and it was most successful. Barbara Coloroso waived her usual speaking fee because of the Bursary. The P.A. gave her an honorarium of U.S. one thousand dollars, they made $8,313.81 Canadian for the Bursary. "A donation to help cover expenses had been given by First Gulf Development Corporation thanks to Appleby parents Maddy and David Gibson."[183]

- Lost and Found was operated in a room under the dining hall. Yvette Dhillon operated the Lost and Found.

- School photos were taken on the front steps of the classroom building and the individual photos in the Chapel. They were ready for Christmas or before. More photos were ordered by families than any other year.

- Pot Luck was held in the gymnasium. Christmas cards were for sale. Sue Tilley, Assistant Headmaster of Student Services, Joanne Orr, Head Nurse and Jane Hilton the College Shop spoke of their respective fields. . Jane Minkhorst, Social convenor, had felt that holding the event on a Thursday rather than a Friday would appeal the parents. She was quite right. There were 110 in attendance, 20 of these being new parents. There were three door prizes – complimentary passes to the fitness centre were given. The winners were delighted.

- Marilyn Freeman, Chapel Guild convenor noted that the new lighting in the Chapel gave a bluish hue to everything. Father Bob Lennox saw that this was rectified. The wooden candle holders were refinished prior to the Carol Services.

- The House Tour Chairs for 2000 were named, Heather Hogarth (Greg'78) and Jane Muddiman. Once Christmas 1999 was over their House Tour work began.

- Lost and Found became a new position on the Executive Committee.

- Sue Martin coordinated volunteers for Public Speaking and Debating.

- The position of New Parent Liaison was ended because of duplication with the Development Office's New Parent Committee.

- The Interguild A.G.M. was held at Bishop Strachan School. It was their 100th anniversary. Appleby delegates attended.

- A pub night was held at Sharkey's on February 16th. It was not a fund raising event but Social convenor, Jane Minkhorst did such a good job they earned $220.00 that night. It was a fun evening with about 70 people in attendance.

- Mary Catherine Acheson organized the Interguild Workshop that was held at Branksome Hall. The title of the workshop was 'How to Get Money and

---

[182] The A.C.P.A. minutes, June 8th, 1999.
[183] The A.C.P.A. minutes, October 5th, 1999.

House Tour - Life Members
Mags Shorey, Lorraine McMullen, Gerry Walters

House Tour Tea
Guy McLean, Guest, Jane Kucey

Influence Friends'. Many compliments were paid to Mary Catherine on the successful event.

- Gale Salema, Math teacher and Housemaster of Walker House underwent treatment for cancer. A number of parents helped support her both physically and emotionally. Physically by delivering meals to her young family and emotionally with e-mails, cards and calls.
- Barbara Lennox and John Mills chaired the auction and rallied parents to assist in another successful venture.
- The A.G.M. was held at the school once again. The meeting was held in Willis Hall (the theatre in the basement of Powell's House) and the lunch in the John Guest Hall. Guy McLean sang the praises of the P.A. and thanked and gifted the outgoing Executive members. Judy Mills, in turn, thanked and gave books for the library to Jinny Flye[♥], Isabel Hodge[*], Kelly McCormack, Ian Roberts and Alana Vickman.

    Terry Guest, (grandson of the school's first Headmaster) Executive Director of Round Square, gave a most informative talk. The parents went away enthused and look forward to the Round Square Conference in the fall.

- Another auction year. "Don Stewart has developed an 'Ultimate Appleby Parents' Package' and has asked the Parents' Association to donate three of the items – no line up at the Bookstore in September, 4 free house tour tickets, and free admission for 2 to the February 2001 social event."[184]

    The P.A. Executive also donated $15.00 each towards wine as a donation to the auction.

    The P.A. gave a set of framed McConnell prints to the auction.

2000-2001
President   **Mary Anne Sarne**

- $30,000.00 to the Bursary Loan Fund.
- $15,000.00 for chairs in the music room.
- $11,000.00 for an outdoor seating area behind the dining hall.
- $5,000.00 for ten exercise stations along the fitness trail[♣].
- $900.00 for an ad in the Argus.
- $2,702.50 for composite grad. photos.
- $500.00 for costume racks for Willis Hall[+]
- Two printers were purchased for the Shops.
- The Bookstore extended its hours for Orientation Day to accommodate as many students as possible.

[♥] Jinny was a past parent, past Executive member and library assistant.
[*] Isabel was also a past parent and the librarian since 1982.
[184] The A.C.P.A. minutes, December 7, 1999.
[♣] The Fitness Trail would be delayed because of changes to the campus, but is anticipated.
[+] The Theatre in the basement of Powell's House was named after Eve and Peter Willis. Peter was Chairman of the Board from 1997-2002. Eve and Peter were generous with their time, talent and funds and did a great deal to see that the theatre was completed, furnished and operational in a short time.

Lunch Volunteers, Round Square Conference, 2000
Making preparations in the kitchen
Foreground L to R: Del Weiglein, Wendy Osmar, Sherry Geisler, Terry Burns, Raff Baldesarra,
Christina Johanssen, Dorothy Harraher, Ellen Budd, Jill Morgan, Angela Lukowski
At back: Judy Mills, Jill Edmonson

A number of boxes of used books were given to the Lion's Club to be forwarded to Africa. Other books were consigned to Canadian School Book Exchange.

Of interest – "We are one of the only private schools that offer a rebate on used texts at the end of the school year."[185] *In the school year 1999-2000 the Bookstore generated a profit of more than $46,000.00.* This year the Bookstore had a profit of $51,804.96.

- Grade Parties took place happily and well attended.

- A kiosk was set up in the foyer of the dining hall to house Lost and Found items. It seems students were reluctant to trek downstairs to the Lost and Found.

- For several years the P.A. had and still has a voice mail at the school. This was initially used as a message centre for the House Tour.

- Steve and Rebecca Hatch, Assistant Headmaster, External Relations and Head of Development and English teacher, respectively moved to Florida in the summer. "Steve Hatch has accepted a new position at a private school in Coconut Grove, Florida and Rebecca Hatch will be departing with him as well. Given the incredible support that the Hatches have given the ACPA, the Executive members asked that M. Freeman purchase a coffee table book on Oakville and present it to the Hatches on our behalf. J. Mills has offered to create a label for the inside front cover."[186]

- Community Service had not been an Executive position in several years but the parent drivers were and are of the utmost importance. John Berriman, Director of Community Services, appealed to the Executive members for more parents to help drive students to and from their community service commitments. "He remarked that this is indeed a major undertaking and one of his first objectives was to stress the philosophical aspect of community service to all of the students. He plans to relay stories of commitment, such as how the seniors in the Lifecare programme consider regular visits by our students to be the highlight of their week and how appreciative they are to have someone read to them or play games with them or just sit and talk to them."[187] "Middle One and Two students must complete ten hours of service throughout the school year whereas Upper One and Two students must complete 25 hours. In Senior School, in one semester, students participate almost everyday in their community service assignments or the arts."[188]

- The 33rd International Round Square Conference was without a doubt the largest and most successful event the school has ever ventured to host. Pages could be written singing the praises of the faculty, staff, parents and students. The parents and their Association outdid themselves and in truth it could not have happened without their support. But that would be true too of the faculty and staff, this was team work at its best.
  Michael DesRoches'62 wrote in the <u>Quarterly</u> "In addition to nearly 400 delegates, dignitaries who attended the conference included Round Square patrons Prince Andrew, The Duke of York and King Constantine of Greece and Prince

---

[185] The A.C.P.A. minutes, November 7th, 2000.
[186] The A.C.P.A minutes, June 6th, 2000.
[187] The A.C.P.A. minutes, September 12th, 2000.
[188] Ibid.

Round Square Conference - Coffee Break in the Dining Hall
The majority of breaks were held outdoors

Round Square Volunteers - Ready to Serve!
At front, L to R: Ellen Pearce, Pat Leblanc, Marsha Baillie, Margaret Bennett, Norma Carusi, Tina Tsallas,
    Elaine Moore
Middle, L to R: Carolyn Bradley, Lynn McLennan, Judy Mills, Monica Virmani, Rosemary Hawkrigg,
    Alex Irish, Terry Stupavski, Sandy Ballios, Anna Robinson
At Back: Lynn McKenzie, and hidden volunteer

Alexander of Schleswig-Holstein. Guest speakers who addressed the conference theme included renowned Canadian author and journalist June Callwood, children's rights activist Craig Kielberger, wheelchair athlete Skip Wilkins, Street Kids International founder Peter Dalglish and War Child Canada founder Dr. Samantha Nutt."[189]

Michael went on to quote a thank you letter, written by Guy McLean, "It was amazing that a mere 185 Appleby homes along with 50 residence beds housed our almost 380 conference delegates. Families opened their doors to our guests, or welcomed their own students home for a week to free up beds in the residence houses.

"In addition, nearly 300 parents, all of our faculty and staff and hundreds of students volunteered their time to ensure that all events and activities ran smoothly.

"We had many volunteer heroes, from the parents and faculty volunteers who stepped in to ensure that the Information and Message Centre ran smoothly, to the volunteers who made sure the delicious meals and essential coffee and snack breaks were ready and waiting for the delegates on demand. We even had volunteers acting as hosts/tour guides during the two days of planned excursions.

"The success of the events reflects well on our school, and the many positive comments and e-mails we received both during and after the events are a testament to your efforts."[190]

The P.A. provided each delegate with a table favour (memento) at the closing Thanksgiving Dinner. "It would be an autograph book with a year 2000 penny set in a square on the front cover. V. Dolegowski has offered to contribute 500 old pennies and A. Boyce will enquire with our bank to see if they will provide us with 500 new pennies in return. K. Schulte will obtain costs for blue and white pens engraved with Appleby College Round Square 2000 on them."[191] The mementos were as planned.

- Even though there was such a great happening at the school other events were planned and took place without missing a beat. Homecoming was held the weekend prior to the conference. It featured the chapel service, a string recital in Willis Hall, "horse drawn wagon rides, the dulcet tones of The Oakville Jazz Band, and a delicious barbecue lunch in the dining hall."[192] There was face painting and other events for children and of course the P.A. sold goods from the College Shop as they have done for years.

  Pot Luck was scheduled for the end of October and House Tour 2000 was in the works. The volunteer work was never ending but always edifying.

- The P. A. was given a filing cabinet to keep their records in. A much needed addition.

- Dede Hacking, Mary Anne Sarne, Midge and Michael DesRoches[62] created a reference guide to benefit all Executive Members. This, too, was long overdue.

---

[189] The Appleby Quarterly, Winter 2000, Volume 22, Issue 2.
[190] Ibid.
[191] The A.C.P.A. minutes, June 6th, 2000.
[192] The Appleby Quarterly, Winter 2000, Volume 22, Issue 2.

Round Square Conference Volunteers
Ready for the Bagged Lunches. Delegates took their lunches and went sightseeing.

Foreground: Jill Edmonson, Sally Ng, Julaine MacNicol, Dorothy Harraher, Margaret Bennett, Sabine Ho, Yvonne Iten-Scott, Carol Erdelyi, Del Weiglein

Middle: Wendy Osmar, Sherry Geisler, Linda Hatch, Raff Baldesarra, Jill Morgan, Ellen Budd, Marie Duggan, Anita Jassani

Background: Veronica Zufelt, Christina Johanssen, Angela Lukowski, Patti Hnatiw, Judy Mills, Liz Goddard, Lisa Forbes, Lesley Weatherhead, Terry Burns

- Class and individual photos were taken pre-Christmas once again. Parents helped and for the first time the pictures were taken in Willis Hall. Four graduating students missed picture and retake day, Ann Ferguson kindly took them directly to the photographer's studio.
- The Gift Wrap sales brought in $7,966.98. Christine Selim and Sharon Tanner did a great job.
- *Of interest - At the October meeting Guy McLean addressed the Executive Committee of the P.A. He spoke about the Round Square Conference and praised and thanked all involved. "Mr. McLean reviewed the changes that had taken place over the summer which included air conditioned classrooms; the refurbishment of the upper level of the Chapel; the installation of new showers in Walker House; the completion of the Weatherhead[+] Terrace behind Powell's; and the enlargement of the Willis Hall foyer.*

  "With regard to the Master Plan, the school's immediate neighbours have participated in an information evening. The first phase, mainly infrastructure, will most likely begin next spring and work will be concentrated on the north end of the campus with respect to the storm sewers, road way and parking.

  "Admissions were excellent this year. The desired ratio of 30 boys to 30 girls was finally achieved with the '00 - '01 Middle One class. In addition, out of the 60 students accepted, 24 are siblings of former and current students; 4 are the children of alumni; and 3 are the children of faculty members. This means that over 50% of the families with children entering Middle One this year have had previous experience with the school.

  "Students from a broader mix of countries (13 in all) are enrolled this year and there has been an increase in the number of boarders in the lower grades. They had hoped to have 20 Upper One boarders and 23 are indeed boarding. This is preferable over having the vast majority of boarders in Senior Two[*]. Appleby is making inroads with respect to broadening their Canadian appeal as well and currently there are students enrolled from British Columbia and Quebec. It was noted that bursary and financial assistance may be required to attract students from other provinces with less economic prosperity.

  "It is the aim of the school to have 60 students each in Middle One and Middle Two. In upper school, the goal is to have 115 to 120 students enrolled in each grade. This uniformity is needed for continuity and staffing purposes. ...

  "Catherine Raaflaub, Assistant Headmaster, Community Relations, is developing a special interests programme for parents to participate in. It will most likely debut this winter and may include a band, a choir, a tech class and a book club. A series of concerts, operated in conjunction with charitable organizations, are also slated for Willis Hall this year. The profits would be divided between the participating charity and the school's bursary fund. ...

  "On a final note, Mr. McLean proposed that students not be the only ones involved in community service work this year on behalf of Appleby College. Plans are underway for parents, faculty and students to work side by side on a

---

[+] Weatherhead Terrace was named after Lesley and John Weatherhead, generous donors.

[*] Senior Two, once called Senior, is the final year of high school.

House Tour Tea
John Baillie'⁶⁷ and wife Patty with her mother Marion Ferris (Frank Baillie'³¹)

variety of projects that the school hopes to undertake in the community in the new year.[193]

- Pot Luck was held on October 27th. Sue Dobson had displayed student art work in the gymnasium and Kip Longstaff helped students prepare a 30 minute presentation to showcase some of their talents. Gingerbread houses were displayed and orders taken. House Tour tickets were also sold. There were 110 people in attendance, 8 of these being faculty and 18 new parents.

- Chapel Guild's Ann Veel held a craft day to make many of the decorations for the Chapel. Not only did the women make a lot of the decorations but Linda Hatch ventured up a ladder outside the Chapel and set up spotlights to shine on the stained glass windows. The Chapel Guild has always done an outstanding job decorating the Chapel particularly for Christmas.

- The Christmas House Tour, chaired by Heather Hogarth (Greg'78) and Jane Muddiman, was a great success - and a sell out, even with an increase of ticket price to $25.00 The ink on the ticket was changed from cranberry to green.

    In November Joanne and Guy McLean graciously hosted a dinner for the homeowners. They also opened their home for the Friday pre-tour crowd.

    The tour was a tremendous success bringing in $43,869.93 after donating $4,460.00 to the Oakville Parent-Child Centre. Incredible

- Nicole Formanek and Dede Hacking co-chaired a bridge tournament in April to foster fellowship and to raise funds for the Bursary. The game was held at the Mississaugua Golf Club and raised $360.00. There was a delicious buffet lunch, great laughter, some good scores and many hands played.

- Anita Boyce, Treasurer, requested that all Executive members fill in expense accounts with accompanying receipts. This would be beneficial to all.

- For several years the P.A. had tried a number of ways to market the McConnell prints. During this year, a framed set was on display in the dining hall and taken to all social events. Jill McIntyre, of the Oakville Arts Council, helped design a flyer to promote sales of the prints. In the past year a framed set had been donated to and sold at the auction.

- Lynn McLennan organized the volunteers for the Debating and Public Speaking event.

- A February Pub Night was held successfully, delicious food and drink, comfortable company - members of the Appleby family.

- The A.G.M. was held at the school, the meeting in Willis Hall and lunch in the John Guest Hall. Peter Willis, Chairman of the Board, was presented with the $30,000. cheque for the Bursary Loan Fund and a cheque for $20,000.00 to complete the Powell's pledge. "P. Willis thanked M. Sarne and the members of the Association for their great support. He noted that we were the first supporters of Powell's building fund and he thanked us for our continued support of the Bursary Fund."[194]

    "M. Sarne asked Michael DesRoches[62] to join her on stage so that the Parents' Association could wish him good fortune upon his retirement following

---

[193] The A.C.P.A. minutes, October 10th, 2000.
[194] The A.C.P.A. minutes, May 3rd, 2001.

Pot Luck - Desserts!
Deborah Sibbald (left) serving

an unparalleled career at Appleby College. It was noted that Michael actually began his student career at Appleby in Grade Two, and he graduated here in 1962. Following his graduation from the U. of T. with a Bachelor of Education degree, Michael returned to Appleby to teach. For 34 years he has served with dedication and devotion, touching the lives of thousands of students."[195]

Guy McLean addressed the assembly, thanked both parents and faculty. "He noted that Appleby College is indeed fortunate to have on staff so many superbly qualified teaching professionals."[196] Guy thanked the retiring Executive members and gave them a gift book for the library.

Traditionally the retiring faculty members were thanked at the meeting and gifted with a library book in their name. This year Mary Anne Sarne thanked and presented the retirees in the dining hall. She made a special presentation to Midge and Michael DesRoches[62]. Midge had served on the Executive since 1999 and had volunteered as a parent since 1987. Mary Anne noted Midge's special status, in that as a daughter of 'Skin' Dewar[+], she was born and brought home to Appleby College and the campus was her playground. This was her home from her birth until 1974.

The guest speaker was Ken Coulter, the manager of the Oakville Centre for the Performing Arts. He spoke on the history of the local theatre.

- A Wine Tasting Bursary fund raiser organized by convenor Val Dolegowski and her husband Rick, was held on June 1st. David Lawrason, an oenophile spoke for over an hour, most informative and truly whet the appetite. A much appreciated $2,500.00 donation was received from BMO Nesbitt Burns and an unknown amount from First Gulf Development Corporation. Approximately $6,500. was made for donation to the Bursary.

- *Of interest – A Tuck Shop was opened in the basement of Powell's House. "It has been very professionally done and Aramark[*] is overseeing it. They brought in the various machines and it is being staffed by the kitchen staff and not the OAC Accounting students as originally thought. In the first fifteen minutes that it was open, $75 in sales were made. Small slushies sell at 99 cents which is cheaper than the Dew. This new school project is being closely monitored and the ladies selling candies etc. to the students do ask them if they have eaten their lunch first! Weatherhead Terrace is getting quite a bit of use as well. There were initial concerns re the cleanliness and this is being monitored as well. Currently it is open during the morning recess and during the lunch hours (11:30 a.m. until 1:30 p.m.) and after school, from 3:30 p.m. to 5:30 p.m. Pizza may be added to the menu but will only be sold after school hours. The Tuck Shop is doing incredibly well and the profits will be put towards 'extras' that would benefit the students."[197]* Karen Shields from the front office said that the Tuck Shop operated March 2001-June 2001, September 2001-June 2002 at which time it was moved

---

[195] The A.C.P.A. minutes, May 3rd, 2001.
[196] Ibid.
[+] D. M. 'Skin' Dewar arrived at Appleby in 1934, he brought his bride Mary to the school in 1943. He retired in 1974. He was a much loved coach, master, housemaster of Powell's and Assistant Headmaster.
[*] Aramark was the school caterer or supplier of meals.
[197] The A.C.P.A. minutes, April 3rd, 2001.

Walkathon, 1998-99

Vanessa Becks '99, Samantha Baillie '99, Marsha Baillie (Aubrey '63), David Suchanek '78

to the dining hall. June, July and August, The Tuck Shop was open for summer sports camp attendees and has operated until the present. It is now overseen by Sodexho, the company which operates the kitchen and replaced Aramark.

2001-2002
President   **Mary Anne Sarne**

- $40,000.00 to the Bursary Loan Fund.
- $20,000.00 final payment to Powell's House pledge.
- $15,000.00 to the Student Travel Bursary.
- $15,000.00 to the library for a laminator.
- $8,000.00 for guest speakers.
- Grade Parties were hosted by parents for Middle Two, Upper Two and Senior One and the McLean's for Middle One, Upper One and Senior Two. Once again these were successful, warm and welcoming for all parents and an opportunity to meet faculty members on a social basis. Over 800 people attended the various parties. Jill and Peter Edmonson attended all parties as Jill was the Grade Party convenor. They were most hospitable.

  Due to the terrorist attack on September 11th the Middle Two Grade Party had to be postponed.

  Of interest – "M. Sarne spoke with Mr. McLean prior to our Executive Meeting with respect to the terrorist attacks in the United States. She conveyed to us that peer counselors and a distress team were working with the students. Any students with family members residing in the U.S. were taken out of class, apprised of the situation and permitted to make any necessary phone calls. The students were not sent home early as there were concerns that some may find themselves home alone watching the events unfold on television. This tragedy has affected everyone in the Appleby community"[198] ...

- Gift Wrap was once again a winner. It generated $9,342.31 in profit. Christine Selim and Sharon Tanner outdid their previous year by $1,375.33. This year they had had a phone blitz and it paid off.
- Lost and Found located a permanent home in the foyer of the dining hall. A most suitable and tasteful cupboard was built in the foyer. It is 7 feet tall with a split door, shelves, wire baskets and a plastic pouch. This can house all kinds of lost items. Terry Burns had a great deal to do with this project. She even drew up the design for it. It was and is open at lunch times.
- Turnover updated and purchased plastic hangers ridding themselves of the old wire ones. In November Turnover had a special sale of roller blades, ice skates and snowboards. A profit of $1,328.66 was made. "Eleven students received community service hours. Some unsold items were sold to 'Play it Again Sports' and the remaining items were donated to the Halton Women's Shelter in Burlington and the Goodwill Store on Dundas in Mississauga."[199]

---

[198] The A.C.P.A. minutes, September 11th, 2001.
[199] The A.C.P.A. minutes, December 4th, 2001.

Chapel Guild, 2001
At Back: Monica Baldesarra, Ann Veel, Linda Hatch, Janie Schwartz, Diane Boston
In Front: Karen Tyres, Oddny Cook, Deborah Brunet

The Turnover added a mirror and change area. Two sandwich boards were acquired to advertise sales. They were now on line at www.appleby.on.ca. David Boyd created their page as he had for the other areas of the P.A. Pearl Lande did such a marvelous job with merchandising in Turnover that they made a profit of over $6,500. that means sales topped $13,000. Certainly a record was made thanks to Pearl Lande.

- The College Shop had quilted vests with the grey hound on them rather than the entire crest. They also carried boxers, Christmas items such as mugs with candy, new key chains, mouse pads and knitted toques. The rings sold well this year 46 versus 19 last year. Parents and students could now order items from the Shop on line.

- *Of interest - For a number of years, parent, Bruce Davies, father of June[00], polished the silver in the trophy cases. It was noted in the minutes of September 11, 2001 that the trophies were in need of some attention. Parents have certainly provided wonderful and diverse service to the school over the years.*

- School photos were taken. Marilyn Freeman and her volunteers oversaw these sittings which lasted a week.

- Sadly, for those who remember the inception of the Bookstore, or volunteered there, it was closed in June 2002. It was not that there would not be book sales but it would be new and different. There had been talk of where to house the Bookstore because the school needed the space for new science labs. Guy McLean offered to get a portable to house the Bookstore until a new building would be built with space to accommodate the store. On top of that, the convenorship had been an incredibly hard position to fill. Every Nominating Committee met this challenge and filled the position. Over the years the most talented and dedicated women were in charge of the Bookstore from Maggie Goh, the first convenor, to Rohani Agnew and Angela Lukowski, the last (see appendix for the other Bookstore heads). The Bookstore was a full time job and particularly labour intensive in September and June. It was a most onerous job. The convenors spent a great deal of time working in the summer finishing off a year and prepping for the next. As the years went by the job expanded and required two heads, one just to organize all the volunteers, the other to operate the Shop. In the fall of 2001 the Bookstore used 45 adult and 20 student (community service) volunteers. In its final year of operation as an on campus store, it earned $52,068.90. It was financially rewarding but Appleby College was now an e-school and it made sense to operate the Bookstore as an on-line system. The Executive agreed to look into the matter and asked Valerie Dolegowski to research on-line book companies. She took this project on and presented her findings. Both the Executive and faculty members felt that this was the way to go. As of July 2002 books were ordered on-line from the Canadian School Book Exchange. There is still a Bookstore convenor, she is the liaison between school and store. She sits on the Executive, trouble shoots, deals with faculty and parents and organizes the book return at the school, for the four days prior to closing. The Association still reaps financial benefits, they do get a percentage of all book sales.

Social - Pub Night
Ain't Appleby Life Grand!
Yasmin Korkis, Jane Muddiman, Andrew Sarne, Rob Muddiman, Greg Hogarth '78, Anne Von Rosenbach

- Karen Wilson ably organized the Pot Luck Luncheon. It was held on Friday, October 26th with a theme of school involvement. Catherine Raaflaub spoke of the Parent Ed 101 courses which she had overseen and Paula Schutz spoke of the school involvement with United Way.

  Catherine Raaflaub, Deb Sewell, Jill Edmonson, Margaret Maich and Karen Wilson put on a cute skit about uniforms – they certainly got the message across to all in attendance.

  David Paul, a fondly regarded teacher and coach at Appleby for a number of years, died of multiple myeloma. He had bravely battled this disease for about seven years. A few words were said on his behalf and in his memory. A donation was made in memory to the Canadian Cancer Society.

- A Bursary fund raiser – Bridge & Games was held on November 12th in the Willis Hall foyer. About $500.00 was made. Bridge players were asked to bring their own tables and chairs.

- The P.A. commissioned an artist, J. David Brown, to paint a portrait of the Chapel. It was auctioned at the Appleby Auction for $6,750. The profit of $3,950. was given to the Bursary.

- The Association hosted the Interguild Suppliers' Day. A number of suppliers, about 25, set up tables in the gymnasium to display their wares. Delegates from the independent schools made purchases for their Shops. Each supplier paid $100.00 for a table. A light lunch was served and tours of the campus given. Marilyn Freeman, as 1st Vice-President organized this successful day.

- Jill Edmonson and Julaine MacNicol oversaw the June Walkathon volunteers.

- *Of interest – Guy McLean spoke to the Executive Committee of the P.A. "A new initiative being introduced at Appleby this year is FACT which stands for Families and Communities Together. It deals with the values of being part of the Appleby community and the expectations of each group within and how to deal with the issues that each of these groups may have. This booklet, which will be distributed to all parents, is designed to help parents become better parents and similarly it will help students to become better students. It will address all the current issues as they relate to parents and students in 2001. Such topics as drugs, alcohol, conflicts, peer pressure etc. will be dealt with in a realistic, age appropriate manner. This booklet will review rules, responsibilities and open communication.*

  "Appleby will be promoting the FACT booklet to various other schools and Mr. McLean asked if the ACPA would like to assist with this promotion. Each booklet costs $3."[200]

- Once again Lynn McLennan oversaw the volunteer recruitment for Debating and Public Speaking. She phoned and organized all the volunteers for the event.

- The chairs for House Tour 2002 were named – Yvonne Iten-Scott and Julaine MacNicol. Their work began at the beginning of the year and would continue until the actual tour on November 30th, 2002.

- A video on ovarian cancer was shown in the dining hall at the behest of Gale Salema. Unfortunately her cancer had recurred. She wanted to inform as many

---

[200] The A.C.P.A. minutes, October 2nd, 2001.

Pot Luck, 2000
Guy McLean, Catherine Raaflaub, Judy Mills

women as possible about the silent killer, ovarian cancer. A survivor of this type of cancer spoke after the screening of the video and told what a frightening experience it was and continued to be. Her chances of further survival were not promising. This video was viewed in January and Gale died of her cancer in the spring. She had been stoic throughout her ordeal.

- The February social, rather than a pub night, was a black tie event called 'An Evening of the Arts'. Cissy Goodridge coordinated the evening. The P.A .looked after ticket sales and the reception. It was held in Willis Hall which seats but 150 and was quickly sold out. It netted about $3,000. that went towards the Bursary.

- Jane Minkhorst attended an Interguild Meeting in Aurora and returned with their online address www.interguild.org.ca. The purpose of the meeting was to discuss way to establish better communication between Interguild and member schools. This started discussion of having an Interguild representative on each Executive Committee of the various parents' associations.

- Dede Hacking and Sue Baillie (Rusty[66]) met with Mary Anne Sarne to discuss plans for the 75th anniversary of the P.A. A motion was made at the next Executive meeting to begin plans for the 75th anniversary.

- The P.A. held a Teacher Appreciation cocktail party at the home of Jill and Peter Edmonson on March 26[th.] A most thoughtful gesture on behalf of the parents and certainly well received by the faculty. A wonderful evening was had by all with the parents already making plans to expand the event next year.

- Catherine Raaflaub spoke to the Executive Committee about the 'Relay for Life' which was already being held in 32 communities in Ontario. Appleby would be the site of such an event on May 31. The event was so successful that Appleby would host another next May 2003 and this will undoubtedly become another Appleby tradition – hosting a 'Relay for Life' each spring. The funds went to the Canadian Cancer Society, over $200,000.00 was made.

- It was once again an auction year. Rosemary Hawkrigg and Christine Selim chaired the event. The P.A. put a half page ad in the auction catalogue at a cost of $500.00. The auction raised $401,000.00.

- *Of interest – Guy McLean once again addressed the Executive Committee, he spoke of a number of things:*

  "An offshoot of the Bursary programme is the 'Travel and Participation' fund which has been established to assist students with their transportation costs if they choose to or have been asked to participate in an Appleby event (cultural, athletic or educational) that requires air travel. For example, this could include the Round Square or a concert band competition in another province. Students who might not otherwise be able to attend out of province school-related events may apply for assistance. ...

  "Mr. McLean noted that the front of the campus will hopefully be realigned over the summer so that vehicular traffic would no longer be permitted behind the school. In addition, the school hopes to start construction of a new gym which will be located towards Lakeshore Road. This new gym would also house the day school lockers. ...

  "Students need to be informed and educated with regards to drugs, tobacco and alcohol. It is not just the role of the school to address this problem

Guy McLean with Alexis Troubetzkoy, June 2003

Orientation Day

and attempt a solution – all parents must become more knowledgeable and do their part with their children at home as well.

"The school wishes to introduce a programme that will be both sensitive and meaningful, one that has validity to the students. There has to be a balance of knowledge and discipline. When the wrong decisions are made, students have to know that they can seek out help or that their peers can help them seek out help without fear of expulsion. It is hoped that more positive peer pressure will be a result of this revised policy. ...

"The school and the parents must be on the same wavelength with respect to our new tobacco, alcohol and drug policy. We all must encourage the students to make better decisions, and when problems do come to light, the parents will now be informed much quicker, even if there is only suspicion of wrong doing."[201]

"Basically the students need to see a fair policy, one where the punishment fits the crime. This new programme will be launched in September 2002."[202]

- The A.G.M. was held at the school. Mary Anne Sarne presented a cheque for $40,000.00 for the Bursary Loan Fund to John See, new Chairman of the Board. John See thanked Mary Anne and the parents for their dedication and support. Other monies were given as listed at the beginning of the term. "Mr. McLean noted that our Association was the first to support the newly established Travel Bursary. It will ensure that all students will be able to travel with their sports teams or arts/music programmes to out of town competitions."[203]

  Guest speaker, Feather Janz, a breast cancer survivor gave a moving and from the heart speech. It was particularly fitting to have cancer as a topic, in view of the fact that the Appleby family had lost two members, David Paul and Gale Salema, in the past school year.

- *Of interest – "J. Minkhorst also reported that Penny Stanbridge (graduate parent) organized the raising of approximately $1,200 from the graduating parents and students to buy a bench with an appropriate plaque and possibly a small tree to be planted alongside. This will be presented at the June 19th Graduating Class Leaving Dinner...."[204]*

2002-2003
President   **Jane Minkhorst**

- $30,000.00 to the Bursary Loan Fund.
- $10,000.00 to the Travel Bursary Fund.
- $20,000.00 to the Appleby College Centennial Capital Campaign ($100,000. pledge over 5 yrs.)
- $10,000.00 for a sound system in the gymnasium.
- $35,000.00 for new and up to date lighting in the Chapel.
- $5,000.00 to the library for research materials.

---

[201] The A.C.P.A. minutes, April 2, 2002.
[202] The A.C.P.A. minutes, March 5th, 2002.
[203] The A.C.P.A. minutes, May 2nd, 2002.
[204] The A.C.P.A. minutes, June 4th, 2002.

Pot Luck, 2001
Guy McLean and Jane Minkhorst

House Tour, 2002
Some of the many Volunteers

- $5,000.00 to the Speakers Series.
- At year end the Lost and Found donated whatever was left to the Salvation Army. Barb Armstrong needed many volunteers to oversee the Lost and Found at lunchtimes.
- Fortunately the College Shop was able to stay in its present locale (near the swimming pool entrance). Space is limited at the school until a new gymnasium is built. Carol Erdelyi added blue crested fleece blankets, a bear dressed in an Appleby tie, leather bookmarks, Appleby crested passport covers, girls' fitted blouses and crystal Inukshuks. The College Shop added new items to its inventory; crested gym bags, Adidas soccer socks, open leg track pants and other gym clothing items. The College Shop webpage offered all items for sale and prices were listed.

  Christine Rennie looked after the ring sales. She also investigated the possibility of using bar codes to expedite the billings – with the use of student cards as well.

- Over the summer the Turnover was moved from the basement of Alumni House to the basement of the dining hall. Jo-Anne Milne, convenor, held a fall Sports Equipment and Clothing Sale in November. Unfortunately the sale was held on mid-term weekend and was financially disappointing, $330.00 but as all Appleby volunteers know it is always fun to work together. Jo-Anne and her volunteers had a pleasant time together and will look at a different date for next year. Turnover moved once again, this time, to the basement of Walker House. This was accomplished after March break.

- Chapel Guild no longer met on Mondays. They would now meet on Wednesdays. A valid point was made by this year's Chapel Guild convenor, Alex Irish. "A. Irish discussed the fact that there seemed to be a lot of competition to keep outdoing the previous year's decorations and that maybe it was time to use a more simplistic approach. She suggested that she would like to go with as much fresh flowers and greenery as possible this year. ..."[205] As wonderful as the idea of fresh was it was laborious. Everything had to be constantly misted to keep it moist and sprayed with fire retardant which is expensive. It required additional clean up. Consideration will be given to having fresh only in a House Tour year but trying to have the Tour as close as possible to the Carol Services.

  Alex Irish also recommended the permanent purchase for outdoor lighting to highlight the stained glass windows. Remember Linda Hatch on the ladder setting up the lights. This explains some of the $35,000.00 noted above for Chapel lighting.

  A Hydrangea and Easter Lily fund raiser was held to raise funds for the Chapel. They raised $890.00, with this money they purchased a plaque to commemorate Chaplains and Head Chapel Wardens, a new Canadian flag and a new altar cloth.

- The Bookstore operated in a very different manner this year but with many benefits. Pearl Lande reported that "ordered books will be delivered directly to the student's home with the exception of the international students. International

---

[205] The A.C.P.A. minutes, June 4th, 2002.

Parents' Association Executive Committee, 2002 - 2003

Back Row: Julaine MacNicol, Carol Erdelyi, Paula Carson-Wood, Pearl Lande, Jo-Anne
Milne, Mary Anne Sarne, Karen Wilson, Jane Minkhorst, Alex Irish, Carol Budd,
Rosemary Hawkrigg, Heather Harris, Liz Goddard, Christine Rennie
Seated: Kathy See, Jill Edmonson, Megan Hanna, Elaine Moore, Yvonne Iten-Scott,
Barb Armstrong, *Absent:* Angela Lukowski

students' books will be delivered to the school and distributed to students on Sept. 4th.

It was pointed out that all old text books could be returned for a 50% refund this year. After the initial year refunds would be 30%. Paperback novels and workbooks cannot be returned however some paper back texts may be returned. The books are bar-coded at time of return and the refund is credited directly to the students account."[206] Wrinkles were ironed out as the year progressed. Next year should be smooth sailing.

- The P.A. agreed "THEREFORE BE IT RESOLVED that the Appleby College Parents' Association recognizes and appoints the Appleby College Archives as the official repository of such of its records as have enduring value for the College for administrative, legal, financial, historical and/or evidentiary purposes."[207]
- The plans for the 75th anniversary were ongoing. Jane Minkhorst often met with fellow committee members Sue Baillie (Rusty[′66]), Dede Hacking and Mary Anne Sarne, and on occasion Jill Edmonson and Pearl Lande. Midge and Michael DesRoches[′62] were often consulted.
- Probably every year, from the birth of the Association to the present time, each President advised, as Jane Minkhorst "advised members that it is absolutely vital that each and every person on all Volunteer lists be contacted and utilized. If you cannot use their help, forward their name to L. Goddard[*] or someone else still looking for help (on the volunteer's approval)."[208]
- The P.A. website was updated and would be kept up to date by Elaine Moore on a two week basis. The opening page 'News and Events' would definitely need a two week check. David Boyd met with pertinent convenors to update their areas of the website.
- The Gift Wrap brochures were mailed out with the newsletter. $8,048.06 was raised. Paula Carson-Wood ably managed this project, in fact more orders were made than in previous years. Paula hopes to have some orders come in on-line next year.
- Grade photos were taken early this year. Group shots on the stairs of the Classroom Building and the individuals in Willis Hall. Often photo day had fallen on Yom Kippur, thus students of the Jewish faith missed having their photos taken. The P.A. would see that this would not happen in the future. *Of interest - a photo day had to be changed because Archbishop Tutu lunched at the school on an anticipated photo day.*
- Kathy See organized the Grade Parties. They were a great success and fortunately no need to change any dates.
- Appleby hosted the International Independent Schools' Public Speaking Competition. This meant billeting, parent volunteers and so on. Anita Boyce, with the help of Jill Edmonson, capably oversaw the details for this event. Anita and Jill needed volunteers for 500 time slots and 190 billets. They looked after all requirements and happily so. Not only did parents billet and volunteer but the

---

[206] The A.C.P.A. minutes, June 4th, 2002.
[207] Ibid.
[*] Liz Goddard was the Volunteer/Life Membership convenor.
[208] The A.C.P.A. minutes, June 4th, 2002.

AGM 2003
Doug Bennett, Guy McLean, Ruth Anne Winter, John See (current Chairman of the Appleby Board)

AGM 2003
Helen and Alexis Troubetzkoy with John See

P.A. provided "funds for the purchase of Appleby College lapel pins and stopwatches, up to a limit of $900.00, for the International Independent Schools Public Speaking Competition."[209]

- Pot Luck was most successful. Karen Wilson invited Steve Poplar to demonstrate how 'Blackboard' operates and the school website. He gave a power point presentation that was much appreciated. House Tour tickets were available and people were asked to sign up for the bake sale. Cookies were sold to add to the bake sale revenue for the House Tour.

- Interguild functions were ongoing. Parents were encouraged to attend the workshops.

- *Of interest – "At the October meeting G. McLean announced that in future, any volunteers with direct contact with the children will have to obtain a Police Clearance. Probably any drivers who are in cars alone with students will get their clearance first. Many public schools already have this policy in place."[210]*

- The Appleby external website now has posting for Life Memberships on the Parents' Association page. They also ran a flyer for the House Tour under events.

- The House Tour out does itself with each new committee. Yvonne Iten-Scott, Julaine MacNicol and their team did fantastically well. Every two years the profits are up and the enthusiasm and goodwill generated is fantastic. This year they brought in $51,570. The P.A. donated $5,000. to the Oakville Cancer Society, especially in memory of Gale Salema.

- Heather Harris looked after photos this year but also monitored the P.A. phone line.

- Rosemary Hawkrigg, Bursary convenor, arranged to have J. David Brown do another painting to be auctioned. David Suchanek[78] suggested a rugby game would be an excellent subject. Photographs of an Appleby/SAC meet were sent off. The painting will be auctioned at the 2004 Appleby Auction.

- A particularly high note of the year was the Staff Appreciation week held at Appleby in the spring. Anita Boyce spearheaded this effort. It was a week long celebration and thanks for the staff. It was terrific team work, and Appleby family fun. The parents and students treated the faculty and staff to a continual round of little surprises. Flowers, lunches, thank you notes, a Friday assembly with the choir, poems, reflections on the positive impact of teachers, and on and on.

- The Executive Committee decided to produce a new cookbook for the 75th anniversary. Carol and Ellen Budd will chair the Committee.

- The A.G.M. was held on May 1st. The meeting was held in Willis Hall. A cheque was presented to the Oakville Unit of the Canadian Cancer Society (House Tour).
  Two amendments to the Constitution were made and are presented as amended: "The Second Vice-President shall assist the President and First Vice-President. The Second Vice-President shall also be the Appleby College Parents' Association Interguild representative and be responsible for the organization of grade and graduate photos. And The Corresponding Secretary shall send to the

---

[209] The A.C.P.A. minutes, September 10th, 2002.
[210] The A.C.P.A. minutes, November 5th, 2002.

Parents' Association Executive Committee, 2003 - 2004

Standing, L to R: Nancy Batchelor, Marla Ashmore, Paula Carson-Wood, Pearl Lande,
Kathy See, Jane Minkhorst, Heather Harris, Alex Irish, Kim Wright, Mary Anne Sarne
Seated, L to R: Jill Edmonson, Megan Hanna, Elaine Moore, Christine Rennie
Absent: Heather Hogarth (Greg'78), Wendy Wootton, Barbara Carrick,
Frances Mantle, Jennifer Clarke

Ruth Anne Winter and John See
on the occasion of Ruth Anne's retirement from the Board of Governors

membership all notices and letters and shall conduct the correspondence of the Association except as otherwise provided. The Corresponding Secretary shall be responsible for relaying and updating information for the 'News and Events' web page to the faculty member in charge of the school's intranet sites."[211]

Jane made presentations to the Foundation and the school. These were accepted by Aubrey Baillie[63] Chairman of the Appleby College Foundation and John See, Chairman of the Appleby College Board, respectively. Both men thanked Jane Minkhorst and the members of the Parents' Association very graciously.

The new Executive Committee was introduced.

It was a wonderful meeting with Jane Minkhorst presenting a survey history of the Association with a different hat for each decade and a detailed list of current events and an accomplishment of the Association in that decade. It was humorous and thought provoking at the same time.

Guy McLean, Headmaster, added his thanks and spoke for several minutes about the Appleby family.

Guy went on to praise Aubrey Baillie[63]. Guy spoke of the contribution he has made to Appleby for so many years. He also spoke of an award Aubrey received this past year. "The Council for Advancement and Support of Education (CASE), the world's largest non-profit education association, selected Aubrey Baillie[63] as the recipient of the Seymour Preston Award, presented annually 'to a school trustee who has exhibited exceptional commitment and leadership in developing voluntary support for his or her institution.' This marks the first time a volunteer from a Canadian independent school has won the award, indicating both the significance of the honour and the truly extraordinary nature of Aubrey's service to Appleby."[212]

Aubrey Baillie[63], the guest speaker, spoke of his association with Appleby. It began with his grandmother, Lady Baillie, the founder of the Women's Association (now the Parents' Association). Aubrey spoke of his grandfather, the Chapel window his grandmother donated to the school in gratitude for all the benefits her sons had from attending Appleby, his own school days at Appleby, his children Aubrey[92] and Samantha[99], (Marsha and Aubrey also have a daughter, Julia, who attended Havergal, prior to Appleby going co-ed) and nieces and nephews who attended Appleby. His talk crossed many years and covered many aspects of Appleby. The audience was most interested and eager to learn more of the history which is exactly what the Executive Committee had hoped.

Lunch was served in the dining hall. A number of Baillies were in attendance. Mr. and Mrs. J. W. Baillie[37], (Jim is the last surviving child of Lady Baillie); Mrs. M. Ferris, mother of Aubrey[63]; Marsha, Aubrey's wife; Diana Howard, sister of Aubrey and of course granddaughter of Lady Baillie; Baillie Howard, daughter of Diana and thus great granddaughter of Lady Baillie. (The Baillie family includes relatives - Belfords, Bensons, Bondens, Ferrises, Greens, Hageys, Harrises, Howards, Osenas, Sersons, Sisokins, Unsworths, Wilsons and Wrights).

---

[211] The A.C.P.A. newsletter, April 2003.
[212] The Appleby Quarterly, Spring 2003, Volume 24, Issue 3.

Appleby College Parents' Association

540 LAKESHORE ROAD WEST
OAKVILLE, ONTARIO
L6K 3P1

July 24, 2002

Mrs. B. H. Collins
2080 Watersedge Drive
Oakville, Ontario L6L 1A4

Dear Mrs. Collins,

We are planning a celebration to mark the 75th anniversary of the founding of the Appleby School Women's Association (presently known as the Appleby College Parents' Association) by Lady Baillie. We hope that you, as a past president of the Association, will not only be able to attend but will also encourage some parents of your era to do so.

We will mark the occasion with a chapel service and luncheon at Appleby on Friday, September 19th, 2003 (invitations to be mailed in the spring of 2003.) Perhaps you might be willing to follow up the formal invitation with a phone call to some of your contemporaries?

Our plans include a display of memorabilia; we would welcome any items you might loan us for the occasion or donate to the Association's archives. In addition, we hope that you will share your recollections with Margaret Bennett (President 1996-97.) who is writing a history of the Association. Her telephone number is 905 849-5594.

Over the years we have shared so many similar experiences and projects that we have forged a significant bond. This commemoration will be a wonderful warm homecoming for the volunteers of the past and present. We certainly look forward to meeting you.

Sincerely,

Jane Minkhorst
President

Telephone: 905-681-8222
e-mail: jminkhorst@hotmail.com

Sample of Letter sent to Association Past Presidents, July, 2002

Jane Minkhorst presented the departing faculty members with the traditional library books and thanked them for their service.

- *Of interest – School Fees for 2003-2004 are $19,750. - Middle School Student; $22,100. - Upper School Student; $24,600. - Senior One; $33,900. - Local Boarders* (i.e. tuition and boarding); Non-Local Boarders - $37,650. These rates are based on the quarterly plan. In addition, there is a technology fee of $2,140.*[213]

2003-2004
President   **Jane Minkhorst**

- Jane Minkhorst will preside for her second term in 2003-2004.

---

* Local Boarders are defined as students whose primary residence is within the 905, 416, 647 and 289 area codes.
[213] 2003-2004 Appleby College Registration Package

Appleby College Parents' Association

540 LAKESHORE ROAD WEST
OAKVILLE, ONTARIO
L6K 3P1

July 24, 2002

Mr. and Mrs. J. Baillie
1100 Westdale Road
Oakville, Ontario L6L 5A2

Dear Mr. and Mrs. Baillie,

We are planning a celebration to ma.. the 5th anniversary of the founding of the Appleby School Women's Association presently known as the Appleby College Parents' Association) by Lady ..illie. As past parents and grandparents we would welcome your help/partic pa.on/..volvement in any aspect of the event.

We will mark the occa.. with a chapel service and luncheon at Appleby on Friday, September 1.th 20.. wh ch we hope you will be able to attend. Our plans include a display of memo.bil. nd we would welcome any items you might loan us for the event or d...... to t e As ciation's archives. In addition, we hope that you will share your recollections with Margaret Bennett (President 1996-97) who is writing a history of the Association. Her telephone number is 905-849-5594.

As this anniversary nears we feel great excitement and pride in our thriving Association and in our founder. Please come and share in this marvelous event.

Sincerely,

Jane Minkhorst
President

Telephone: 905-681-8222
e-mail: jminkhorst@hotmail.com

Sample of Letter sent to Members of the Baillie Family

APPENDIX

Executive Committees   *The Executive Committees for the early years may not be totally accurate. Data was scarce.*

1928-1929

Honorary President	Mrs. J. S. H. Guest
President	Lady Baillie
Vice-President	Mrs. E. F. Osler
Secretary	Mrs. E. V. Brown
Committee Members	Mrs. E. H. Ambrose
	Mrs. W. S. Davis
	Mrs. W. T. Marlatt
	Mrs. J. B. McLeod

1929-1930

Honorary President	Mrs. J. S. H. Guest
President	Lady Baillie

No other information is available, would imagine the committee may have remained the same.

1930-1931

Honorary President	Mrs. J. S. H. Guest
President	Lady Baillie

Again, no further information is available.

1931-1932

Honorary President	Mrs. J. S. H. Guest
President	Lady Baillie
Vice-President	Mrs. E. F. Osler
Secretary Treasurer	Mrs. F. Robin
Committee Members	Mrs. B. P. Alley
	Mrs. E. H. Ambrose
	Mrs. W. S. Davis
	Mrs. A. F. Jennings
	Mrs. W. T. Marlatt
	Mrs. J. B. McLeod

1932-1933   **same as the previous year with the change**
Secretary Treasurer   Mrs. D. F. Benson

1933-1934   **same as the previous year**

1934-1935   **not sure of the makeup of the committee the top three positions remain the same**

Prize Day, 1939
Lady Baillie handing out prizes and awards

1935-1936   **added to the committee**
                                      Mesdames J. McPherson and H. W. Weis
1936-1937   **added to the committee**
                                      Mrs. Crawford Gordon, Mrs. W. D. Ross
                                      Mrs. W. D. Marlatt resigned

1937-1938
Honorary President   Mrs. J. S. H. Guest resigned and nominated
                                      Mrs. J. A. M. Bell
President, etc.   **same as above**

1938-1939
Honorary President   Lady Baillie
Honorary President   Mrs. J. A. M. Bell
President   Mrs. Donald Benson
Vice-President   Mrs. E. F. Osler
Hon. Secretary-Treasurer   Mrs. Henry Hill
Committee Members   Mrs. B. P. Alley
                                      Mrs. E. H. Ambrose
                                      Mrs. Alfred Bunting
                                      Mrs. Hugh Denison
                                      Mrs. J. W. Little
                                      Mrs. W. D. Ross

1939-1940
Honorary President   Lady Baillie
Honorary Vice-President   Mrs. J. A. M. Bell
President   Mrs. Donald Benson
Vice-President   Mrs. J. W. Little
Hon. Secretary-Treasurer   Mrs. E. E. Finch Noyes
Committee Members   Mrs. Alfred Bunting
                                      Mrs. J. W. Crashley
                                      Mrs. J. C. Davidson
                                      Mrs. Hugh Denison
                                      Mrs. Henry Hill
                                      Mrs. R. T. Williams

1940-1941
Honorary President   Lady Baillie
Honorary Vice-President   Mrs. J. A. M. Bell
President   Mrs. Donald Benson
Vice-President   Mrs. J. W. Little
Hon. Secretary-Treasurer   Miss E. E. Finch Noyes
                                      Mrs. Alfred Bunting
                                      Mrs. J. W. Crashley
                                      Mrs. J. C. Davidson

Covered Rink, circa 1940

Mrs. Henry Hill
Mrs. J. A. Huston and Mrs. R. T. Williams

1941-1942

Honorary President	Lady Baillie
Honorary Vice-President	Mrs. J. A. M. Bell
President	Mrs. Donald Benson
Vice-President	Mrs. Ronald Hart
Hon. Secretary-Treasurer	Mrs. Alfred Bunting
Committee	Mrs. A. S. Auld
	Mrs. J. C. Davidson
	Mrs. Henry Hill
	Mrs. J. B. Holden
	Mrs. S. N. Lambert

1942-1943

Honorary President	Lady Baillie
Honorary Vice-President	Mrs. J. A. M. Bell
President	Mrs. R. R. Hart
Vice-President	Mrs. B. Green
Secretary-Treasurer	Mrs. A. Bunting
Committee	Mrs. A. S. Auld
	Mrs. J. D. Davis
	Mrs. J. B. Holden
	Mrs. S. N. Lambert
	Mrs. R. K. Slater
	Mrs. H. W. Weis

1943-1944

Honorary President	Lady Baillie
Honorary Vice-President	Mrs. J. A. M. Bell
President	Mrs. R. R. Hart
Vice-President	Mrs. A. Bunting
Hon. Secretary-Treasurer	Mrs. J. D. Davis
Committee	Mrs. G. A. K. Boomer
	Mrs. C. D. Magee
	Mrs. F. S. Milligan
	Miss Barbara Stone

1944-1945

Honorary President	Lady Baillie
Honorary Vice-President	Mrs. J. A. M. Bell
President	Mrs. C. B. Green
Vice-President	Mrs. A. Bunting
Hon. Secretary-Treasurer	Mrs. G. A. K. Boomer
Committee	Mrs. L. Davis
	Mrs. C. D. Magee

Appleby College Women's Association
Oakville, Ontario

March 1st. 194.

Dear *Mrs Tomlinson*

A general meeting of the Appleby College Women's Association was held on October 31st at the College.

The President, Mrs. Bellingham, announced the appointment of Mrs. J. H. Gairdner to the Executive Committee as the representative of the mothers of new boys.

At the suggestion of Mr. Bell, it has been decided that, since there is no immediate need for books for the Library, the $50.00 which has been donated by the Association for that purpose will be held until spring and used at that time for some special purpose.

A discussion followed as to the best means of raising money in the Association for the furnishing of one room in the new buildings. It was decided that each member will be responsible for a minimum of $5.00 per year for five years, this amount to be raised in any way the member chooses and to be payable annually or, if preferred, the entire amount at one time. These payments will be due before or at the Spring Meeting. The Executive Committee feels that, in view of the outstanding contribution to the Building Fund being made by the Old Boys, wives of old boys should not be asked to contribute this $5.00 per year unless they are also mothers of boys at the school.

Letters were read from Mr. Bell and from Mr. Walker, Chairman of the Board of Governors, thanking the members of the Association for their donation of pews for the gallery of the Chapel.

Mr. Bell then addressed the meeting, giving us a very interesting picture of activities at the school and telling us of the progress being made in the drive for funds for the new buildings.

After Mr. Bell's address, the meeting adjourned and the members were guests of the College for luncheon.

Yours truly,

Frances A Bull

(Mrs. John Bull)
Acting Secretary

1948 Letter from Frances Bull (Acting Secretary) to Mrs. Tomlinson

Mrs. H. P. Bellingham
Mrs. A. P. Reid, Miss B. Stone and Mrs. H. W.
Weis

1945-1946

Honorary President	Lady Baillie
Honorary Vice-President	Mrs. J. A. M. Bell
President	Mrs. F. S. Milligan
Vice-President	Mrs. H. P. Bellingham
Hon. Secretary-Treasurer	Mrs. G. A. K. Boomer
Committee	Mrs. A. Bunting
	Mrs. L. Davis
	Mrs. Monahan
	Mrs. A. P. Reid
	Mrs. H. W. Weis

1946-1947

Honorary President	Lady Baillie
Honorary Vice-President	Mrs. J. A. M. Bell
President	Mrs. F. S. Milligan
Vice-President	Mrs. H. P. Bellingham
Hon. Secretary-Treasurer	Mrs. G. A. K. Boomer
Committee	Mrs. John Bull
	Mrs. Hugh Cayley
	Mrs. L. Davis
	Mrs. J. A. Gairdner
	Mrs. J. Tomlinson
	Mrs. Jack Townsend

1947-1948

Honorary President	Lady Baillie
Honorary Vice-President	Mrs. J. A. M. Bell
President	Mrs. H. P. Bellingham
1st Vice-President	Mrs. J. A. Gairdner
2nd Vice-President	Mrs. Joseph Tomlinson
Treasurer	Mrs. Jack Crashley
Secretary	Mrs. Jack Townsend
Committee	Mrs. Aubrey Baillie
	Mrs. C. A. Birge
	Mrs. John Bull
	Mrs. Hugh Cayley
	Mrs. Clarke Wallace

1948-1949

Honorary President	Lady Baillie
Honorary Vice-President	Mrs. J. A. M. Bell
Past President	Mrs. Frank Milligan (ex officio)

Appleby School
Women's
Association

Women's Association Membership Invitation - Cover

President	Mrs. H. P. Bellingham
1st Vice-President	Mrs. Joseph Tomlinson
2nd Vice-President	Mrs. A. W. Baillie
Secretary	Mrs. John Bull
Treasurer	Mrs. Hugh Cayley
Committee	Mrs. C. A. Birge
	Mrs. Ross Blaikie
	Mrs. Jack Crashley
	Mrs. J. H. Gairdner
	Mrs. H. G. Pepall
	Mrs. N. Clarke Wallace

1949-1950

Honorary President	Lady Baillie
Honorary Vice-President	Mrs. J. A. M. Bell
Past President	Mrs. H. P. Bellingham (ex officio)
President	Mrs. Joseph Tomlinson
1st Vice-President	Mrs. H. G. Pepall
2nd Vice-President	Mrs. Clarke Wallace
Secretary	Mrs. W. F. R. Smith
Treasurer	Mrs. G. M. Cayley
Committee	Mrs. Ross Blaikie
	Mrs. John Bull
	Mrs. D. Brouse
	Mrs. F. H. Chisholm
	Mrs. R. R. Manbert

1950-1951

Honorary President	Lady Baillie
Honorary Vice-President	Mrs. J. A. M. Bell
Past President	Mrs. Joseph Tomlinson (ex officio)
President	Mrs. H. G. Pepall
1st Vice-President	Mrs. R. R. Manbert
2nd Vice-President	Mrs. Clarke Wallace
Secretary	Mrs. W. F. R. Smith
Treasurer	Mrs. A. L. Stagg
Committee	Mrs. A. W. Baillie
	Mrs. Ross Blaikie
	Mrs. John Bull
	Mrs. D. Brouse
	Mrs. F. H. Chisholm
	Mrs. G. Holden
	Mrs. J. D. Terryberry
	Mrs. R. Wace

1951-1952

THE APPLEBY SCHOOL
WOMEN'S ASSOCIATION
was formed in order that the Mothers of
the boys at Appleby might be able to take
a personal interest in their physical com-
forts and surroundings. It was felt that
members of the Association could make
suggestions to the Headmaster, which
would assist him in the care of the boys,
especially in matters pertaining to the cultural side of school life. The funds of the
Association are used for the boys in providing extra equipment, which, though
desirable, the Board of Governors do not
think it possible to supply.

Membership to the Association is
open to all Mothers and Sisters of past and
present pupils, wives of Masters and of Old
Boys, also to others who would be interested. As your son has recently been
enrolled as a student at Appleby School
the Women's Association cordially invites
you to become one of its members.

There are two types of Membership:

The Sustaining Member, pays an
annual fee of $5, with no other obligation.

The Associate Member pays an annual
fee of $1, but also gives a certain amount
of time each year to the work of the sewing
committee.

The Association holds its Annual
Meeting at the home of the President,
Lady Baillie, in February. For the rest of
the year the Committee is in close touch
with the Headmaster.

We sincerely hope that you may find
it possible to join the Association.

Yours sincerely,

Hon. Secretary-Treasurer
30 Roxborough St. E., Toronto.

Women's Association Membership - Inside Invitation

Honorary President	Lady Baillie
Honorary Vice-President	Mrs. J. A. M. Bell
Past President	Mrs. Joseph Tomlinson (ex officio)
President	Mrs. H. G. Pepall
1st Vice-President	Mrs. J. P. Curran
2nd Vice-President	Mrs. S. B. Douglas
Secretary	Mrs. R. G. Wace
Treasurer	Mrs. Mrs. E. L. Taylor
Committee	Mrs. A. W. Baillie
	Mrs. Ross Blaikie
	Mrs. T. R. Deacon
	Mrs. G. H. Holden
	Mrs. T. Marshall
	Mrs. F. Smith
	Mrs. J. A. Whalen

1952-1953

Honorary President	Lady Baillie
Honorary Vice-President	Mrs. J. A. M. Bell
Past President	Mrs. H. G. Pepall (ex officio)
President	Mrs. T. R. Deacon
1st Vice-President	Mrs. J. P. Curran
2nd Vice-President	Mrs. S. B. Douglas
Secretary	Mrs. R. G. Wace
Treasurer	Mrs. Mrs. E. L. Taylor
Committee	Mrs. A. W. Baillie
	Mrs. Ross Blaikie
	Mrs. Fraser
	Mrs. G. H. Holden
	Mrs. T. Marshall
	Mrs. D. Robertson
	Mrs. W. F. R. Smith
	Mrs. F. M. Sperry
	Mrs. J. A. Whalen

1953-1954

Honorary President	Lady Baillie
Honorary Vice-President	Mrs. J. A. M. Bell
Past President	Mrs. H. G. Pepall (ex officio)
President	Mrs. T. R. Deacon
1st Vice-President	Mrs. T. Marshall
2nd Vice-President	Mrs. J. G. Middleton
Secretary	Mrs. R. G. Wace *(for an extended term of 1 year)*
Treasurer	Mrs. E. L. Taylor *(for an extended term of 1 year)*
Committee	Mrs. J. P. Curran
	Mrs. Fraser

APPLEBY COLLEGE WOMEN'S ASSOCIATION

Through the years 1930 to 1954 the Association has directed its energies and resources where it was felt the best results might be obtained.

While the amounts of the expenditures have not been great, they have been timely and persistent.

The following is a summary of expenditures on various projects.

Chapel   - Altar Curtains, Brass Lamps, Roof Beams,
                 Tinted Windows, Cupboard, Credence Bracket,
                 Grilles, Cassocks for Junior Choir Boys,
                 Choir and Gallery Pews, Hymn Books.   2,648.00

Hospital   - Painting and Decorating, Equipment, Trays,
                 Lamps, etc.   599.00

Library   - Reading Lamps, Books, Book Shelves.   438.00

Recreation   - Stage Curtain, Dramatic Club, Billiard
                 Table Repairs, Cadet Corps, Cinema Screen
                 Cinema Films, Manual Training.   749.00

General   - Including Dining Room, Kitchen and Dor-
                 mitories.
                 Painting and Decorating, Vegetable Peeler,
                 Lights, Tiling Shower Baths.   1,082.00

                                      Total:-   5,516.00

Added to above from 1950-1954:
               Pews for Chapel   822.96
               Library   677.49
               Tape Recorder   290.75
               Cassocks for Choir   306.70
               Gramophone   120.00
               Cadet Colours   212.58
               Records for Gramophone   75.00
               Bursary   300.00   2,805.48

               1955 - Bursary   300.00

               Silver Trumpets   250.00

               Repayment to Library Fund   260.00
                                                     ─────────────
                                      Total:- $9,131.48

Summary of Association Expenditures, 1955

Mrs. G. Holden, Mrs. McKendrick,
Mrs. D. Robertson and Mrs. J. T. Scarlett

1954-1955

Honorary President	Lady Baillie
Honorary Vice-President	Mrs. J. A. M. Bell
Past President	Mrs. T. Marshall (ex officio)
President	Mrs. J. P. Curran
1st Vice-President	*unknown*
2nd Vice-President	*unknown*
Secretary	Mrs. R. G. Wace
Treasurer	Mrs. E. L. Taylor
Committee	Mrs. E. K. G. Burden
	Mrs. J. B. Smith
	Do not know the make up of the committee.

1955-1956

Honorary President	Lady Baillie
Honorary Vice-President	Mrs. J. A. M. Bell
Honorary Member*	Mrs. H. T. Jamieson
Past President	Mrs. J. P. Curran (ex officio)
President	Mrs. R. G. Wace
Vice-President	Mrs. E. L. Taylor
Secretary	Mrs. W. H. Stanton
Treasurer	Mrs. J. R. Winchell
Committee	Mrs. E. K. G. Burden
	Mrs. F. H. Davies
	Mrs. L. N. Drynan
	Mrs. H. D. Hendershot
	Mrs. H. J. Lang
	Mrs. J. B. Smith

*representing mothers of boys who served overseas.

1956-1957

Honorary President	Lady Baillie
Honorary Vice-President	Mrs. J. A. M. Bell
Honorary Member*	Mrs. H. T. Jamieson
Past President	Mrs. J. P. Curran (ex officio)
President	Mrs. R. G. Wace
Vice-President	Mrs. E. L. Taylor
Secretary	Mrs. W. H. Stanton
Treasurer	Mrs. J. R. Winchell
Committee	Mrs. F. W. Baillie
	Mrs. H. G. Bennett
	Mrs. H. D. Hendershot
	Mrs. H. J. Lang

The Appleby College Parents' Association
cordially invites you to the

ANNUAL MEETING and LUNCHEON
Wednesday, May 5, 1993

GLEN ABBEY GOLF CLUB
RR 2. Oakville, Ontario

Special Guests
MICHAEL and ROSALIND NIGHTINGALE
The Peacock and the Beaver

R.s.v.p. by April 21   10:30 Arrival & Coffee
Margaret Bennett   11:00 Meeting
849-5594   12:00 Speaker/Lunch

Celebrate the publication of "A Taste of Appleby"

Invitation to Annual Meeting and Luncheon, 1993

Mrs. D. W. Newlands

representing mothers of boys who served overseas.

1957-1958

Honorary President	Lady Baillie
Honorary Vice-President	Mrs. J. A. M. Bell
Honorary Member*	Mrs. H. T. Jamieson
Past President	Mrs. J. P. Curran (ex officio)
President	Mrs. R. G. Wace
Vice-President	Mrs. E. L. Taylor
Secretary	Mrs. F. B. Brooks-Hill
Treasurer	Mrs. J. R. Winchell
Committee	Mrs. F. W. Baillie
	Mrs. H. G. Bennett
	Mrs. David Guest
	Mrs. H. J. Lang
	Mrs. A. J. Little
	Mrs. D. W. Newlands
	Mrs. C. Tugwell

representing mothers of boys who served overseas.

1958-1959

Honorary President	Lady Baillie
Honorary Vice-President	Mrs. J. A. M. Bell
Honorary Member*	Mrs. H. T. Jamieson
Past President	Mrs. R. G. Wace (ex officio)
President	Mrs. E. L. Taylor
Vice-President	Mrs. David Guest
Secretary	Mrs. F. B. Brooks-Hill
Treasurer	Mrs. J. R. Winchell
Committee	Mrs. A. J. Little, Mrs. D. W. Newlands
	Mrs. Donald Ross and Mrs. F. T. Smye

1959-1960

Honorary President	Lady Baillie
Honorary Vice-Presidents	Mrs. J. S. H. Guest, Mrs. J. A. M. Bell
Honorary Member*	Mrs. H. T. Jamieson
Past President	Mrs. R. G. Wace (ex officio)
President	Mrs. E. L. Taylor
Vice-President	Mrs. David Guest
Secretary	Mrs. F. W. Baillie
Treasurer	Mrs. C. Cooper
Dramatic Club Costume Convenor	Mrs. H. G. Bennett
Infirmary Convenor	Mrs. H. Lang
Ash-tray Convenor	Mrs. R. G. Wace
Committee	Mrs. J. D. Harrison, Mrs. A. J. Little,
	Mrs. D. W. Newlands, Mrs. Donald Ross,

1961

Appleby College Women's Association
The president and members of the executive
invite you to attend

the

Annual Meeting

of the
Appleby College Women's Association
to be held in the School Gymnasium

on

Thursday, April 6th, at 10:45 a.m.

Buffet lunch $1.00

Invitation to Annual Meeting, 1961

Mrs. F. T. Smye and Mrs. G. M. C. Wright

representing mothers of boys who served overseas.

1960-1961

Honorary President	Lady Baillie
Honorary Vice-Presidents	Mrs. J. S. H. Guest, Mrs. J. A. M. Bell
Honorary Member*	Mrs. H. T. Jamieson
Past President	Mrs. E. L. Taylor (ex officio)
President	Mrs. David Guest
Vice-President	Mrs. G. M. C. Wright
Secretary	Mrs. F. W. Baillie
Treasurer	Mrs. C. F. W. Cooper
Dramatic Club	Mrs. H. G. Bennett
Hospital	Mrs. Ross Ryrie
Wedgewood Plates	Mrs. R. G. Wace
Matches	Mrs. F. T. Smye, Mrs. A. J. Little
Dancing Class	Mrs. J. T. Scarlett, Mrs. D. S. Watson
Nominating	Mrs. K. M. Tewes
Committee	Mrs. L. W. Cole
	Mrs. B. H. Collins, Jr.
	Mrs. M. H. Gibson
	Mrs. J. D. Harrison
	Mrs. D. W. Newlands
	Mrs. C. T. Wood

representing mothers of boys who served overseas.

1961-1962

Honorary President	Lady Baillie
Honorary Vice-Presidents	Mrs. J. S. H. Guest, Mrs. J. A. M. Bell
Honorary Member*	Mrs. H. T. Jamieson
Past President	Mrs. E. L. Taylor (ex officio)
President	Mrs. David Guest
Vice-President	Mrs. G. M. C. Wright
Secretary	Mrs. F. W. Baillie
Treasurer	Mrs. J. F. Isard
Dramatic Club	Mrs. H. G. Bennett
Hospital	Mrs. Ross Ryrie
Wedgewood Plates	Mrs. R. G. Wace
Matches	Mrs. F. T. Smye, Mrs. A. J. Little
Dancing Class	Mrs. J. B. Essery, Mrs. P. Redgrave
Committee	Mrs. B. H. Collins
	Mrs. M. H. Gibson
	Mrs. J. D. Harrison
	Mrs. D. Watson
	Mrs. C. T. Wood

representing mothers of boys who served overseas.

Two 'Old Boys' !!

Ian Grant'⁶⁰ and Mark Bennett'⁶⁴

1962-1963

Honorary President	Lady Baillie
Honorary Vice-Presidents	Mrs. J. S. H. Guest, Mrs. J. A. M. Bell
Honorary Member*	Mrs. H. T. Jamieson
Past President	Mrs. David Guest
President	Mrs. B. H. Collins, Jr.
1st Vice-President	Mrs. J. R. Winchell
2nd Vice-President	Mrs. L. R. Lever
Secretary	Mrs. F. W. Baillie
Treasurer	Mrs. J. G. Isard
Committee	Mrs. S. G. Fearman
	Mrs. M. H. Gibson
	Mrs. J. D. Russell
	Mrs. D. Watson
	Mrs. H. Wilson

representing mothers of boys who served overseas.

1963-1964

Honorary President	Lady Baillie
Honorary Vice-Presidents	Mrs. J. S. H. Guest, Mrs. J. A. M. Bell
Honorary Member*	Mrs. H. T. Jamieson
Past President	Mrs. David Guest
President	Mrs. B. H. Collins, Jr.
1st Vice-President	Mrs. J. R. Winchell
2nd Vice-President	Mrs. D. W. Newlands
Secretary	Mrs. T. A. Gordon
Treasurer	Mrs. A. Phillips
Committee	Mrs. J. W. Baillie
	Mrs. S. G. Fearman
	Mrs. C. G. Page
	Mrs. J. T. Scarlett
	Mrs. H. P. Wilson

representing mothers of boys who served overseas.

1964-1965

Honorary President	Lady Baillie
Honorary Vice-Presidents	Mrs. J. S. H. Guest, Mrs. J. A. M. Bell
Honorary Member*	Mrs. H. T. Jamieson
Past President	Mrs. B. H. Collins, Jr.
President	Mrs J. R. Winchell
1st Vice-President	Mrs. D. W. Newlands
2nd Vice-President	Mrs .S. G. Fearman
Secretary	Mrs. J. W. Baillie

APPRECIATION FOR FORTY YEARS OF SERVICE
Retiring president Mrs. D. W. Newlands, new president Mrs. G. L. Waters
retiring headmaster Dr. J. A. M. Bell, and Mrs. Bell

Appleby Women's Association Says Goodbye To Headmaster

OAKVILLE — The fortieth annual meeting of the Appleby College Women's Association heard its final address from retiring headmaster Dr. J. A. M. Bell yesterday afternoon, and as a parting gift, presented Dr. and Mrs. Bell with a cheque for $1,000.

The money, donated by parents of Appleby students and by graduates of the College, came with an inscribed scroll with the request that Dr. and Mrs. Bell buy a color television set of their choice.

Close to 200 mothers and grandmothers attended the Women's Association spring meeting in the school gymnasium. The meeting was chaired by retiring president Mrs. D. W. Newlands, of Burlington.

Reports were given on the WA's $500 bursary to the school, prizes and repairs, as well as furniture for the common room of New House. Treasurer Mrs. P. K. Hanley's report revealed total receipts of $1,109 during the year with disbursements of $1,103.

NEW OFFICERS

Mrs. G. H. Greenhough, chairman of the nominating committee, reported on the new executive. Mrs. J. A. M. Bell and Mrs. J. S. H. Guest are honorary vice-presidents; Mrs. Newlands is p a s t - president; Mrs. G. L. Waters, Dundas, is president; Mrs. Gurth Bramell, Oakville, is vice-president; Mrs. P. K. Hanley, Oakville, is treasurer; and Mrs. H. W. Angus, Port Credit, is secretary.

The executive board consists of Mrs. G. T. Wright, Mrs. G. E. Grundy, Mrs. G. M. Hagey, Mrs. W. W. Drinkwater and Mrs. N. F. Batchelder.

Dr. Bell, in his final speech before the WA, outlined his career at the College since joining as a junior master in 1928. He became headmaster in 1937 and has held the position since then.

Dr. Bell stressed the need for parents to teach their young people self-discipline, and to inspire them to finer achievements. "It's not easy to grow up," he said, adding that young people today need a great amount of understanding.

After Mrs. Newlands presented the scroll, Dr. Bell was given a standing ovation.

Following a sherry party in the gymnasium, the mothers were guests of the school for luncheon.

Newspaper Clipping - March 28, 1968 - Daily Journal-Record

Treasurer	Mrs. A. Phillips
Committee	Mrs. A. L. Ambrose
	Mrs. E. J. Muir
	Mrs. R. L. Onkey
	Mrs. C. G. Page
	Mrs. J. T. Scarlett

representing mothers of boys who served overseas

Lady Baillie deceased, March 14, 1965.

1965-1966

Honorary Vice-Presidents	Mrs. J. S. H. Guest, Mrs. J. A. M. Bell
Honorary Member*	Mrs. H. T. Jamieson
Past President	Mrs. B. H. Collins, Jr.
President	Mrs J. R. Winchell
Vice-President	Mrs. D. W. Newlands
Secretary	Mrs. J. W. Baillie
Treasurer	Mrs. H. W. Angus
Committee	Mrs. C. N. P. Blagrave
	Mrs. J. A. Botterell
	Mrs. J. H. Disher
	Mrs. R. L. Onkey
	Mrs. G. L. Waters

representing mothers of boys who served overseas

1966-1967

Honorary Vice-Presidents	Mrs. J. S. H. Guest, Mrs. J. A. M. Bell
Honorary Member*	Mrs. T. A. Jamieson
Past President	Mrs. J. R. Winchell
President	Mrs. D. W. Newlands
Vice-President	Mrs. G. L. Waters
Secretary	Mrs. J. W. Baillie
Treasurer	Mrs. H. W. Angus
Committee	Mrs. C. N. P. Blagrave
	Mrs. J. A. Botterell
	Mrs. J. H. Disher
	Mrs. K. B. MacNaughton
	Mrs. R. L. Onkey

representing mothers of boys who served overseas

1967-1968

Honorary Vice-Presidents	Mrs. J. S. H. Guest, Mrs. J. A. M. Bell
Honorary Member*	Mrs. T. H. Jamieson
Past President	Mrs. J. R. Winchell
President	Mrs. D. W. Newlands
Vice-President	Mrs. G. L. Waters

Appleby College Women's Association autumn meeting
Wednesday October 22 nd. 1969
1p.m. Sherry Party at the Home of Mr. and Mrs. E. R. Larsen

Luncheon and Short Business Meeting to follow
in the
John Guest Hall   – $2.00

Membership Fee $5.00 payable at the meeting
    or send to   Mrs. H. W. Angus
                          541 Comanche Rd., Port Credit

Notice of Autumn Meeting, 1969

Secretary	Mrs. P. K. Hanley
Treasurer	Mrs. H. W. Angus
Committee	Mrs. H. C. Arrell
	Mrs. G. Bramall
	Mrs. J. A. Botterell
	Mrs. G. E. Grundy
	Mrs. K. B. MacNaughton
	Mrs. G. T. Wright

representing mothers of boys who served overseas

1968-1969
Honorary Vice-Presidents	Mrs. J. S. H. Guest, Mrs. J. A. M. Bell
Honorary Member*	Mrs. T. H. Jamieson
Past President	Mrs. D. W. Newlands
President	Mrs. G. L. Waters
Vice-President	Mrs. G. Bramall
Secretary	Mrs. P. K. Hanley
Treasurer	Mrs. H. W. Angus
Committee	Mrs. N. F. Batchelder
	Mrs. W. W. Drinkwater
	Mrs. G. E. Grundy
	Mrs. G. M. Hagey
	Mrs. G. T. Wright

representing mothers of boys who served overseas

1969-1970
Honorary Vice-Presidents	Mrs. J. A. M. Bell, Mrs. J. S. H. Guest,
	Mrs. E. R. Larsen
Past President	Mrs. D. W. Newlands
President	Mrs. G. L. Waters
Vice-President	Mrs. G. Bramall
Secretary	Mrs. E. W. Stone
Treasurer	Mrs. H. W. Angus
Committee	Mrs. W. W. Drinkwater
	Mrs. J. Hetherington
	Mrs. L. McAlister
	Mrs. T. P. Snowden
	Mrs. B. Wells

1970-1971
Honorary Vice-Presidents	Mrs. J. A. M. Bell, Mrs. J. S. H. Guest,
	Mrs. E. R. Larsen
Past President	Mrs. G. L. Waters
President	Mrs. G. Bramall
Vice-President	Mrs. I. Jamieson
Secretary	Mrs. E. W. Stone

Appleby family members at Miss Chamberlain's Retirement Party

Left to Right: Cam MacArthur'60, Jamie Gairdner'58, Tom Menzies (Honorary Old Boy),
Peter Baillie'68, Janet and Dave Manbert'57

More party guests....

John Baillie'67, Bert Hardwick, Fran Richardson (Honorary Old Boy),
Peter Baillie'68, Jamie MacArthur'68, Stu Sloane'57

Treasurer	Mrs. H. W. Angus
Committee	Mrs. W. G. Colville
	Mrs. H. Fisker
	Mrs. J. Hetherington
	Mrs. L. McAlister
	Mrs. B. Wells

1971-1972

Honorary Vice-Presidents	Mrs. J. A. M. Bell, Mrs. J. S. H. Guest,
	Mrs. E. R. Larsen
Past President	Mrs. G. L. Waters
President	Mrs. G. Bramall
Vice-President	Mrs. I. Jamieson
Secretary	Mrs. J. G. Lloyd
Treasurer	Mrs. D. Pegg
Committee	Mrs. J. Burn
	Mrs. W. G. Colville
	Mrs. B. Green
	Mrs. L. McAlister
	Mrs. A. Platt
	Mrs. B. Wells

1972-1973

Honorary Vice-Presidents	Mrs. J. A. M. Bell, Mrs. J. S. H. Guest,
	Mrs. E. R. Larsen
Past President	Mrs. G. Bramall
President	Mrs. I. Jamieson
1st Vice-President	Mrs. J. C. Platt
2nd Vice-President	Mrs. D. I. Gallagher
Secretary	Mrs. J. G. Lloyd
Treasurer	Mrs. S. B. McLaughlin
Committee	Mrs. A. C. Abbott
	Mrs. J. Burn
	Mrs. W. G. Colville
	Mrs. B. B. Green

1973-1974

Past President	June Bramall
President	Shirley Jamieson
1st Vice-President	Diana Thomson
2nd Vice-President	Angela Platt
Secretary	Cay Lloyd
Treasurer	Pat McLaughlin
Jewellery	Marnie Green
Members at Large	Barbara Gibson, Pat Lytle
New Mothers' Rep.	Gretchen McCullough

Appleby Family celebrating Miss Chamberlain's Retirement
Friends of Miss C., Miss Chamberlain, Mary Isard, Nancy Baillie (Jim '37)

More friends and celebrants...
Mr. D. 'Skin' Dewar, his wife Mary, David and Betty Newlands

Heather Strucken

1974-1975
Past President	Shirley Jamieson
President	Diana Thomson
Vice-President	Heather Strucken
Secretary	Connie Dorion
Treasurer	Barbara Gibson
Committee	Mrs. A. C. Abbott
	Mrs. J. Burn
	Mrs. W. G. Colville
	Mrs. B. B. Green
	Mrs. A. Platt

1975-1976
Past President	Shirley Jamieson
President	Diana Thomson
1st Vice-President	Heather Strucken
2nd Vice-President	Joan Schmidt
Secretary	Connie Dorion
Treasurer	Barbara Gibson
Jewellery and Membership	Maureen Morrison
New Mothers' Rep.	Mary McCarter

1976-1977
Honorary Member	Marion Larsen
Past President	Diana Thomson
President	Barbara Gibson
1st Vice-President	Connie Dorion
2nd Vice-President	Heather Strucken
Secretary	Mary McCarter
Treasurer	Betty Ross
Members at Large	Gaye Bateman
	Anna Gardner
	Eleanor Gaskin
	Eleanor Hueton
	Barbara Powis

1977-1978
Honorary Member	Marion Larsen
Past President	Barbara Gibson
President	Connie Dorion
1st Vice-President	Heather Strucken
2nd Vice-President	Mary McCarter
Secretary	Eleanor Hueton

Cafe in the Arena for the Giant Booksale
Heather Armstrong (Chair of the event) at the ready!

Children's Section at the Giant Book Sale

Treasurer	Betty Ross
Members at Large	Louise Cartotto
	Anna Gardner
	June Gregory
	Katie MacKay

1978-1979

Honorary Member	Marion Larsen
Past President	Barbara Gibson
President	Connie Dorion
1st Vice-President	Louise Cartotto
2nd Vice-President	Katie MacKay
Secretary	Elinor Hueton
Treasurer	June Gregory
Members at Large	Gail Bascombe
	Betty Distlemeyer
	Ronnie Easson
	Peggy Mann
	Barbara Skinner
	Marjorie Stacie

1979-1980

Honorary Member	Marion Larsen
Past President	Connie Dorion
President	Libby DalBianco
1st Vice-President	Barbara Skinner
2nd Vice-President	Gail Bascombe
Recording Secretary	Peggy Mann
Corresponding Secretary	Trudy Davidson
Treasurer	June Gregory
Assistant Treasurer	Ray Strachan
Membership Secretary	Betty Distlemeyer
Social Convenor	Judy Leach
Jewellery	Sue Crawford-Brown
Appleby Turnover	Anne Mann
Telephone Committee	Shirley Barr
New Mother Liaison	Pat Jelinek
Members at Large	Lynn Batty
	Paula Smith

1980-1981

Past President	Libby DalBianco
President	Judy Leach
1st Vice-President	Trudy Davidson
2nd Vice-President	Marcia Hays
Recording Secretary	Anne Lewitt

Pot Luck, 1997
Yola Rager, Claudia Jaecklin

Corresponding Secretary	Lynn Batty
Treasurer	Ray Strachan
Assistant Treasurer	Joan Milburn
Membership Secretary	Asse Husebye
Social Convenor	Marilynne Grant
Jewellery	Sue Crawford-Brown
Appleby Turnover	Anne Mann
Telephone Committee	Shirley Barr
New Mother Liaison	Ann Bell
Members at Large	Monique Buysschaert (Dominion Tapes)
	Inge Macham (Assistant Social Convenor)
	Barbara Wood

1981-1982

Past President	Judy Leach
President	Trudy Davidson
1st Vice-President	Joan Milburn
2nd Vice-President	Ann Bell
Recording Secretary	Anne Lewitt
Corresponding Secretary	Jane Buckland
Treasurer	Ray Strachan
Assistant Treasurer	Marcia Hays
Membership Secretary	Shirley Barr
Social Convenor	Evie Magill
Jewellery	Jocelyn King
Appleby Turnover	Peggy Manning
Telephone Committee	Inge Machan
New Mother Liaison	Vesna Walmsley
Members at Large	Maria McDonnell
	Audrey Norrey
	Enid Palmeer

1982-1983

Past President	Trudy Davidson
President	Joan Milburn
1st Vice-President	Ann Bell
2nd Vice-President	Evie Magill
Recording Secretary	Alice Fournier
Corresponding Secretary	Sarah Thompson
Treasurer	Marcia Hays
Assistant Treasurer	Peggy Manning
Membership Secretary	Katie Way
Social Convenor	Valerie Burke
Jewellery	Jocelyn King
Turnover	Carol Barcados
Telephone Committee	Maria McDonnell

English Pub Night - February Social in the John Guest Hall, 1998
Andrew and Mary Anne Sarne, Jeremy Hacking, Patti Hnatiw

New Mother Liaison   Ann Mann
Members at Large   Bonnie Wace (Chapel)

Con.)   Suzanne de Josselin de Jong (Assistant Social

      Margaret Howie (Dominion Store Tapes)

1983-1984

Past President	Trudy Davidson
President	Joan Milburn
1st Vice-President	Evie Magill
2nd Vice-President	Liz Durdan
Recording Secretary	Ann McJannet
Corresponding Secretary	Barbara Humeniuk
Treasurer	Marcia Hays
Assistant Treasurer	Judy Rowntree
Membership Secretary	Bonnie Wace
Social Convenor	Maureen Sauve
Jewellery	Valerie Burke
Turnover	Carol Barcados
Telephone Committee	Donna Piaseke
New Mother Liaison	Libby MacAulay
College Shop	Katie Way
Chapel	Zsa Zsa Koves

1984-1985

Past President	Joan Milburn
President	Barbara Humeniuk
Vice-President	Sharon Maich
Recording Secretary	Ann McJannet
Corresponding Secretary	Maggie Larock
Treasurer	Ann Lewitt
Assistant Treasurer	Judy Rowntree
Membership Secretary	Irene Glyn-Jones
Social Convenor	Jane Moore
Jewellery	Valerie Burke
Turnover	Shirley Krug
Telephone Committee	Jean Hufton
New Mother Liaison	Marcia Hays
College Shop	Betty Moore
Chapel	Debbie Kern

1985-1986

Past President	Barbara Humeniuk
President	Sharon Maich
Vice President	Anne Lewitt

Distribution of Gift Wrap, November, 1997
Mary Anne Sarne handing out gift wrap in Alumni House

Recording Secretary	Ann McJannet
Corresponding Secretary	Maggie Larock
Treasurer	Anne Lewitt
Assistant Treasurer	Eleanor Lewis
Membership Secretary	Irene Glyn-Jones
Social Convenor	Jane Moore
Jewellery	Valerie Burke
Stationery	Mary Coleman
Turnover	Elizabeth Denyar
Telephone Committee	Helen Barnes
New Mother Liaison	Jeanette Cooke
College Shop	Betty Moore
Chapel	Colleen Baumler

1986-1987

Past President	Barbara Humeniuk
President	Sharon Maich
1st Vice-President	Mary Coleman
2nd Vice-President	Maggie Larock
Recording Secretary	Rosalind Nightingale
Corresponding Secretary	Betty Moore
Treasurer	Anne Lewitt
Assistant Treasurer	Eleanor Lewis
Membership Secretary	Irene Glyn-Jones
Social Convenor	Jane Moore
Jewellery	Valerie Burke
Turnover	Elizabeth Denyar
Telephone Committee	Linda Bignell
New Mother Liaison	Jeanette Cooke
College Shop	Valerie Burke
Chapel	Colleen Baumler

1987-1988 (*no slate found for this year, possibly as listed*)

President	Mary Coleman
Past President	Sharon Maich
Vice-President	Maggie Larock
Recording Secretary	Rosalind Nightingale
Corresponding Secretary	Betty Moore
Treasurer	Kathy Stewart
Assistant Treasurer	Eleanor Lewis
Membership Secretary	Sue Scott
Social Convenor	Maggie Larock
Jewellery	Valerie Burke
Turnover	Liz Denyar
Telephone Committee	Phyllis Good
New Mother Liaison	Jeanette Cooke

Writing Grade Party Invitations at Convenor Barbara Barone's Home
Olga Harper, Nancy Barone, Debbie Cunningham, Sheila Sarraino, Julie Samuels,
Sue Bailey and Terry Burns with back to camera

| College Shop | Valerie Burke |
| Chapel | Carol Milne-Smith |

1988-1989

President	Mary Coleman
Past President	Sharon Maich
1st Vice-President	Liz Denyar
2nd Vice-President	Christine Apted
Recording Secretary	Rosalind Nightingale
Corresponding Secretary	Pam Bishop
Treasurer	Kathy Stewart
Assistant Treasurer	Brenda Bisiker
Life Membership	Liz Denyar
Social Convenor	Jenny Ransom
College Shop	Kelly Beales
Stationery	Sue Scott
Jewellery	Marg. Shorey
Turnover	Lorraine McMullen
Telephone Committee	Phyllis Good
Chapel Guild	Carol Milne-Smith
Grade Party Convenor	Colleen Baumler

1989-1990

President	Maggie Larock
Past President	Mary Coleman
1st Vice-President	Pam Bishop
2nd Vice-President	Christine Apted
Recording Secretary	Kathy Stewart
Corresponding Secretary	Kelly Beales
Treasurer	Sharon Campbell
Life Membership	Lorraine McMullen
Social Convenor	Teena McDiarmid
Turnover	Carol Milne-Smith
Telephone Committee	Phyllis Good
College Shop	Kelly Beales
Stationery	Ann Ghirardi, Jeannie Osmak
Jewellery	Marg. Shorey
Chapel	Sue Wu
Grade Parties	Colleen Baumler
Bookstore	Maggie Goh

1990-1991

President	Maggie Larock
Past President	Mary Coleman
1st Vice-President	Maggie Goh

Women's Health Day, 1998
Organizers Judy Mills & Nora Curran-Blaney
(Appleby's in house physician)

Women's Health Day, January, 1998
Mags Shorey, Jana Gray, Heather Christensen, Margaret Bennett (Mark '64)

2nd Vice-President	Pam Bishop
Recording Secretary	Kathy Stewart
Corresponding Secretary	Pam Olley
Treasurer	Sharon Campbell
Social Convenor	Erica Smith
Grade Party Convenor	Jinny Flye
Life Membership	Libby Heisey
College Shop	Stefa Williams
Stationery	Jeannie Osmak
Jewellery	Marg Shorey
Chapel	Sue Wu
Telephone Committee	Christine Apted
Turnover	Anne Harvey
Bookstore	Maggie Goh

1991-1992

President	Maggie Goh
Past President	Maggie Larock
1st Vice-President	Pam Olley
2nd Vice-President	Marg Shorey
Recording Secretary	Francine Johnston
Corresponding Secretary	Pam Olley
Treasurer	Jim Valade
Social Convenor	Erica Smith
Grade Party Convenor	Jinny Flye
Life Membership	Libby Heisey
College Shop	Stefa Williams
Stationery	Jeannie Osmak
Jewellery	Isabel Fox
Chapel	Sue Wu
Telephone Committee	Christine Apted
Turnover	Gerry Walters
Bookstore	Colleen Balders

1992-1993

President	Maggie Goh
Past President	Mary Coleman
1st Vice-President	Marg Shorey
2nd Vice-President	Stefa Williams
Recording Secretary	Pam Olley
Corresponding Secretary	Eve Willis
Treasurer	Jim Valade
Social Convenor	Margaret Bennett
Grade Party Convenor	Jinny Flye
Life Membership	Libby Heisey
College Shop	Stefa Williams

Pre-House Tour Baking Party in Mags' Kitchen
Marsha Baillie (Aubrey '63), Mags Shorey, Libby Heisey

Stationery	Jeannie Osmak
Jewellery	Isabel Fox
Chapel	Ann Sinclair
Telephone Committee	Christine Apted
Turnover	Gerry Walters
Bookstore	Colleen Balders

1993-1994

President	Marg Shorey
Past President	Maggie Goh
1st Vice-President	Stefa Williams
2nd Vice-President	Libby Heisey
Recording Secretary	Pam Olley
Corresponding Secretary	Eve Willis
Treasurer	Jim Valade
Social Convenor	Margaret Bennett
Grade Party Convenor	Jane Tilley
Life Membership	Jeannie Osmak
College Shop	Wendy Smith
Stationery	Isabel Fox
Jewellery	Barb Lewis
Chapel	Ann Sinclair
Telephone Committee	Hilary Maile
Turnover	Dede Hacking
Bookstore	Pat Chiang

1994-1995

President	Mags Shorey
Past President	Maggie Goh
1st Vice-President	Stefa Williams
2nd Vice-President	Libby Heisey
Recording Secretary	Eve Willis
Corresponding Secretary	Hilary Maile
Treasurer	Stefa Williams
Social Convenor	Margaret Bennett
Grade Party Co-ordinator	Jane Tilley
Volunteer Co-ordinator	Elaine Mahoney
College Shop	Wendy Smith
Stationery	Isabel Fox
Jewellery	Barbara Lewis
Chapel	Caroline Morrow
Turnover	Dede Hacking
Bookstore	Pat Chiang

1995-1996

President	Stefa Williams

House Tour Tea
Marsha Baillie, Margaret Bennett, Rana Gupta

House Tour Tea - Serving Hot Mulled Cider
Peter Dennett of 'SecondCup', and Baillie Howard

Past President	Mags Shorey
1st Vice-President	Margaret Bennett
2nd Vice-President	Wendy Smith
Treasurer	Dede Hacking
Recording Secretary	Barbara Lewis
Corresponding Secretary	Hilary Maile
College Shop	
Clothing	Barbara Lennox
Stationery	Isabel Fox
Jewellery	Sue Baillie
Bookstore	Hilary Selby
Turnover	Vicki Lydall
Chapel	Caroline Morrow
Social Convenor	Mary Catherine Acheson
Grade Party Co-ordinator	Patti Hnatiw
Volunteer/Life Membership	Lorraine Shrigley
Member at Large/Bookfair	Debbie Cunningham

1996-1997

President	Margaret Bennett
Past President	Stefa Williams
1st Vice-President	Dede Hacking
2nd Vice-President	Lorraine Shrigley
Treasurer	Ann Ferguson
Recording Secretary	Barbara Lewis
Corresponding Secretary	Vicki Kennan
College Shop	
Clothing	Barbara Lennox
Stationery	Heather Armstrong
Jewellery	Sue Baillie
Bookstore	Hilary Selby
Turnover	Vicki Lydall
Chapel	Susan Mactaggart
Social Convenor	Mary Catherine Acheson
Grade Party Convenor	Patti Hnatiw
Life Members / Volunteers	Charlotte Riddell
Members at Large	
Bookfair	Deborah Cunningham
Community Service	Eve Willis
Gift Wrap	Ann Hepburn

1997-1998

President	Dede Hacking
Past President	Margaret Bennett
1st Vice-President	Mary Catherine Acheson
2nd Vice-President	Hilary Selby

House Tour
Ian Bradley and Baillie Howard

Independent Schools Fashion Show, 1998
Rusty Baillie '66, with attendees, Dorothy Leonard and Eveline Dear

Treasurer	Ann Ferguson
Recording Secretary	Vicki Lydall
Corresponding Secretary	Vicki Kennan
College Shop	
Clothing	Heather Armstrong
Stationery	Karin Schulte
Jewellery	Lynn Brown
Bookstore Administration	Jana Grey
Bookstore Volunteer Coordinator	Nalini Paul
Bursary Raffle	Judy Mills
Turnover	Irene Carley
Chapel Guild	Susan Mactaggart
Social Convenor	Barb Barone
Volunteers/Membership	Charlotte Riddell
Community Service	Eve Willis

1998-1999

President	Mary Catherine Acheson
Past President	Dede Hacking
1st Vice-President	Judy Mills
2nd Vice-President	Sue Baillie
Treasurer	Bev Peat
Recording Secretary	Vicki Lydall
Corresponding Secretary	Terry Burns
College Shop	
Clothing	Rebecca Lalani
Stationery	Karin Schulte
Jewellery	Lynn Brown
Bookstore Administration	Jana Grey
Bookstore Volunteer Coordinator	Nalini Paul
Turnover	Irene Carley
Chapel Guild	Marilyn Freeman
Social	Barb Barone
Volunteers/Membership	Linda Lucas
Community Service	Eve Willis
Grade Parties	Mary Anne Sarne

1999-2000

President	Judy Mills
Past President	Mary Catherine Acheson
1st Vice-President	Mary Anne Sarne
2nd Vice-President	Sue Baillie
Treasurer	Bev Peat
Recording Secretary	Ann Ferguson
Corresponding Secretary	Terry Burns
College Shop Clothing	Karin Schulte

Intranet Seminar, September, 1997

Dr. Clifford Sampson presenting an Appleby Intranet Seminar to parents Jackie Yundt,
Liz Prescott, Lorraine Shrigley, Nalini Paul, Sue Bailey, Hilary Selby

1998 Oakville Independent Schools Fashion Show
Midge DesRoches, Dede Hacking, Michael DesRoches'62

College Shop Stationery	Jane Hilton
Bookstore Administration	Amber Ing
Bookstore Volunteers	Rohani Agnew
Turnover	Diane Treharne
Chapel Guild	Marilyn Freeman
Social Events	Jane Minkhorst
Volunteers/Membership	Midge DesRoches
Community Service	Eve Willis
Grade Parties	Heather Hogarth
Bursary Fundraiser	Wendy Osmar
New Parent Liaison	Valerie Dolegowski

2000-2001

President	Mary Anne Sarne
Past President	Judy Mills
1st Vice-President	Marilyn Freeman
2nd Vice-President	Ann Ferguson
Treasurer	Anita Boyce
Recording Secretary	Heather Harris
Corresponding Secretary	Wendy Osmar
College Shop Clothing	Karin Schulte
College Shop Stationery	Jane Hilton
Bookstore Administration	Amber Ing
Bookstore Volunteers	Rohani Agnew
Turnover Shop	Diane Treharne
Chapel Guild	Ann Veel
Social Events	Jane Minkhorst
Volunteers/Membership	Midge DesRoches
Grade Parties	Jill Edmonson
Bursary Fundraiser	Valerie Dolegowski
Lost and Found Shop	Terry Burns

2001-2002

President	Mary Anne Sarne
Past President	Judy Mills
1st Vice-President	Jane Minkhorst
2nd Vice-President	Marilyn Freeman
Treasurer	Anita Boyce
Recording Secretary	Heather Harris
Corresponding Secretary	Wendy Osmar
College Shop Clothing	Carol Erdelyi
College Shop Stationery	Karin Schulte
Bookstore Administration	Rohani Agnew
Bookstore Volunteers	Angela Lukowski
Turnover Shop	Pearl Lande
Chapel Guild	Ann Veel

Bursary Bookfair at Bookers, November, 1997
Paul McCulloch leading the Appleby String Ensemble

Bursary Bookfair at Bookers
Parent Volunteers gift wrapping purchases at the Bookfair, November, 1997

Social Events	Karen Wilson
Volunteers/Membership	Jane Muddiman
Grade Parties	Jill Edmonson
Bursary	Rosemary Hawkrigg
Lost and Found Shop	Terry Burns

2002-2003

President	Jane Minkhorst
Past President	Mary Anne Sarne
1st Vice-President	Jill Edmonson
2nd Vice-President	Heather Harris
Treasurer	Megan Hanna
Recording Secretary	Carol Budd
Corresponding Secretary	Elaine Moore
College Shop Clothing	Carol Erdelyi
College Shop Stationery	Christine Rennie
Bookstore Administration	Pearle Lande
Bookstore Volunteers	Angela Lukowski
Turnover Shop	Jo-Anne Milne
Chapel	Alex Irish
Social Events	Karen Wilson
Volunteers/Membership	Liz Goddard
Grade Parties	Kathy See
Bursary	Rosemary Hawkrigg
Lost and Found Shop	Barb Armstrong

2003-2004

President	Jane Minkhorst
Past President	Mary Anne Sarne
1st Vice-President	Pearl Lande
2nd Vice-President	Heather Harris
Treasurer	Megan Hanna
Recording Secretary	Kim Wright
Corresponding Secretary	Elaine Moore
College Shop Clothing	Christine Rennie
College Shop Stationery	Marla Ashmore
Bookstore Administration	Heather Hogarth
Volunteer Co-ordinator	Jennifer Clarke
Turnover Shop	Frances Mantle
Chapel	Alex Irish
Social Events	Nancy Batchelor
Volunteers/Membership	Paula Carson-Wood
Grade Parties	Kathy See
Bursary	Wendy Wootton
Lost and Found Shop	Barb Carrick

Independent Schools Fashion Show, 1998
Organizers Dede Hacking and Margaret Bennett receive floral tributes

Committees throughout the years – not complete by any means!

1936 Committee to decorate masters sitting room

Convenor   Mrs. Weis
Lady Baillie
Mrs. Crawford Gordon
Mrs. W. D. Ross

1937 Committee to decorate the hospital

Convenor   Mrs. McPherson
Lady Baillie
Mrs. R. T. Williams (to consult with Miss Niblett & Mr. Wickens)

1938 First Telephone Committee, taken on by members of the Executive

1941 Dance Committee

Mrs. Bell
Mrs. Grant
Mrs. Green
Mrs. Hart
Miss Stone

1953 Dance Committee

Mrs. Cooper
Mrs. New

1954 Dance Committee

Mrs. Brooks-Hill

1956 Dance Committee

Mrs. R. H. Macdonald
Mrs. T. B. Lartice?

1958 Dance Committee

Mrs. J. D. Wood

1959 Dance Committee

Mrs. Newlands
Mrs. Ryrie

1960 Dance Committee

Mrs. Scarlett

1962 Dance Committee

Mrs. P. Redgrave

Fashion Show for Rugby
Organized by Anne Sinclair for the Appleby Rugby Team
Looking on: Marilynne Grant, Jana Heins, Susan Nicholas, Jane Moore and Rosemary Corcoran

1963 Dance Committee
> Mrs. J. W. Baillie
> Mrs. M. Gibson

1964 Dance Committee
> Mrs. Blagrave
> Mrs. Phillips

1965 Dance Committee
> Mrs. Blagrave
> Mrs. Hall

1966 Dance Committee
> Mrs. Botterell
> Mrs. Tewes

1968 Dance Committee
> Mrs. Kilmer

1950 Library Fund Furniture Committee
> Mrs. R. W. Blaikie – Chair
> Mrs. D. Brouse
> Mrs. F. H. Chisholm
> Mrs. H. G. Pepall
> Mrs. J. Terryberry

1952 Publicity Committee
> Mrs. Holden – Chair

1962 Publicity Committee
> Mrs. John Botterell – Oakville
> Mrs. Roger Clarkson – Toronto
> Mrs. Murray Proctor – Hamilton

1953 Coronation Tree Committee
> Mrs. Graydon
> Mrs. Soanes
> Mrs. Stanton

1953 Match Books – Sales Committee
> Mrs. F. Brooks-Hill
> Mrs. Eaton Burden
> Mrs. Hughes
> Mrs. Winchell

1954 Match Books – Sales Committee

February Social, 2000
David Batchelor, John and Vicki Lydall, Nancy Batchelor

Chapel Guild
Carol Morrow dusting, 1997

Mrs. A. W. Baillie - Toronto
Mrs. Eaton Burden – Toronto
Mrs. F. Brooks-Hill – Oakville
Mrs. E. Windeler – Oakville

1955 Match Books – Sales Committee
Mrs. E. Windeler – Oakville
Mrs. D. Newlands – Burlington
Mrs. Smith – Toronto

1958 Match Books – Sales Committee
Mrs. Smye – Oakville
Mrs. Little – Toronto

1959 Match Books – Sales Committee
Mrs. Gibson – Oakville
1959 Match Books – Sales Committee continued…
Mrs. Smye – Oakville
Mrs. Cole – Toronto
Mrs. Little – Toronto

1966 Match Books – Sales Committee
Mrs. Depew

1958 Committee for Recreational Supplies for the Hospital
Mrs. Tewes – Oakville
Mrs. Little – Toronto
Mrs. Lang – Burlington

1962 Cultural Committee
Mrs. J. A. Stewart – Oakville
Mrs. N. Pilkey – Burlington

1972-1973 Champagne and Strawberries Committee
Pat Lytle
Pat McLaughlin
Angela Platt
Diane Thomas

Fall Fair Committee 1975

Convenor	Joan Schmidt
Food	Connie Dorion, Shirley Jamieson
Games	Sue Reid
Prizes and Decorations	Sharon Bates
Decoration	Executive
Tickets	Diana Thomson
Bake Table	Betty Distelmeyer

Some College Shop Volunteers, 1998
Jackie Yundt, Lynn Brown, Rebecca Lalani

Sewing	Shirley Stewart
Telephone	Marylyn Leggat
Crafts	Donne Parker
Plants	Audrey Wilson, Shirley Stewart
Auctioneer	Tom Parker
Finances	Barbara Gibson
Candy Table	Heather Strucken
Publicity	Sheila Kishino
Helpers	Betty Caird, Sue Crawford-Brown, Eleanor Hueton, MarylynLeggat, Betty Ross, Greta Senst, Nancy Vernon, Mary Wood

Fall Fair Committee 1977

Co-Convenors	Katie MacKay and Kay Petkovich
Attic Treasures	Barbara Cooper, Maj Dickens, Barbara Skinner
Baking and Candy	Patsy Halliday, Marjorie Stacey
Books and Toys	Janet Manbert, Darlene Moffat
Cook Book	Angela Platt, Mary Tarbett
Crafts	Donna Piasecki
Plants and Flowers	Anna Hayward, Rosalind Nightingale
Preserves and Pickles	Betty Distelmeyer, Maria Sopinka
Telephone Committee	
Tickets	Freda Manifould, Jean Pamenter

Fall Fair Committee 1979

Convenor	Kay Petkovich
Tickets	Susie Federchuk, Barbara Humeniuk
Publicity	Kathryn Mahoney, Paula Smith
Prizes and Donations	Carol Pollock, Ray Strachan, Beryl Sustronk
Crafts	Judy Leach, Libby MacAulay
Decorating	Marcia Hays, Gail Volterra
Bakery	Libby DalBianco, Asse Husebye
Country Store	Monique Buysschaert, Barbara Holland
Food	Marilynne Grant, Darlene Moffat
Drinks	Shirley Barr
Lemonade	Margot Seferian
Coffee	Lu Horwood
Books, Used Toys, Attic Treasures	Trudy Davidson
Picture Booth	Gail and Gerry Bascombe
Finances	Joanna Kay, Enid Palmeer report to June Gregory
Door Prizes and Raffles	Janis Altman
Candy Floss	Molly Fuller, Rita MacKinnon
Games	Anne Mann
Telephone Committee	Barbara Skinner
Tea Room	Gloria Anderson, Jean McDougall

Turnover - September, 1997
Irene Carley measures up at Turnover
in the basement of Alumni House

Attic Treasures	Pat Locke, Peggy Mann
Plant and Flowers	Anna Hayward
Food Tickets	Sue Crawford-Brown
Signs and Posters	Maj Dickens

Fall Fair Committee 1983

Co-Convenors	Liz Durdan, Sharon Maich
Antiques	Suzanne de Josselin de Jong
Books, Games & Collectibles	Rosalind Nightingale
Decorating	Maureen Sauve
Staffing	Sharon Maich
Pick up of items	Wendy Davies
Country Store	Donna Piasecki, Suzanne de Josselin de Jong
Preserves	Marcia Hays
Bake Table	Maria McDonnell
Tickets	Rianne Merry
Food	Jane Moore
Games	Roberta Butcher, Betty Moore
Tea Room	Zsa Zsa Koves
Plant and Bulbs	Jenny Balmer, Jeanne McFarlane
Finance	Judy Rowntree
Publicity	Joanne Bromley

1976 Appleby Family Picnic

Co-convenors	Eleanor Gaskin and Anna Gardiner

1978 Appleby Family Picnic

Co-convenors	Gail Bascombe and Peggy Mann
Tickets	Elaine Stoneham
Games	Joey Follows and Ann Mann
Desserts/Condiments	Gail Bascombe, Elinor Hueton, Sue Crawford-Brown
Beverages	Pat Locke and Freda Manifould
Money Tree/Pillow Raffle	Jo Schneider
Guessing Games	Barbara Edgecombe and Ann Lewitt
Tickets for food	Pat Jelinek
Posters	Helen Hendry
Decorating	Gail Bascombe and Peggy Mann

1977 Cookbook Committee

Bon Appetit Appleby

Isobel Johnson
Angela Platt
Mary Tarbett

APPLEBY COLLEGE WOMEN'S ASSOCIATION SHOP
APPLEBY COLLEGE
OAKVILLE, ONTARIO L6K 3P1

ORDER FORM

QUANTITY	ITEM	SIZE/COLOUR	PRICE PER UNIT	TOTAL COST
			POSTAGE AND HANDLING	2.50
			TOTAL	

75th Anniversary Necktie

☐ PLEASE SEND ME A 75th ANNIVERSARY NECKTIE FOR WHICH I ENCLOSE $14.00 PLUS $1.50 FOR POSTAGE AND HANDLING

NAME _____

ADDRESS _____

_____

TELEPHONE _____

PLEASE MAKE CHEQUES PAYABLE TO "APPLEBY COLLEGE WOMEN'S ASSOCIATION".
PRICES SUBJECT TO CHANGE WITHOUT NOTICE.

Order Form for Appleby's 75th Aniversary Necktie, 1986

Dedication in Cook Book reads

Our Heartfelt thanks
To
President Barbara Gibson
Margaret Ford
Tryphena Flood
Paul Jackson

Cover by John McConnell

In memory of Hilda Chattaway ♥

1993 Cookbook   **A Taste of Appleby**
Committee at the direction of Mags (Marg) Shorey

Verna Andrews	Tricia Munce
Debbie Cunningham	Pam Olley
Becky Dent	Bev Peat
Midge Des Roches	Tammy Racette
Isabel Fox	Sheila Roche
Susan Freeman	Marg. Shorey
Dede Hacking	Wendy Smith
Libby Heisey	Renate Sommer
Lillian Johannsen	Marjorie Ward
Maggie Levy	Missie Williamson
Barbara Lewis	Eve Willis
Jill Mark	Diana Wise
Teena McDiarmid	Kathie Zimmerman

Front Cover Art   Glenn Man, Senior
Sketches by: Daniel Ling, Junior
                   Glenn Man, Senior
                   Alf Plessow, Upper I
                   Kirsten Ostberg, Upper II
                   Veronica Kan, Upper I
                   Gary Poon, UpperII
                   Michael Lee, Junior

2003 75ᵗʰ Anniversary Cookbook
Co-chairs   Carol and Ellen Budd

─────────────────

♥ Hilda Chattaway was the much loved cook at Appleby from 1928 to 1985.

A

The Headmaster and Parents' Association

cordially invite

_____

to attend the _____

at the Headmaster's House, Appleby College

on _____

at _____

R.s.v.p.

B

The Headmaster and Parents' Association

cordially invite

_____

to attend the _____

at _____

_____

on _____

at _____

R.s.v.p.

C

Paul Hung

Senior

C

A. Invitation to attend a function at the Headmaster's Residence
B. General Invitation to an Appleby College function
C. Parent Name Tag (A.G.M. 1993)

1980 Dinner Dance – Art Auction Committee
Convenor	Evie Magill
	Gail Bascombe
	Ann Bell
Treasurer	Marcia Hays
	Judy Leach
	Libby MacAulay
	Peggy Mann

1982 Appleby Spring Fever
Co-Convenors	Evie Magill, Enid Palmeer
	Gail Bascombe
	Marcia Hays
	Asse Husebye
	Hugh Magill
	Freda Manifould
	Margo Safarian
	Katie and Bob Way

1988 The Bursary Ball
Co-convenors	Maggie Larock and Eleanor Lewis
Publicity	Jane Moore
Tickets	Jenny Ransom
Decorating Committee:	
Co-ordinator	Brenda Bisiker
	Christine Apted
	Linda Franklin
	Tony Giglio
	Phyllis Good
	Astride James
	Rosalind Nightingale
	Karla Scheel
	Mary Sutherland
Auction Committee:	
Co-ordinators	Sally Caty and Maggie Larock
	Verna Andrews
	Jocelyn Bennett
	Pam Bishop
	Liz Dormon
	Jackie Haroun
	Jane McCurdy
	Marg Shorey
	Kathy Stewart
	Susan Verdon
	Shirley Walters

Afternoon Bridge, 2000

At the First Table: Kathleen Vipond, Nicole Formanek, Lisa Blyler, Vicki Kennan

In the Background: Ann Ferguson, Dede Hacking

Planning Consultant	Janet Marshall
Display Consultant	Marion Snodgrass

1989 Library Plant Committee

Valerie Burke
Barbara Humeniuk
Eve Riekers
Stefa Williams (to water plants in the summer)

1990 Friday the 13th Barbecue

Linda Alexander
Lorraine McMullen
Wendy Smith
Kathy Stewart

1992 House Tour

Co-Chairs	Lorraine Chapman and Stefa Williams
Ticket Design, posters, flyers	Mariella Holmes and Diana Jones
Ticket Sales	Jeannie Osmak
Publicity	Hilary Maile
Acquisitions (raffle), advertising	Gerry Walters
House Captains	Patti Hnatiw and Jane Tilley
Bake Sale	Marjorie Alliston
Tea	Margaret Bennett

1994 House Tour

Co-Chairs	Patti Hnatiw and Jill Mark
Ticket Design, posters, flyers	Mariella Holmes and Diana Jones
Ticket Sales	Rose Copeling and Debbie Cunningham
Publicity	Sue Baillie and Hilary Maile
Acquisitions (raffle), advertising	Anne Sinclair and Eve Willis
House Captains	Barbara Lennox and Jane Tilley
Bake Sale	Marjorie Alliston and Lynn Brown
Tea	Margaret Bennett and Carla Hanna
Baking Parties	Maggie Levy
Gift Wrap/Gift Sale	Dede Hacking

1996 House Tour

Co-Chairs	Hilary Maile and Judi Vincent
Ticket Design, posters, flyers	Leslie Clubb and Mariella Holmes
Ticket Sales	Debbie Cunningham and Judy Nestmann
Publicity	Sue Baillie and Barb Lewis
Acquisitions (raffle), advertising	Eve Willis
House Captains	Rose Copeling and Barbara Lennox
Bake Sale	Marjorie Alliston and Susan Mactaggart
Tea	Mary Catherine Acheson and Margaret Bennett
Cider Stop	Carla Hanna

Pot Luck - Fitness Prize Winners

Back Row: Mary Catherine Acheson, Lynn McLennan, Ann Veel, Jane Minkhorst
In Foreground: Lisa Blyler, Magdalene Poon, Ann Ferguson, Jenny Stranges

1998 House Tour

Co-Chairs	Barbara Lennox and Charlotte Riddell
Ticket Design and Printing	(Mariella Holmes) Jane Muddiman and Denise Reeve
Ticket Sales	Mary Anne Curtis and Judy Mills
Treasurer	Stefa Williams
Publicity	Susan Little and Jane Raham
Acquisitions (raffle), advertising	Sue Baillie and Eve Willis
Designer Liaison	Joan Jones and Hilary Maile
House Captains	Linda Lucas and Mary Anne Sarne
Bake Sale	Rebecca Lalani, Julie Samuel and Jackie Yundt
Tea	Marsha Baillie and Margaret Bennett
Cider Stop	Liz Goddard

2000 House Tour

Co-Chairs	Heather Hogarth and Jane Muddiman
Ticket Design and Printing	(Gren Weis) Alison Meinert and Diane Treharne
Ticket Sales	Valerie Dolegowski
Treasurer	Jane Connor
Publicity	Heather Harris and Evelyn Sloan
Acquisitions (raffle), advertising	Julaine MacNicol and Wendy Osmar
Designer Liaison	Cindy Cottrelle and Val Letwin
House Captains	Pat LeBlanc and Veronica Zufelt
Bake Sale	Janis Benson, Yasmin Korkis and Anne Von Rosenbach
Tea	Margaret Bennett
Cider Stop	Karen Tyers

2002 House Tour

Co-Chairs	Yvonne Iten-Scott and Julaine MacNicol
Ticket Sales	Ann McComb
Treasurer	Anita Boyce
Publicity	Heather Harris
Advertising	Marla Ashmore and Christine Rennie
Raffle	Joan Walters
Design/Layout	Ann Veel
House Captains/Volunteers	Heather Hogarth
Bake Sale	Pearl Lande
Tea	Jill Edmonson
Cider Stop	Noelle Parsons
Student Liaison	Jane Connor
Music	Sara Thomson

1999 Used Book Fair

Chair	Heather Armstrong

Gift Wrap Sales

Christine Selim, Carol Small, Ann McComb

Cash Desk	Maggie Levy
Children's Area	Heather Christensen
Pricing/Labels	Nicole Formanek and Vicky Kennan
Publicity	Dede Hacking and Wendy Osmar
Refreshments	Vicki Lydall
Secretary	Judy Mills
Set-up and Display	Marsha Baillie, Margaret Bennett and Lynn McLennan
Sorting	Denise Reeve
Storage	Barb Barone
Transportation	Patti Hnatiw and Eve Willis
Treasurer	Ann Ferguson
Volunteers	Sue Baillie and Bev Paul

Round Square Lunch, Dinner and Breaks Committee

Co-chairs	Patti Hnatiw and Eve Willis
Lunches and Breaks Captain	Margaret Bennett
Dinner Captains	Yvette Dhillon
	Madeleine Gibson
	Heather Harris
	Hilary Maile
	Karen Wilson
Decorating	Marilyn Freeman
	Janie Schwartz
	Sandra Tucker
Parents' Association	Marilyn Freeman
	Judy Mills

Please note – there were many other areas in which parents were involved.

2003 Staff Appreciation Week Committee

Chair	Anita Boyce
	Barb Armstrong
	Jill Edmonson
	Carol Erdelyi
	Alex Irish
	Pearl Lande
	Angela Lukowski
	Jane Minkhorst
	Julaine MacNicol
	Elaine Moore
	Christine Rennie
	Kathy See
	Karen Wilson

1990 The Phantom of the Auction

Honorary Chairman	Guy McLean

Appleby Auction
Karin and Carol Schulte
John and Vicki Lydall in background

Co-Chairs	Douglas MacKenzie and Stuart Smith
Executive Manager	David Singer
W.A. Liaison – Advisor	Maggie Larock
Acquisitions Coordinators	Glen Moore, Roger Shorey and Andy Prozes
Treasurer	Stefa and Les Williams
Public Relations	Phil Johnson
Dinner Committee	Marg Shorey
Brochure Coordinators	Rosemary and Roger Verrall
Auction Night Coordinators	Harry Henderson and Peter Ward

1992 An Elegant Auction Cruise

Honorary Chairman	Guy McLean
Chairman	Terry Whalen
Executive Director	Don Stewart
Acquisitions Coordinators	Eve and Peter Willis
Treasurer	Ann and Jim Anas
Brochure Coordinators	Rosemary and Roger Verrall
Advertising	Giulio Carlin
Decorating Coordinator	Lorraine McMullen
Dinner Coordinator	Janice Weir
Auction Night Coordinator	Paul Bundschuh
Silent Auction Coordinator	Jinny Flye
Tickets	Catherine Duddeck

1994 Up, Up and Away

Honorary Chairman	Guy McLean
Chairman	Terry Whalen
Executive Directors	Dave Singer and Don Stewart
Acquisitions Coordinators	Brenda Cundill and Gerry Walters
Treasurer	Jim Anas
Brochure Coordinators	Cathy Whalen
Advertising	Les Williams
Publicity	Jennifer Kay
Decorating Coordinator	Lorraine McMullen
Dinner Coordinator	Janice Weir
Auction Night Coordinator	Paul Bundschuh
Silent Auction Coordinator	Jinny Flye
Tickets	Becky Dent, Catherine Duddeck and Barbara Lennox

1996 A Magical Evening

Honorary Chairman	Guy McLean
Co-Chairs	Mags Shorey and Eve Willis
Executive Director	Don Stewart
Acquisitions Coordinators	Charlotte Riddell and Lorraine Shrigley
Treasurer	Jeremy Hacking

Appleby Auction, 2000
Another of the Memorable Auction Events at Appleby College

Paul & Jane Moore

**Susan Martin
John & Vicki Lydall**

Eve Willis, Jamie Bradley *'01*,
Simon Carmichael-Willis *'01*,
Peter Willis

Brochure Coordinators	Jinny Flye and Cathy Whalen
Advertising	Irene and Brian Carley
Publicity	Jane Hamilton
Decorating Coordinator	Lorraine McMullen
Dinner Coordinator	Janice Weir
Auction Night Coordinator	Fran Richardson
Silent Auction Coordinators	Debbie Cunningham and Barb Lewis
Tickets	Catherine Duddeck and Barbara Lennox

1998 Saturday Night Fever

Honorary Chairman	Guy McLean
Co-Chairs	Patti Hnatiw and Charlotte Riddell
Executive Director	Don Stewart
Acquisitions Co-Chairs	Joan Jones and Hilary Maile
Treasurer	Jeremy Hacking
Advertising and Brochure Co-Chairs	Mags Shorey and Eve Willis
Decorating Co-Chairs	Sue Baillie, Yvonne Pajak and Sandra Tucker
Dinner Co-Chairs	Mary Catherine Acheson and Liz Belford
Auction Night Coordinator	Fran Richardson
Silent Auction Coordinators	Rose Copeling and Bev Paul
Ticket Co-Chairs	Barbara Lennox and Jeannie Osmak
Publicity	Jane Hamilton
Business Office Liaison	Susan Forsey and Joan Lapointe

2000 Lights, Camera, Auction

Honorary Chairman	Guy McLean
Co-Chairs	Barbara Lennox and John Mills
Executive Director	Don Stewart
Acquisitions	Anita Boyce and Colleen Mackay
Treasurer	Joan LaPointe
Advertising	Sue Baillie and Lesley Weatherhead
Brochure	Nicole Formanek and Dede Hacking
Communications	John Simpson
Decorations	Marilyn Freeman and Sandra Tucker
Dinner	Patti Hnatiw, Charlotte Riddell and Eve Willis
'Night of' Manager	Steve Poplar
Secretary	Judy Mills
Silent Auction	Kathy Mundy and Julie Samuel
Tickets	Jane Hilton and Nancy Zavitz

2002 Viva Las Vegas

Honorary Chairman	Guy McLean
Co-Chairs	Rosemary Hawkrigg and Christine Selim
Acquisitions	Alex Irish and Kathy See
Advertising	Heather Harris and Karen Wilson
Balloons	Pearl Lande and Donna McCarthy

Guy and Joanne McLean attending a Hindu wedding in India, 2003

Auction, 2000
Guy McLean, Margaret and Mark'⁶⁴ Bennett

Decorating	Jayne Cruise and Colleen Mackay
Food and Beverage	Sheila Sarraino
Night Of	Tara George and Steve Poplar
Secretary	Heather Harris
Silent Auction	Lynn Beach and Kathy Mundy
Special Events	Meghan Graham
Tickets	Hilary Maile and Julie Samuel
Volunteers	Jill Edmonson and Christine Rennie

2004 All That Jazz

Honorary Chairman	Guy McLean
Co-Chairs	Anita Boyce and Jill Edmonson
Advertising	Pam Graham and Christine Rennie
Decorating	Catherine Bobesich, Gay Longo and Andrea Williamson
Tickets	Rachel Fowler, Yvonne Iten-Scott and Julaine MacNicol
Auctioneer	Don Stewart
Silent Auction	Hilary Maile and Julie Samuel
Auction Adviser	Christine Selim
Volunteer Coordinator	Heather Hogarth
Food and Beverage	Sheila Sarraino and Andrea Williamson
Promotions	Anita Griffiths and Andrea Williamson
Logistics	Mike Hourahine, Steve Poplar and Andrea Williamson
Catalogue	Carol Erdelyi, Anita Griffiths, Alex Irish, Megan Hanna and Kathy See
Secretary	Shevawn Adams and Nadja Bindon
Acquisitions	Barb Armstrong, Rosemary Hawkrigg and Kathy Mueller

Appleby College Chapel, 2003
The Chapel is the heart of the College, featuring classic Gothic design,
and a number of marvellous stained glass windows,
including the Lady Baillie window
which is featured in detail at the end of this book

The School Prayer (written by Dr. Bell)

Almighty and everlasting God, who makest us both to will and to do those things that be that be good and acceptable unto Thy Divine Majesty; we make our humble supplications unto Thee for those to whom Thou has committed the charge of this School, and for all boys of the same. Let Thy Fatherly hand, we beseech Thee, ever be over them: let Thy Holy Spirit ever be with them; and so lead them in the knowledge and obedience of Thy Word, that in the end they may obtain everlasting life; through our Lord Jesus Christ. Amen.

The School Prayer (written by Reverend Lennox)

Lord, help us to make Appleby College a community of consideration and cooperation, where everyone helps others to learn and learns from others. Help us to stretch our minds, our bodies, our talents, our hearts and our spirits. Help us to be a school that nourishes and cares neither rashly nor fearfully. Amen.

In
gratitude for all
that Appleby had done for
her three sons, Aubrey'27, Frank'31,
and James'37; Lady Baillie donated and had a
hand in the design of this gorgeous stained glass
window. See picture on opposite page.

"**On June 24, 1945**, a beautiful stained glass window, the gift of Lady Baillie, was presented to the School. Among those present at the dedication were the Headmaster [Dr. Bell], Lady Baillie, Frank Baillie and Mr. Aubrey Baillie.

The window is, in itself, a masterpiece, with six appropriate parables centered around its basic theme. In the first panel the upper medallion illustrates the story of Lazarus and the Rich Man. The lower part portrays the decision of the Prodigal Son to return home. Between the medallions is the Crown of Eternal Life. In the window-head is placed the Lamp, symbol of Faith, and the Tower, symbol of Strength.

"The centre panel illustrates the parable of the Good Shepherd, in the upper medallion. In the lower is pictured the Pharisee and the Publican. Between these is the Baillie Crest. In the window-head is the star representing Guidance, and the Sword and the Breastplate representing the Armour of Righteousness.

"In the third panel the upper medallion portrays the Sower in the Field. In the lower is Jesus' exhortation to do as the Good Samaritan has done. Between these is the Book, representing the word of God. Running through the three lights is the inscription: 'Unto you it is given to know the mysteries of the Kingdom of God.'

"On the left side of the tracery is the Cross and Crown of Thorns; in the centre is the Dove, or the Holy Spirit of God. To the right, the Resurrection is depicted as a Phoenix. These symbols are superimposed on the Rainbow, Symbol of Hope.

"In tribute to the three sons of Lady Baillie, the bases of the window represent the three services [in which her sons served] and the commemorative inscription. The left panel represents the 48th Highlanders [Aubrey'27], the centre the Volunteer Reserve [Jim'37], and the right panel the R.A.F. Ferry Command [Frank'31]." [1]

[1] *The Argus, June 1946, No. 54.*

LADY BAILLIE COMMEMORATIVE STAINED GLASS WINDOW
APPLEBY COLLEGE CHAPEL